Slavery and the Catholic Church in the United States

Slavery and the Catholic Church in the United States: Historical Studies

David J. Endres, Editor

The Catholic University of America Press
Washington, DC

Copyright © 2023
The Catholic University of America Press
All rights reserved

Cataloging-in-Publication Data available from the Library of Congress
ISBN 978-0813236759

Contents

Foreword: Archbishop Shelton J. Fabre vii

Introduction: David J. Endres ix

Contributor Biographies xiii

I. Enslaved Persons and Slaveholders

A National Legacy of Enslavement: Jesuits and
   Enslaved Persons
   Kelly L. Schmidt 1

U.S. Catholic Religious and Slavery: Seeking Truth,
   Justice, and Reconciliation
   James Fitz, S.M. 33

Catholic Slaves and Slaveholders in Central Kentucky:
   Reconstructing a Relationship
   C. Walker Gollar 63

II. Debating Abolition and Emancipation

American Reaction to Gregory XVI's Condemnation
   of the Slave Trade
   John F. Quinn 89

An Antislavery Archbishop: John B. Purcell and the
   Slavery Controversy among Border State Catholics
   David J. Endres 125

Catholic Responses to Lincoln's Emancipation
   Proclamation
   Robert Emmett Curran 155

III. Historians and Historiography

The Church and Slavery: A Historical Chronology, 1452–2023
Ronald LaMarr Sharps 189

Uncomfortable Entries: Documenting Enslaved and Free Persons of Color in Sacramental Records
Emilie Gagnet Leumas 211

Contending with a Slaveholding Past: Slavery and U.S. Catholic Historiography
David J. Endres 237

Selected Bibliography 269

Index 277

Foreword

As an African American Catholic bishop in the United States, the issue of race is deeply personal to me and should be important to all Catholics as we strive to be a part of healing the hurt and pain that endure because of racism. Racism is an evil and a sin and has persisted far too long in our country and even within our Church. It is essential that we know our history, both its triumphs and its heartbreaks. To know our history regarding racism can help us to move beyond it, to seek to rise above it, and not repeat it.

In 2018, the United States Conference of Catholic Bishops published a pastoral letter on racism, "Open Wide Our Hearts: The Enduring Call to Love." The pastoral letter challenges us all to conversion of heart from the evil and sin of racism. The letter noted that "examining our sinfulness—individually, as the Christian community, and as a society—is a humbling experience. Only from a place of humility can we look honestly at past failures, ask for forgiveness, and move toward healing and reconciliation." And yet, how do we begin to acknowledge and reconcile our sins if we do not know our past? We rely on the work of researchers and scholars to make the past better known and understood.

In this book, Father David Endres has gathered a group of essays by notable scholars who explore the history of the Catholic Church and its relationship with enslaving human beings. This work is part of a broader dialogue about the sins of racism that is taking place in the United States today. These studies open our eyes to a past in the Church that many of us may not be familiar with and will find very painful. This book addresses the issue with transparency and truthfulness and can thus lead us to an awakening, or an ongoing awakening, about the Church's painful history regarding racism.

But such an awakening to the evil and sin of racism must not only lead us to identify with the pain and suffering of another but also lead us to do something about it. Knowing our history, we can become instruments of God's justice who seek to respond to the suffering of others. We cannot be afraid to enter courageous conversations about racism in the Church. The work to end racism is hard and slow, but seeking to overcome it advances our efforts to bring about healing and reconciliation among the races.

This book assists us in learning about the Church's history regarding racism. Reflecting on our past can invite us to open our hearts wide to dismantle the evil and sin of racism as it continues to exist in our Church and society.

Archbishop Shelton J. Fabre
Archbishop of Louisville, Kentucky
Chair, U.S. Conference of Catholic Bishops' Ad Hoc Committee
   Against Racism

Introduction

"We warn and adjure earnestly . . . that no one in the future dare to vex anyone, despoil him of his possessions, reduce to servitude, or lend aid and favor to those who give themselves up to these practices, or exercise that inhuman traffic by which the Blacks, as if they were not men but rather animals [are] bought, sold, and devoted sometimes to the hardest labor. . . . We reprove, then, by virtue of Our Apostolic Authority, all the practices abovementioned as absolutely unworthy of the Christian name."
—Pope Gregory XVI, *In Supremo Apostolatus* (1839)

"The world of today reveals itself as at once powerful and weak, capable of achieving the best or the worst. There lies open before it the way to freedom or slavery, progress or regression, brotherhood or hatred."
—Second Vatican Council, *Gaudium et Spes* (1965)

IN 1839, THROUGH THE PAPAL PROCLAMATION *In Supremo Apostolatus*, Pope Gregory XVI condemned the slave trade as an offense against humanity and slavery's supporters as "unworthy of the Christian name." Few U.S. Catholics, including the nation's bishops, took much notice, and if they did, it was to argue that the pronouncement did not apply to slavery in this country—the importing of enslaved persons having been abolished in 1807. Anti-Catholics seized the opportunity to condemn the Church as abolitionist, even as most Catholics, whether in the North or the South, refused to consent to such a strict interpretation. The proclamation's equivocal reception led to confusion about whether Catholics should consider slavery immoral and under what conditions—a confusion that continued for decades. On the eve of the Civil War, there was little unanimity of opinion among U.S. Catholics and few pronouncements from the American hierarchy.

In Supremo Apostolatus's reception—or lack thereof—could be seen as emblematic of the U.S. Church's engagement with the troubling issue of slavery. Long after enslavement was abolished by the thirteenth amendment to the Constitution, Catholic historians and theologians were slow to probe the Church's entanglement in hereditary, race-based slavery. Even today, the relationship of the U.S. Catholic Church to slavery has yet to be explored in depth. Many historians have shied away from the uncomfortable topic, whether due to the subject matter itself or lack of access to archival sources. In recent years, however, this has begun to change as historians and the public at large have been awakened to the pervasive and lingering effects of slavery in the United States. While all forms of racism are not linked to the nation's practice of slavery, the experience of slavery is foundational for understanding structures of racial injustice—from Jim Crow to the Civil Rights era to the present.

This compilation of essays highlights the place of religion, and in particular the Catholic Church, in the institution of slavery. It shows the varied roles of Catholics: as enslaved persons, as enslavers, as proponents of slavery's status quo, but also occasionally as advocates of emancipation. It also suggests how historians might approach such studies—not only topically but in terms of methods, contexts, and resources—and through their own scholarship, deepen our knowledge of the topic.

This volume's first section contains three studies focused on enslaved persons and the Catholics who held them. The first essay by Kelly L. Schmidt explores the Jesuits' ownership of bondspeople, highlighting the enslaved persons taken to the religious order's western and southern missions. James Fitz, S.M., follows with a theologically-informed study of men and women religious who held slaves, suggesting how this difficult history might be acknowledged and its legacy repaired. C. Walker Gollar offers a case study of lay Catholic slave owning in Kentucky, suggesting the kind of careful archival work that is necessary for a fuller understanding of the Church's role in race-based enslavement and the community of persons who members of the Church enslaved.

The second section on abolition and emancipation provides three perspectives on antislavery efforts—and the responses they received. John F. Quinn explores the reception of Pope Gregory

XVI's antislavery bull *In Supremo Apostolatus*. He explains how the pronouncement was used by those on both sides of the slavery issue—even as most American Catholics presumed the pope's words did not apply to them. The next chapter focuses on the evolution of the thought of Cincinnati's Archbishop John B. Purcell, who was among a small number of U.S. bishops that could be considered antislavery. Purcell called slavery the nation's "fatal contrast," whereby it failed to live up to the Declaration of Independence's ideals. Robert Emmett Curran follows with an examination of Catholic reaction to President Lincoln's 1863 Emancipation Proclamation, explaining that for Catholics "hostility to abolitionism became a test of tribal loyalty"—and indeed they were loyal.

The third section titled "Historians and Historiography" includes Ronald LaMarr Sharps' historical chronology of the Church and slavery, highlighting events from the fifteenth century through the present. Emilie Gagnet Leumas then explores the "uncomfortable entries" found within Catholic sacramental records. Focusing on the extensive records of the Archdiocese of New Orleans, she shows how these records can be useful for understanding slavery's religious and social implications. Lastly, a contribution from the editor examines how U.S. Catholic historians have assessed slavery, ranging from its acceptance in the nineteenth century to modern approaches that seek to retrieve enslaved persons' experiences and explore the racist underpinnings of the institution.

These contributions assembled herein witness to the fragility of a humanity that is and was—in the words of the Second Vatican Council—capable of "freedom or slavery, progress or regression, brotherhood or hatred." Yet each study offers a ray of hope, pointing beyond their subjects to new understandings. May these essays contribute to a broader recognition of Catholicism's role in race-based slavery, and in doing so, assist scholars, teachers, and students in the contemporary task of remembering and addressing this painful history.

David J. Endres

Contributor Biographies

Robert Emmett Curran

Robert Emmett Curran is emeritus professor of history at Georgetown University, Washington, D.C. A prolific scholar, Curran's works include *American Catholics and the Quest for Equality in the Civil War Era* (2023); *For Church and Confederacy: The Lynches of South Carolina* (2019); *Intestine Enemies: Catholics in Protestant America, 1605–1791* (2017); *Papist Devils: Catholics in British America, 1574–1783* (2014); *Shaping American Catholicism: Maryland and New York, 1805–1915* (2012); and *John Dooley's Civil War: An Irish American's Journey in the First Virginia Infantry Regiment* (2011).

David J. Endres

David J. Endres, a priest of the Archdiocese of Cincinnati, is academic dean and professor of church history and historical theology at Mount St. Mary's Seminary of the West/The Athenaeum of Ohio. He is editor of the quarterly *U.S. Catholic Historian*. He has edited several volumes, including the *Native American Catholic Studies Reader: History and Theology* (2022); *Black Catholic Studies Reader: History and Theology* (2021); and *Soldiers of the Cross: The Heroism of Catholic Chaplains and Sisters in the American Civil War* (2019).

James Fitz, S.M.

James Fitz, a member of the Society of Mary (Marianists), is vice president for mission and rector of the University of Dayton (Ohio). He has served in administration and formation in the Marianists as well as appointments to the University of Dayton as director of campus ministry and instructor in religious studies.

C. Walker Gollar

C. Walker Gollar is professor of theology at Xavier University, Cincinnati, Ohio. He holds a doctoral degree in historical theology from the University of Saint Michael's College, Toronto. His publications include *American and Catholic: Stories of the People Who Built the Church* (2015) as well as numerous journal articles on the antebellum Church and slavery.

Emilie Gagnet Leumas

Emilie Gagnet Leumas, a consultant in archives and records management, is an adjunct professor at Louisiana State University's School of Library and Information Science. She is past director of archives and records at the Archdiocese of New Orleans. She coauthored *Speaking French in Louisiana, 1720-1955: Linguistic Practices of the Catholic Church* (2018); *Managing Diocesan Archives and Records: A Guide for Bishops, Chancellors, and Archivists* (2012); and *Roots of Faith: History of the Diocese of Baton Rouge* (2009). She was inducted as a Fellow of the Society of American Archivists in 2022.

John F. Quinn

John F. Quinn is professor of history at Salve Regina University, Newport, Rhode Island. He holds a doctorate from the University of Notre Dame. His published research includes numerous journal articles on abolitionism, slavery, ethnicity, and nineteenth-century social questions. He is also the author of *Father Mathew's Crusade: Temperance in Nineteenth-Century Ireland and Irish America* (2002).

Kelly L. Schmidt

Kelly L. Schmidt is a postdoctoral research associate for the WashU & Slavery Project at Washington University in St. Louis, Missouri, affiliated with the African and African-American Studies Department and the Center for the Study of Race, Ethnicity, and Equity. She is the former research coordinator of the Slavery, History, Memory, and Reconciliation Project, an initiative of the Jesuit Conference of Canada and the United States in partnership with Saint Louis University. She holds a doctorate in U.S. and public history from Loyola University Chicago. Her research and writing has focused on the experiences of people enslaved to members of the Catholic Church and the moral implications of Catholic slaveholding.

Ronald LaMarr Sharps

Ronald LaMarr Sharps is an associate dean of the College of the Arts at Montclair State University (New Jersey). He earned a doctoral degree in American studies from George Washington University and has taught courses in American history, art history, and arts management. He contributed to the *Black Catholic Studies Reader: History and Theology* (2021).

A National Legacy of Enslavement: Jesuits and Enslaved Persons

KELLY L. SCHMIDT*

THREE COUPLES, THOMAS (ca. 1780s–bet. 1833 and 1852) and Mary (called Polly or Molly, ca. 1781–1852) Brown; Isaac (ca. 1798–1864) and Susanna (called Succy or Susan, ca. 1800–1850) Queen-Hawkins; and Moses (ca. 1777–1862) and Nancy (ca. 1770s–bef. 1865) Queen, huddled together in a flatboat that at times drifted and at other moments careened down the Ohio River in May 1823.[1] They had already walked on foot for a month as the "rearguard" of a hierarchically arranged band of twelve Jesuit priests, novices, and brothers while crossing the approximately 273-mile mountainous terrain of the Cumberland Road from the Jesuits' White Marsh plantation in Maryland to Wheeling, Virginia. They drove heavy wagons laden with the goods with which the Jesuits intended to found a new mission in the West. When the party reached the Ohio River, their enslaver, Father Charles Van Quickenborne (1788–1837), hoping to spare the expense of taking a steamboat, ordered that two flatboats be lashed together by a double cord. Most could not swim, and none

---

* This essay was originally published as "A National Legacy of Enslavement: An Overview of the Work of the Slavery, History, Memory, and Reconciliation Project," *Journal of Jesuit Studies* 8, no. 1 (2021): 81-107. Reprinted with permission.

1 Tom, Mary, Moses, and Nancy were in their forties. Isaac and Susan were in their twenties. Gilbert J. Garraghan, S.J., *The Jesuits of the Middle United States* (Chicago: Loyola University Press, 1938), 84–85; Peter De Meyer, "Reminiscences of Pioneer Life," 1868, box 2.0013, folder 4, General Governance Collection MIS.2.001, Jesuit Archives and Research Center, St. Louis, Missouri (hereafter JARC); Felix Verreydt, "Memoirs," ca. 1870, Felix Verreydt Personnel file, JARC; Walter Hill, "Historical Sketches by Walter Hill, SJ," n.d., Walter Hill Personnel files, JARC; Peter Verhaegen, "History of the Missouri Mission of the Society of Jesus," ca. 1840s–1880s, 20, box 2.0013, folder 2, General History Collection, JARC.

knew how to navigate the river. Rather than hire a pilot, Van Quickenborne purchased a river guidebook and commissioned Brother Charles Strahan (b. 1796) to navigate. Cargo themselves, Tom, Molly, Isaac, Succy, Moses, and Nancy sat in one overloaded flatboat separated by a small partition wall from four horses and the baggage, while the Jesuits shared the other boat. The three couples clung to one another as the boats snagged on driftwood and were caught in trees. Isaac frequently came to the Jesuits' aid in rowing the group out of trouble when the boats drifted out of the current, especially at night.[2] On one occasion, the small flotilla nearly collided with a passing steamboat.[3] "A clamor arose from the slaves; all jumped out of bed awoken by the rapid striking together of the beams and strongly agitated by the dim of the horses," Jesuit Felix Verreydt (1798–1883), one of the novices on the journey, later reflected. All hurried to save their own lives, until the calamity passed.[4]

On less eventful days, the enslaved passengers and their Jesuit enslavers saw little of one another, since a partition wall divided the two boats. Though he could not see them, Verreydt assumed, "As they were good people, I do not doubt, they were saying their beads in a corner of their boat."[5] Some of what Jesuits such as Verreydt thought is known because they wrote it down. The thoughts of the enslaved people were not recorded, but it can be surmised that as they prepared meals for their enslavers and assisted in navigation, the three couples prayed, yearned for the family and community they left behind, and worried about the unknown future before them. Moses and Nancy grieved over their separation from their children, who remained in Maryland.[6] Isaac and Susan, newlyweds, wondered what it would be like to start a new family in an unfamiliar region far from their kin who remained in Mary-

---

2 Verhaegen, "History of the Missouri Mission." Verreydt writes, "One boat was laden with all our moveables, four horses were staked in it [. . .]. Beside this heavy load, that did almost far to out balance our boat, were the six colored people, making a pretty heavy load by themselves."
3 Verhaegen, "History of the Missouri Mission," 23.
4 Verhaegen, "History of the Missouri Mission."
5 Verreydt, "Memoirs."
6 Hill, "Historical Sketches by Walter Hill, SJ," 23.

land.[7] All had left behind close relatives, including brothers and sisters.[8] None knew whether they would ever see their families again. They must have dreamed of the freedom that was so close, on the northern bank of the river they traversed. Once settled for several years at their destination in Missouri, Verreydt commented, "We heard sometimes their earnest desire to be free in a free country, it was difficult not to say almost impossible to convince them of their happiness."[9]

Jesuit historians have long known that Jesuits brought with them six enslaved people from their White Marsh plantation in Maryland to their new novitiate and missionary headquarters in Missouri in 1823. When Louis William Valentine DuBourg (1766–1883), bishop of Upper Louisiana and the Two Floridas, requested in 1823 that the Maryland Jesuits come to Missouri to establish a novitiate and farm in Florissant, he stipulated that they bring with them "at least four or five or six negroes, to be employed in preparing & providing the additional Buildings, that may be found necessary, and in cultivating the land of the above mentioned Farm."[10] In response, on April 10, 1823, the Corporation of Roman Catholic Clergymen of Maryland (the Society of Jesus in Maryland) transferred to Van Quickenborne, "Tom & Polly his wife, Moises & Nancy his wife, Isaac & Succy his wife all of whom are the property of the above Corporation, with permission to transport them into the State of Missouri and there employ them in his service."[11]

---

7 "Register of Baptisms, White Marsh," Maryland Province Archives, Georgetown University, Washington, D.C. (hereafter MPA).

8 Father James Van de Velde wrote that the enslaved people sold from Georgetown to Louisiana in 1838 "have near relations, brothers, sisters &c at Florissant." James Van de Velde to Thomas Mulledy, March 28, 1848, MPA (Georgetown Slavery Archive, https://slaveryarchive.georgetown.edu/items/show/3); Hill, "Historical Sketches."

9 Verreydt, "Memoirs."

10 Concordat regarding the Missouri Mission between Charles Neal and William DuBourg, handwritten duplicates, ca. 1823, 1886, box 2.0021, folder 1, General Governance Collection, MIS.2.001, JARC; Maryland Provincial's Instructions to Charles Felix Van Quickenborne, 1823, box 2.0018, folder 2, General Governance Collection, MIS.2.0018, JARC.

11 Transfer of Slaves by Corporation of Roman Catholic Clergymen of Maryland to Father Charles Felix Van Quickenborne, Contract, April 10, 1823, box 2.0018, folder 1, General Governance Collection, MIS.2.001, JARC.

Yet, while more contemporary Jesuits have been aware of the presence of slavery in its Midwestern and Southern missions, few have given it much attention. Nor has this history been widely known beyond the Jesuits. The Slavery, History, Memory, and Reconciliation (SHMR) Project acknowledges records the Jesuits left behind about their slaveholding, and pushes beyond them, aiming to more thoroughly uncover and understand the lived experiences of the people held in slavery to the Jesuits. The project began as a joint initiative of the Jesuits USA Central and Southern Province and Saint Louis University in 2016 and has since grown into a national effort supported by the Jesuit Conference of Canada and the United States. Jesuits have recognized the need to understand and share more fully their history of slaveholding throughout the United States. Thus, this essay offers an overview of the lesser-known lives of people whose enslavement sustained the Jesuits beyond Maryland and Pennsylvania. At present, it has been determined that nineteenth-century Jesuits owned, rented, and borrowed more than 189 individuals in their Missouri, Kentucky, Louisiana, Alabama, and Kansas missions. That number grows, sometimes daily, as the investigation progresses. Through historical and genealogical research, the project also works to connect with living descendants of people the Jesuits held in slavery so that they can lead the Jesuits toward a path forward in acknowledging historical harms, repairing relationships, and working within communities to address the legacies of slavery that persist in the form of racial inequities today.

Slavery was a total institution; it did not operate in isolation. Jesuit slaveholding was interconnected across parishes, missions, and schools throughout the nineteenth-century United States. Enslaved people were borrowed from and loaned to other religious orders, diocesan bishops and clergy, lay people, and non-Catholics. Jesuit institutions relied on other institutions, like contractors, banks, and benefactors, that benefited from enslaved labor. In this way, Jesuits were no different from their contemporaries: they were participants in local, national, and global systems of slavery that were—that are—inextricably bound to the origin story of the United States and tied to the participation of the Society of Jesus and the Catholic Church in slavery and the slave trade worldwide. Parishes, schools, and other works of the Catholic Church and its members share in this complicity of slaveholding. Likewise, the legacies of enslavement endure: just as descendant communities continue to be affected by slavery's consequential structural racism, so too have Jesuit institutions continued to benefit.

The first step toward reconciliation in a Catholic context is confession and acknowledgement of one's sins, so the project has begun by sharing its findings, as Jesuits express their remorse. When the project began, all that was known were the first names of about eight individuals in Missouri. Now it is known that the Jesuits owned, rented, or borrowed closer to two hundred people, in what is now the Central and Southern United States. Moreover, researchers have identified surnames for most of the enslaved people held by the Jesuits in these regions, which assists in efforts to connect with descendants of the enslaved today. The project's findings have been shared with descendants and the public, including the website: https://www.jesuits.org/our-work/shmr/ and on social media (@SHMRJesuits) on Facebook, Instagram, and Twitter. The project has advanced through contact with descendants who have shared their stories and contributed to efforts to address the legacies of slavery present today.

Project Findings

Enslaved people supported the growth of the Jesuit order in the expanding United States. They were at the heart of the running of the Jesuits' parishes, their missions to Native Americans and European-American settlers, as well as the development of their institutions of higher learning, including those established in the North. Although the Jesuits had established regulations intended to ensure more humane treatment of enslaved people, these regulations had more to do with conforming Jesuit slaveholding to Catholic teaching and moral law and justifying holding people in bondage as a means to lead them to salvation. In reality, the experiences of people enslaved to the Jesuits hardly differed from those of other bondspeople, because the Jesuits were no different in how they treated enslaved people than other enslavers. Jesuits frequently broke their own regulations about physically punishing bondspeople, splitting up families, and providing basic necessities such as adequate food and shelter.

Nevertheless, although the Jesuits attempted to dictate enslaved people's lives, they did not fully control the boundaries of these enslaved communities; enslaved people interacted with fellow bondspeople and other settlers and Indigenous people around them, establishing roots in each area that endured even after they became free. Enslaved people used these networks to survive, surmount, and resist their enslavement. The Catholicism many bondspeople practiced, often inherited from previous generations who had the faith imposed on them from clergy enslavers, did not result in blind adherence to Jesuit enslavers, as some scholars have argued. Instead, enslaved people used their conceptions of their faith, as well as their enslavers' understanding of Catholicism, to resist their enslavement and to build and protect their families and kin communities.[12]

Thomas and Molly Brown, Moses and Nancy Queen, and Isaac and Susan Queen-Hawkins were six of the thousands of people the Jesuits held in slavery globally over the course of their history. Their forced journey to Missouri extended the presence of Jesuit slaveholding beyond Maryland, bringing it back to a region where the Jesuits had held people in bondage previously. Prior to the Jesuits' suppression, English Jesuits relied on indentured and enslaved labor in Maryland and Pennsylvania at sites including White Marsh, Fingale, Saint Thomas, Port Tobacco, Newtown, Saint Inigos, Saint Joseph, Bohemia, Tuckahoe, Deer Creek, Queenstown, Conewago, and Goshenhoppen beginning in the seventeenth century.[13] French Jesuits

---

12   Randall M. Miller, "The Failed Mission: The Catholic Church and Black Catholics in the Old South," in *Catholics in the Old South: Essays on Church and Culture* (Macon, GA: Mercer University Press, 1999). For more on how enslaved people owned by the Jesuits in Missouri may have regarded their faith, and used religious services and the sacraments to solidify and protect kin communities, see Kelly L. Schmidt, "Enslaved Faith Communities in the Jesuits' Missouri Mission," *U.S. Catholic Historian* 37, no. 2 (Spring 2019): 49–82.

13   Nicholas P. Cushner, *Soldiers of God: The Jesuits in Colonial America, 1565–1767* (Buffalo, NY: Language Communications, 2002), 147. See Sharon M. Leon, "Life and Labor under Slavery: The Jesuit Plantation Project," https://jesuitplantationproject.org/s/jpp/page/welcome; Edward F. Beckett, *Listening to Our History: Inculturation and Jesuit Slaveholding* (St. Louis, MO: Seminar on Jesuit Spirituality, 1996); Robert Emmett Curran, *The Bicentennial History of Georgetown*

had exploited enslaved labor most extensively on cash crop plantations in the Caribbean, but also relied on enslaved people in Canada and the Great Lakes region, and on plantations in what are now Kaskaskia, Illinois, and New Orleans, Louisiana. French Jesuits became among the largest enslavers on the sugar island of Martinique, and were influential in shaping the *Code Noir*, the Black Codes that dictated enslaved lives in the French colonies.[14] In 1727, they also forced bondspeople from their plantations in Saint-Domingue to their newfound New Orleans plantation to cultivate sugarcane, figs, oranges, and other crops that would supply the Jesuits funds to expand their missionary efforts toward Native Americans as well as their educational institutions in colonial North America. The Jesuits in Louisiana held an estimated 140 people in slavery on their New Orleans plantations at the time of their suppression in 1763. They also forcibly conveyed forty-eight of the people they held in enslavement in Kaskaskia on a treacherous journey to New Orleans in response to the royal decree of their expulsion. Adults and children, among them Ursula, Stanislaus, Borgia, Joachim, Rosalie, Jerome, Cyprian, Christopher, Bazile, Chrysostom, and Gabriel, were auctioned away.[15]

University (Washington, DC: Georgetown University Press, 1993); Thomas Murphy, *Jesuit Slaveholding in Maryland, 1717–1838* (New York: Routledge, 2001); Robert Emmett Curran, "Peter Kenney: Twice Visitor of the Maryland Mission (1819–21, 1830–33) and Father of the First Two American Provinces," in *With Eyes and Ears Open: The Role of Visitors in the Society of Jesus*, ed. Thomas M. McCoog, Jesuit Studies 21 (Leiden: Brill, 2019), 191–213, here 205.

14   Robert W. Harms, *The Diligent: A Voyage through the Worlds of the Slave Trade* (New York: Basic Books, 2002), 24–28.

15   Albert Hubert Biever, *The Jesuits in New Orleans and the Mississippi Valley: Jubilee Memorial* (New Orleans: Society of Jesus in Louisiana, 1924), 35–36; Reuben Gold Thwaites, ed., *The Jesuit Relations and Allied Documents: Travels and Explorations of the Jesuit Missionaries in New France, 1610–1791* (Cleveland: Burrows Bros., 1900), 70: 243–425; "Expulsion of the Jesuits from Louisiana in 1763," *Woodstock Letters* 6 (1877): 19–24; Roger Baudier, *The Catholic Church in Louisiana* (New Orleans: n.p., 1939): 164–165; Stephan Lenik, "Mission Plantations, Space, and Social Control: Jesuits as Planters in French Caribbean Colonies and Frontiers," *Journal of Social Archaeology* 12, no. 1 (February 1, 2012): 51–71; Eric Hinderaker, *Elusive Empires: Constructing Colonialism in the Ohio Valley, 1673–1800* (New York: Cambridge University Press, 1999), 98.

The Society of Jesus participated extensively in slaveholding and the slave trade globally, almost since the order's founding, and remained involved until slavery's abolition as it occurred in different parts of the world. Early Jesuits, including co-founders Ignatius Loyola (ca. 1491–1556) and Diego Laínez (1512–1565), discussed the use of enslaved labor in India and Japan. Simão Rodrigues (1510–1579), Francis Xavier (1506–1552), Matteo Ricci (1552–1610), and many other Jesuits relied on Indigenous and African enslaved people in Portugal, India, Japan, and China. Jesuits were extensively involved in the slave trade in Angola, as elsewhere, and enslaved 5,100 people on their estates in Mozambique. Jesuits were especially large enslavers in the Caribbean and South America, and even when they did not directly hold people in slavery, collaborated with European governments in expanding slavery in their colonial missions.[16] As such, all Jesuits and their

---

16 The following citations are a selection of the plentiful scholarship on Jesuit slaveholding globally: Rômulo da Silva Ehalt, "Jesuit Arguments for Voluntary Slavery in Japan and Brazil," *Revista brasileira de história* 39, no. 80 (April 2019): 87–107, here 7; Dauril Alden, "Those Who Also Served: Bondsmen and Lay Servants," in *The Making of an Enterprise: The Society of Jesus in Portugal, Its Empire, and Beyond: 1540–1750* (Stanford, CA: Stanford University Press, 1996), 502–527; letter from Francis Xavier to Gaspar Barzeas, October 25, 1552, M. Costelloe, trans., published in M. Joseph Costelloe, *The Letters and Instructions of Francis Xavier* (St. Louis, MO: Institute of Jesuit Sources, 1992), 445–447; Matteo Ricci, *Della entrata della Compagnia di Giesù e Christianità nella Cina*, ed. Piero Corradini and Maddalena del Gatto, trans. Nicholas Lewis and Philip Gavitt (Macerata: Quodlibet, 2000); Festo Mkenda, "Jesuits and Africa," *Oxford Handbooks Online*, August 3, 2016, https://doi.org/10.1093/oxfordhb/9780199935 420.013.56; Festo Mkenda, "Jesuit Historiography in Africa," *Jesuit Historiography Online*, ed. Robert A. Maryks, https://referenceworks.brillonline. com/entries/jesuit-historiography-online/jesuit-historiography-in-africa-COM_192529; William Francis Rea, "Agony on the Zambezi: The First Christian Mission to Southern Africa and Its Failure 1580–1759," *Zambezia* 1, no. 2 (1970): 46–53, here 50; Nicholas P. Cushner, "Slave Mortality and Reproduction on Jesuit Haciendas in Colonial Peru," *The Hispanic American Historical Review* 55, no. 2 (1975): 177–199; Brendan J. M. Weaver, "Perspectivas para el desarrollo de una arqueología de la diáspora africana en el Perú: Resultados preliminares del proyecto arqueológico haciendas de Nasca," *Allpanchis* 43, no. 80, 2 (2012): 85–120; Brendan Weaver, "Rethinking the Political Economy of Slavery: The Hacienda Aesthetic at The Jesuit Vineyards of Nasca, Peru," *Post-Medieval Archaeology* 52, no. 1 (2018): 117–133; Yannick Le Roux, Réginald Auger, and Nathalie Cazelles, *Loyola, les jésuites et l'esclavage l'habitation des jésuites de Rémire en Guyane française*

institutions are inheritors of the Jesuit legacy of slaveholding. The pages that follow examine the history of the enslaved people the Jesuits exploited in the Central and Southern United States, to illuminate one piece of this global history of enslavement and its legacies.

The Missouri Mission

The Browns, Queens, and Hawkinses were relieved when their flatboat navigating the Ohio River landed at last in Shawneetown, Illinois, though their relief was fleeting. The conditions they left in Maryland were abysmal, their trip terrifying, and their new, foreign situation promised to be difficult as well.[17] The band of bondspeople and Jesuits walked on foot through Illinois, which had been a free state for fewer than five years, to Saint Louis, where, with the permission of DuBourg, they settled on a farm in Florissant, Missouri, a village northeast of Saint Louis, where the Jesuits named their new novitiate Saint Stanislaus. The Jesuits took the farmhouse, while Tom, Molly, Moses, Nancy, Isaac, and Susan shared a small cabin that also served as the kitchen and washhouse, and had no loft.[18] From this space, the three enslaved couples began to build the Jesuits' missionary outpost in the West. Susan prepared meals, and Molly and Nancy performed domestic work such as sewing and laundering. Moses served as a "jack of all trades," and along with others performed additional labor at night for pay, while Thomas, Isaac, and others hewed logs and stone to build new structures on the farm, and began cultivating the farmland.[19] As they worked the land and attended Mass at the nearby Saint Ferdinand Church, they encountered unfamiliar creole populations of French, Spanish, Native American, and African heritage.

(Québec: Presses de l'Université du Québec, 2009); Sherwin K. Bryant, "Enslaved Rebels, Fugitives, and Litigants: The Resistance Continuum in Colonial Quito," *Colonial Latin American Review* 13, no. 1 (June 1, 2004): 7–46; Herman W. Konrad, *A Jesuit Hacienda in Colonial Mexico: Santa Lucía, 1576–1767* (Stanford, CA: Stanford University Press, 1980).

    17 See Curran, *Bicentennial History of Georgetown University*, 130–131.

    18 Peter De Meyer, "Reminiscences of Pioneer Life," 1868, 25–26; Verreydt, "Memoirs"; Hill, "Historical Sketches," 35–37.

    19 Garraghan, *Jesuits of the Middle United States*, 100; Verreydt, "Memoirs"; Hill, "Historical Sketches," 41.

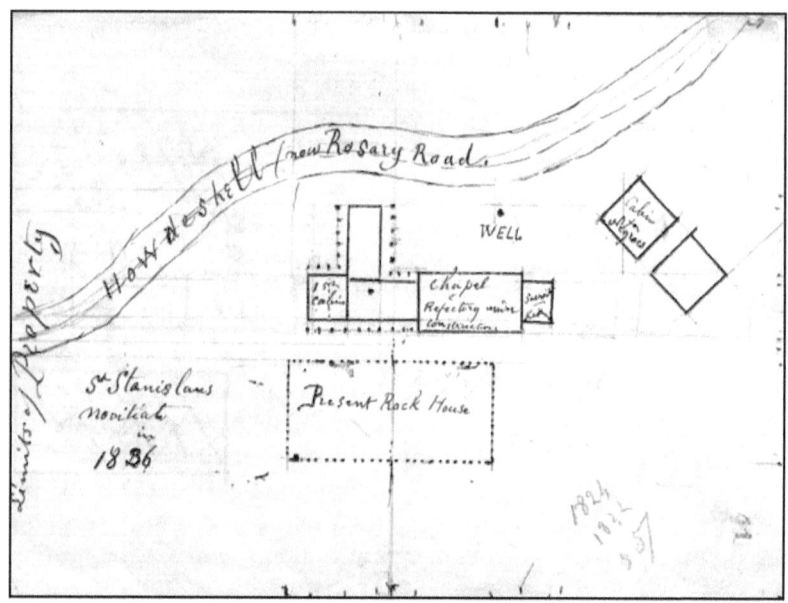

Aerial sketch showing the Jesuits' Saint Stanislaus Seminary in 1836, including the cabin (marked as "cabin for Negroes") where the Brown, Queen, and Hawkins families lived. Their cabin also served as the seminary's kitchen and washhouse for many years because the Jesuit superior neglected the construction of new facilities (Jesuit Archives and Research Center, St. Louis, Missouri).

Over time, their community grew, by birth, marriage, purchase, and the arrival of more families from Maryland. Moses and Nancy Queen, Isaac and Susan Queen-Hawkins, and Thomas and Molly Brown rejoiced when reunited with relatives in 1829, when Van Quickenborne personally conveyed two families, Proteus (ca. 1750s–1869) and Anny (unknown–1841) Queen-Hawkins, and Jack (unknown–1850) and Sally (ca. 1797–1857) Queen, and the children of both couples—about sixteen to twenty people total—from White Marsh to Florissant.[20] Although overjoyed at their

---

20 Jesuits recorded Proteus Hawkins to be between 100 and 120 years of age at his death, based on Proteus's own claims about his age and that he was "a ploughboy" during the American Revolution. Verreydt, "Memoirs"; Garraghan, *Jesuits of the Middle United States*, 613; Joseph Zwinge, "Jesuit Farms

reunion, their arrival evoked a mixture of other emotions: while the Queens and Hawkinses were related to most of the first six enslaved people who had helped found the mission in Missouri, their reunion was bittersweet because it also meant separation from brothers, sisters, and other family in Maryland, many of whom were among the more than 272 enslaved people sold by the Jesuits of the Maryland Province in 1838 to pay off growing debts.[21] Moses and Isaac, among others, frequently requested to go home to see their loved ones, but most were never to see their families again.[22]

By 1829, when the Missouri Jesuits took over operation of Saint Louis College (which became a university in 1832) in downtown Saint Louis, they enslaved at least twenty-six people. By 1830, about six people, including Thomas and Molly Brown, had been sent to work at the new college, while most remained on the Jesuits' seminary and farm in Florissant to support the school and local Jesuit parishes. A few bondspeople labored at Saint Ferdinand Parish in Florissant, and Saint Charles Borromeo Parish in Saint Charles, Missouri. A few others involuntarily joined the Jesuits on missionary ventures to Portage des Sioux, Missouri, and to Potawatomi missions in Sugar Creek, Kansas.[23]

The Jesuits also shared enslaved people with local enslavers, Catholic bishops and clergy, and the Sisters of the Sacred Heart and

---

in Maryland: Facts and Anecdotes, the Negro Slaves," *Woodstock Letters* 41 (1912): 276–291; Hill, "Historical Sketches," 51.

21 There were also smaller sales that may have broken up their families. Van de Velde to Mulledy, March 28, 1848.

22 Charles Van Quickenborne to unidentified, October 11, 1826, Maryland State Archives film about Missouri Mission/Province (hereafter MSA), MSA M 1320, JARC; Charles Van Quickenborne to Francis Dzierozynski, November 17, 1828, MSA M 1320, JARC; Charles Van Quickenborne to Francis Dzierozynski, November 24, 1828, MSA M 1320, JARC.

23 Missouri Mission Varia, box 2.0157, item 2, Office of the Treasurer Collection, unprocessed collection, JARC; 1830 United States Federal Census for St. Louis, St. Louis, Missouri, M19, roll 72, Records of the Bureau of the Census, Record Group 29, National Archives and Records Administration (hereafter NARA), Washington, D.C., 336; "Tertius Liber Archivii Domus Probationis Sti. Stanislai Missionis S.J. Missourianae," 1832–73, box 3.0148, vol. 3, Saint Stanislaus Seminary Collection, MIS.3.008, JARC; Verreydt, "Memoirs."

Sisters of Loretto, among other religious orders.[24] One such individual was Charles Nesbit (ca. 1791–unknown), whom Saint Louis bishop Joseph Rosati (1789–1843) considered his property. Nesbit had been sent to paint, whitewash, and plaster the convent of the Sisters of Saint Joseph of Cahokia, Illinois, and sued Rosati for his freedom. Soon after, Rosati made Jesuit Missouri Vice-Provincial Peter Verhaegen (1800–1868) administrator of his estate, including the people he held in slavery, while he was abroad. Thus, Charles refiled the suit naming Verhaegen as the defendant, claiming Verhaegen had assaulted and falsely imprisoned him "with force and arms."[25] Another was Edmund (ca. 1810–aft. 1844), whom the Religious of the Sacred Heart and the Jesuits brought with them to Sugar Creek, where Edmund assisted with the construction of buildings and taught the Potawatomi farming and carpentry.[26] Because the Missouri Compromise of 1820 had outlawed slavery in the Louisiana Territory west of Missouri north of the 36° 30′ latitude line, Edmund was legally free after both orders brought him to labor in Kansas. One of the sisters remarked, "Edmund showed the Indians where to put the gate in the center of the fence around the cemetery. I don't tell him he's free in Kansas, even though he would probably stay. I am being very careful not to let him learn that he is free here, for even though he is content and perhaps too pious to take advantage of [his free

---

24 The Society of the Sacred Heart and the Sisters of Loretto, among other orders of women religious, have both been involved in projects to investigate their slaveholding. See "Our History of Slaveholding," https://rscj.org/history-slaveholding; "Motherhouse History," *Loretto Community*, https://www.lorettocommunity.org/about/history/motherhouse-history/. The involvement of women religious and slaveholding has received attention in the *New York Times*: Rachel L. Swarns, "The Nuns Who Bought and Sold Human Beings," August 2, 2019, https://www.nytimes.com/2019/08/02/opinion/sunday/nuns-slavery.html.

25 "Charles, a man of color, vs. Peter Verhaegen," 1840, 1841, case files 203 and 75, St. Louis Circuit Court Records, Missouri State Archives-St. Louis.

26 Garraghan, *Jesuits of the Middle United States*, 205–207; Lucille Mathevon, "Commencement de la Mission Indienne par les Religieuses du Sacré Coeur partie de St. Louis le 29 juin 1841," Archives of the United States-Canada Province of the Society of the Sacred Heart (hereafter RSCJ); Catherine de Tardieu, "Journal Sacred Heart Convent. St Mary's. Kan." (1872), RSCJ; Verreydt, "Memoirs."

status], he is nonetheless more certain (if that is possible) to leave it alone, if he remains ignorant of it."[27] Meanwhile, back at the novitiate, bondspeople labored alongside Native American boys at the Jesuits' Saint Regis Indian School, both groups suffering beatings at the hands of the Jesuits when their labor did not meet Superior Van Quickenborne's expectations.[28]

Bondspeople continued to endure physical punishment, arduous labor, and poor housing conditions. Edmund's unstable cabin was susceptible to whirlwinds and almost destroyed by a tornado. Wood for new cabins at the Florissant novitiate lay rotting in a field.[29] At Saint Louis University, Thomas Brown remarked in 1833 that the shelter provided by the Jesuit rector Peter Verhaegen for himself and his wife, Molly, was so poor that Brown had "not a doubt but cold will kill both me and my wife here." Advocating that "I have been a faithful servant in the Society going on 38 years, & my wife, Molly, has been born & raised in the Society, She is Now about 52 years of Age," Brown lamented, "Now we have not a place to lay our heads in our old age after all our Service."[30]

Although the Jesuits mistreated them, the people they enslaved were resilient. Bondspeople in Missouri frequently resisted their enslavement, and several sought to obtain their freedom. Members of the Brown, Hawkins, and Queen families in Missouri were part of a larger extended family experienced at pursuing their freedom. They descended from a network of active freedom-seekers who sued for their freedom in the courts of Washington, D.C.[31] Several sustained this agency in Missouri.

---

27 Mathevon, "Commencement de la Mission Indienne par les Religieuses du Sacré Coeur partie de St. Louis le 29 juin 1841"; De Tardieu, "Journal Sacred Heart Convent. St Mary's. Kan."

28 Garraghan, *Jesuits of the Middle United States*, 147–169; Pierre-Jean De Smet to Peter Verhaegen, Florissant, June 11, 1830, MSA M 1320, JARC.

29 Verreydt, "Memoirs"; *Miss.*, 1001-IV, fols. 215r–217r, trans. Timothy Kieras, Archivum Romanum Societatis Iesu (hereafter ARSI).

30 Thomas Brown, October 21, 1833, MPA.

31 For more on the freedom suits of the Queen, Hawkins, and Brown families, see William G. Thomas, III, et al., "Queen Family Network," *O Say Can You See: Early Washington, D.C., Law & Family*, University of Nebraska-Lincoln, http://earlywashingtondc.org/families/queen.

When Thomas Brown wrote his letter regarding his and Molly's inadequate housing conditions, he petitioned Jesuit leadership in Maryland to allow him to buy their freedom for one hundred dollars, "as much as I can raise, & as much as our old bones are worth."[32] Another bondsman, Peter Queen-Hawkins (1824–ca. 1907), had made an arrangement with the Jesuits to purchase the freedom of himself and his wife, Margaret (ca. 1839–ca. 1869). Saint Louis University had purchased Margaret in 1862 from Charles G. McHatton (1811–1895) for $800 at Peter's request as a reward for being "the best slave." In allowing Peter to buy their freedom, the Jesuits stipulated that Peter must pay back Margaret's purchase price. In 1864, Peter complained that what the Jesuits were asking of him was too difficult to achieve. The Jesuits, in turn, grumbled that other bondspeople must have influenced Peter to be so dissatisfied. However, they agreed that Peter and Margaret either take their furnishings and go live as free people, sending back the remaining $400 owed on Margaret's purchase as they earned it, or the couple could remain for two more years and pay off the cost with their labor. Peter and Margaret chose to stay. When the Jesuits decided to make contracts for the hired labor of four remaining families who had become free with Missouri's abolition of slavery in January 1865, Peter and Margaret were among them, but did not receive pay until April 1867, effectively held in a state of debt peonage.[33] In 1866, Peter had requested that the Jesuits grant him a ten-acre plot of their land in Florissant for his own use, but the Jesuits denied it to him, deeming that it was inefficient. Nevertheless, Peter remained with the Jesuits in Florissant until close to the time of his death around 1907.[34]

---

32   Thomas, "Queen Family Network."
33   "Day book for the House and Farm," 1855–65, box 3.0144, folder 1, Saint Stanislaus Seminary Collection, MIS.3.008, JARC.
34   "Consultors Meeting Minutes for the Missouri Vice Province" (1832), Missouri Province Collection, unprocessed collection, JARC; "Bill of Sale for Margaret," December 26, 1862, box 3.0223, folder 7–Slavery 1850, 1862, 1872, Saint Louis University Collection, MIS 3.002, JARC; Status Temporalis St. Louis, St. Joseph College, and St. Francis Xavier College, 1855–6, folder D, vol. 6, 404–406, JARC; William J. Grace, "Photographs of Brother Peter, in Album 25, Scrapbook by William J. Grace, S.J.," 1905, box 2.0125,

Peter Queen-Hawkins, pictured here ca. 1905, was the first enslaved person born at the Saint Stanislaus Seminary and the last of formerly enslaved people to remain on the property, despite his efforts to purchase his freedom and the freedom of his wife, Margaret (Jesuit Archives and Research Center, St. Louis, Missouri).

Saint Mary's College, Lebanon, Kentucky

As the Missouri mission expanded into a vice-province in 1840 and a province in 1863, so too grew its slaveholding. In addition, French Jesuits had begun reestablishing their presence as missionaries in the United States, also supported by enslaved labor. In 1831, French Jesuits from Lyon accepted an offer from the bishop in Bardstown, Kentucky, to take over Saint Mary's College from the diocese. There, they relied upon enslaved labor to support the college, until its leadership left to take over

---

Missouri Province Scrapbook Collection, JARC; 1870 United States Federal Census for Saint Ferdinand, Saint Louis, Missouri, M593, roll 809, NARA, Washington, D.C., 265B; Baptisms, living Rosary, Rosary Sorority, Apostleship of Prayer, and Sacred Heart Devotion record book, 1864–1871, box 3.0148, folder 12, Saint Stanislaus Seminary Collection, MIS.3.008, JARC.

Fordham University (then Saint John's College) in New York in 1846, and from there, founded the Canada Province.[35]

The enslaved laborers at Saint Mary's College regularly worked alongside the college's students. The Jesuits prided themselves on the work ethic of their students, for whom it had been a rule since Saint Mary's founding to support the cash-strapped college with manual labor once a week, "to work upon the college farm in plowing, driving teams, chopping and sawing wood, assisting in harvesting and engaging in any other species of manual labor incident to life upon the farm."[36] Enslaved laborers, however, continued to do the bulk of the work. Seventeen enslaved people supported the college as farm laborers and domestics according to the 1840 census.[37] Bondspeople and students hewed trees to make fences and pens, raised cattle and horses, and tended to the cornfields.[38] Bondspeople also supplied Jesuits and students with their meals. Writing of Saint Mary's College in 1843, Michael Nash, S.J. (1825–1895), commented, "Hog killing time was a feature of every year. During this time our negro cooks gave us fine specimens of their culinary skill. They served us pork in every style, together with the inevitable, but always relished 'Corn-dodger'; and we grew healthy and contented on the plain but abundant fare."[39] In 1838, the Jesuits expanded the college farm with the purchase of a neighboring farm.[40] Enslaved people held by enslavers in the area attended Saint Charles Church, near Saint Mary's College, with their enslavers.[41] The people the Jesuits enslaved likely took these Sunday opportunities to intermingle with neighboring bondspeople, as they also did in Missouri and Louisiana.

---

35 "Kentucky: Lebanon, St. Mary's College," n.d., Missouri 3.0111, JARC.
36 "Kentucky: Lebanon, St. Mary's College."
37 Sixth Census of the United States, 1840, for Marion, Kentucky, M704, roll 118, NARA, Washington, D.C, 343.
38 Augustus J. Thebaud, *Forty Years in the United States of America (1839–1885)* (New York: The United States Catholic Historical Society, 1904), 72.
39 Michael Nash, "Reminiscences of Father Michael Nash," *Woodstock Letters* 26, no. 2 (1897): 257–286, here 263.
40 "Kentucky: Lebanon, St. Mary's College."
41 Thebaud, *Forty Years*, 90.

On July 4, 1839, Saint Mary's College hosted an Independence Day celebration. Bondspeople worked under the direction of a few white carpenters to construct a spacious stage in a shady grove of trees big enough for all the members of the county to gather, using their labor to create a space where white attendees could leisurely enjoy presentations on American freedom, while the enslaved people served them food and drink. The irony was likely not lost on the enslaved people present. There, beginning at ten in the morning, the students paraded, gave speeches, performed dramatic acts, and sang patriotic songs. As a student commenced the event with a reading of the Declaration of Independence to the crowd of hundreds, Jesuit Augustus Thebaud (1807–1885) observed "a great number of jolly negroes, who had come with their masters and mistresses, stood on the extreme limits of the assemblage and attentively listened to the reading."[42] He commented that he

> could not distinguish on their faces the effect produced on them when the words of Thomas Jefferson were read declaring that *man* has inalienable rights, and among them life, liberty, and the pursuit of happiness. But it is very probable that they drew no conclusions from those words as to their own rights. They appeared to be very happy, and when called on to bring refreshments to their masters they were not too closely watched nor prevented from taking their share of them.[43]

Thebaud assumed the enslaved people were ignorant, denying their intelligence and cultural acuity. However, the enslaved attendants likely did hear this language about freedom and discussed what this rhetoric of freedom meant for them with one another, even if they did not let their sentiments show on their countenances to the white enslavers present. While it is unknown what they discussed, it is clear that the people enslaved by the Jesuits in each region took steps to resist their enslavement and achieve freedom. Such was the case of Peter Queen at Saint Joseph College in Bardstown.

---

42 Thebaud, *Forty Years*, 141–144.
43 Thebaud, *Forty Years*, 141–144.

Saint Joseph College, Bardstown, Kentucky

Jesuits from the Missouri Vice-Province returned to Kentucky in 1848 to take over Saint Joseph College, where, through their operation of the college until 1864, they relied upon the forced labor of up to twenty enslaved people at any given time. Some the Jesuits owned; others were loaned to them by the diocese and the local bishop and clergy. Some they hired from neighboring lay people, and some were loaned to the Jesuits on behalf of students in payment of their tuition. Jesuit John Baptist Duerinck wrote that "the Black boys sweep the house and mind the boys refectory," and commented that Peter Verhaegen (1800–1868; as president of Saint Louis University, 1829–1836; as president of Saint Joseph's College, 1845–1851) used to grumble and scold the enslaved boys when the college's pigs got into the yard outside his window, and he would call upon one of them to drive them away.[44]

Near the 1850s, the Jesuits also took two enslaved people from their novitiate in Missouri to Bardstown, Kentucky. One of these was a man named Peter Queen. "Big" Peter, as he was called in Jesuit records, had been sold away from his family on the Jesuits' farm in 1830, and was the son of either Proteus and Anny Queen-Hawkins or Jack and Sally Queen, forced with the families from Maryland to Missouri in 1829. Van Quickenborne had sold seventeen-year-old Peter in about 1830 for allegedly having threatened his life, though no other Jesuit had heard the threat. Van Quickenborne's successor, Theodore De Theux, repurchased Peter in 1832 from Louis Barada (1792–1852) of Saint Charles, Missouri, because Peter's grieving and angry parents had never ceased

---

44 John Baptist Duerinck to John Baptist Druyts, September 21, 1848, box 3.011, folder 1, St. Joseph College Collection (hereafter SJC), MIS.3.007, JARC; "Register of Students, 1848–1861," bin 3.0110, SJC, MIS.3.007, JARC; Account Book 1, 1848–52, box 3.0111, SJC, MIS.3.007, JARC; Account Book 2, 1849–54, box 3.0111, SJC, MIS.3.007, JARC; Ledger, 1848–61, box 3.0111, SJC, MIS.3.007, JARC; "St. Joseph's College, Financial Records," 1827–62, Saint Louis University Archives and Special Collections (hereafter SLU); "St. Joseph's College, Financial Records," 1848–56, SLU; "St. Joseph's College Financial Records," 1849–61, SLU.

pressuring De Theux to buy their son back. Parts of Peter's purchase price of $513 had been paid for and secured from donations raised by De Theux's mother in Belgium. Peter labored on the Jesuits' farm, where he met Marian (b. ca. 1827), a woman enslaved to Major Richard Graham (1780–1857), who owned a farm nearby. Peter and Marian married and had three children: Elizabeth (b. 1845), Gabriel (b. 1847), and Thomas William (b. 1849).[45]

In 1849, within the same year of the birth of Peter and Marian's youngest child, the Missouri Jesuits sold Peter away from his kin and made him work at the Jesuits' Saint Joseph College in Bardstown, Kentucky. Forced to leave his wife and children behind, Peter left a small sum of money for Marian to support herself and their three children, the oldest of whom was three years old.[46] The Jesuits claimed that Peter and Marian's "presences greatly harm the other slaves in the house of probation."[47] It is possible that Peter and Marian, discontented with their treatment, were encouraging their kin to resist the Jesuits, and that the Jesuits, feeling threatened, sold Peter away to prevent further unrest. Or, as the Jesuits frequently expressed in letters as a justification for sale, it is also possible Peter and Marian were behaving "immorally," and were, in the Jesuits' view, setting a bad example for other bondspeople. Jesuits had

---

45 Garraghan, *Jesuits of the Middle United States*, 291; Theodore De Theux to his mother, June 16, 1832, De Theux Personnel File, JARC; "Consultors Meeting Minutes for the Missouri Vice Province" (1832), Missouri Province Collection, unprocessed collection, JARC; "Ledger of Saint Stanislaus House, 1840–57," box 3.0146, vol. 1, St. Stanislaus Collection, JARC; Ledger of the Missouri Mission 1836–51, box 2.0147, item 5, Office of the Treasurer Collection, unprocessed collection, JARC; Pierre-Jean De Smet to Peter Verhaegen, May 2, 1830, MSA M 1320, JARC; *Miss.*, 1001-IV, 215-217, ARSI; Louis Barada, "Bill of Sale for Peter," May 1, 1832, box 3.0136, folder 26 "Office of Indian Affairs regarding Saint Francis Indian Seminary, 1819–1832," Saint Stanislaus Collection, JARC; Register of Marriages and Burials, box 3.0373, item 38, St. Ferdinand's Collection in the Missouri Province Collection, unprocessed collection, JARC; "Old St. Ferdinand Records" (St. Ferdinand Parish, 1792–1856), Archdiocese of St. Louis Office of Archives and Records.
46 "Day Book, 1848–1854," box 3.0143, vol. 4, St. Stanislaus Collection, JARC.
47 "Consultors Meeting Minutes for the Missouri Vice Province."

rules against separating enslaved families, but nevertheless they broke up families constantly. In part they did not fully recognize the extent of enslaved family and kin networks. While Jesuits were permitted to sell people who had acted immorally, and used this as justification for many such decisions, they often sold people because they felt threatened, or due to financial need.[48]

A few weeks after Peter Queen's forced arrival in Bardstown, he ran away. Peter's separation from his family and the proximity of freedom in Indiana may have prompted him to take the calculated risk to run. He headed north toward Louisville, likely either to find freedom in Indiana, or reach the Ohio River to make his way back to his family.[49] Verhaegen posted an ad in local papers offering a fifty-dollar reward for Peter "for his apprehension and safe confinement in the Bardstown jail." According to Verhaegen, Peter was "somewhat more polished than a common negro, and his vigorous frame shows that he has been well fed in Missouri." He "speaks fluently and smartly," perhaps evidence of his influence among bondspeople at the Florissant farm.[50] Peter was caught, for on the same day as the publication of this advertisement, the consultors of the Missouri Vice-Province questioned in their minutes, "whether we ought to sell the slave Peter, who ran away and is now spending time in prison [in] (Louisville)." All agreed that "he should be sold." Peter was sold, and we do not know if he and his family ever saw one another again.[51]

About a month later, the consultors, trying to decide what to do with the revenue from Peter's sale, agreed to use the money to purchase an enslaved woman named Mary Hoppins Queen (bef.

---

48 "Tertius Liber," 1832–73; *Miss.*, 1001-1, 39–42, trans. Timothy Kieras, ARSI.

49 On the opportunities and risks involved in escaping slavery in the borderlands, see Matthew Salafia, *Slavery's Borderland: Freedom and Bondage along the Ohio River* (Philadelphia: University of Pennsylvania Press, 2013); R. J. M. Blackett, *The Captive's Quest for Freedom: Fugitive Slaves, the 1850 Fugitive Slave Law, and the Politics of Slavery* (New York: Cambridge University Press, 2018).

50 Peter Verhaegen, "$50 Reward," *The Louisville Daily Courier*, November 13, 1849.

51 "Consultors Meeting Minutes for the Missouri Vice Province."

> **$50 REWARD.**
> RAN AWAY, from St. Joseph's College, a Negro man, called PETER. He is about 32 years of age, 5 feet 3 inches high, wears a long beard, had on when he started, a blue blanket coat and pants of the same color, speaks fluently and smartly. He is somewhat more polished than a common negro, and his vigorous frame shows that he has been well fed in Missouri, whence he just arrived. A reward of $50 will be given for his apprehension and safe confinement in the Bardstown jail. P. J. VERHAEGEN,
> nov10 d3   President of St. Joseph's College.
> [Louisville Daily Courier will give the above three insertions and charge this office. —*Bardstown Visitor.*]

Advertisement offering a reward for the capture of Peter Queen, who sought freedom on foot from Saint Joseph College in Bardstown, Kentucky (*The Louisville Daily Courier*, November 13, 1849).

1830–aft. 1861), who was married to the Jesuits' bondsman Augustine Queen (ca. 1826–1886), but was enslaved to a lay Catholic, to prevent the possibility of the couple being broken apart in the future. In such a way, one man's sale and forced separation from his family ensured the preservation of another family.[52]

Second middle passages like Peter's were common.[53] Another woman, Mary (dates unknown), was forced from family in Missouri to labor in Bardstown in 1850.[54] And in Grand Coteau,

---

52   Mary Hoppins Queen was the widow of Gabriel Queen, who was also held in slavery to the Jesuits. "Consultors Meeting Minutes for the Missouri Vice Province"; "Register of Marriages, 1813–1862; Register of Burials, 1813–1876," box 3.0373, item 38, St. Ferdinand Parish Collection, JARC; "Bill of Sale of Mary," October 28, 1850, box 3.0223, folder 7–Slavery 1850, 1862, 1872, Saint Louis University Collection, MIS 3.002, JARC.

53   In describing Peter's forced journey as a "second middle passage," I employ Ira Berlin's concept of Second Middle Passages, which he uses to describe the forced migrations of the internal slave trade in the United States. Ira Berlin, *Generations of Captivity: A History of African-American Slaves* (Cambridge, MA: Belknap Press of Harvard University Press, 2003), 161–162.

54   "St. Joseph's College Financial Records," 1848–56, SLU.

Louisiana, sales and the stability of families depended upon the health of the Jesuit college.

Saint Charles College, Grand Coteau, Louisiana

Lyon and Missouri Province Jesuits relied upon enslaved labor in Grand Coteau, Louisiana, where they ran Saint Charles College beginning in 1837. They borrowed people held by local enslavers and teachers at the college, as well as from the bishop and the Religious of the Sacred Heart. In 1839, the Jesuits purchased three bondspeople of their own to support the college and the Jesuit community. Jesuits obtained Philodie, about age fifty (ca. 1789–1855), and Rachel (b. ca. 1830), her nine-year-old daughter, from Charles Napoleon Olivier (1811–1858) and later sold them to two different enslavers: Rachel, about fourteen in 1844, to Nicholas Charles Grimmer (1814–1854), music teacher at Saint Charles College, and Philodie to a Mr. Gora (dates unknown) in 1847, in clear disregard of their rules against separating families. The Jesuits also bought Ignatius Gough (ca. 1818–1861), a young man of about twenty-one years of age who had been sold by Stephen H. Gough (a graduate of Georgetown University in 1830, dates unknown) in Maryland when Ignatius was seventeen. Ignatius endured his middle passage to the port of New Orleans packed in a hold alongside 142 other enslaved people on the brig *Isaac Franklin* in 1835.[55]

After his arrival at Saint Charles College, Ignatius Gough met and married a woman named Sally Grayson (ca. 1816–aft. 1900),

---

55 "Fr. Carbery requests a tax deduction for the value of seventeen slaves sold by the Maryland Jesuits, 1836," *Georgetown Slavery Archive*, from MSA, https://slaveryarchive.georgetown.edu/items/show/311; *Slave Manifests of Coastwise Vessels Filed at New Orleans, Louisiana, 1807–1860*, M1895, 30 rolls, Records of the U.S. Customs Service, Record Group 36, NARA, Washington, D.C.; Robert S. Smith, "Bill of Sale of Ignatius Gough," February 13, 1839, New Orleans Province Collection, unprocessed collection, JARC. "Bill of Sale for Philadie and Rachel," September 8, 1848, New Orleans Province Collection, unprocessed collection, JARC; Wendell Holmes Stephenson, *Isaac Franklin: Slave Trader and Planter of the Old South* (Baton Rouge: Louisiana State University Press, 1938), 38; Garraghan, *Jesuits of the Middle United States*, 153–156; "Minister's Diary, St. Charles College"; "Historia Domus" (1837–1942), New Orleans Province Collection, unprocessed collection, JARC.

enslaved to Pierce (1804–1883) and Cornelia Connelly (1809–1879), who taught English, music, and drawing at the college and nearby Academy of the Sacred Heart. Cornelia, who later became foundress of the Society of the Holy Child Jesus, is now considered venerable and a candidate for canonization in the Catholic Church. Ignatius and Sally had nine children together, about six of whom lived to adulthood. After the birth of their first child, James Henry (b. 1840), local sheriffs imprisoned Ignatius Gough for suspected involvement in a plotted slave revolt. According to Pierce Connelly, Gough had been one of the several local enslaved people arrested because a loaded pistol had been "unluckily . . . put in his possession" by a brother running away from the Society, which was "accidentally discovered in his hands."[56] After being incarcerated and interrogated for eight days, Ignatius, deemed innocent, returned to his family in time to see his son's baptism. Thirty others who were hanged were not as fortunate.[57]

It is not known to what extent Ignatius Gough may have been actually involved in plans for widespread resistance among the local enslaved population. Bondspeople near Saint Charles College had previously attempted uprisings, all of which had resulted in their apprehension and extensive court-ordered hangings and vigilante executions. By this point, it was not clear whether white reactions were to a real plot or were the result of mass hysteria. Solomon Northup (1808–1863), however, in describing an enslaved conspiracy that had occurred in the region where Gough lived three years earlier, recounted that he had been part of multiple consultations over the course of his enslavement near Bayou Boeuf about the feasibility of renewed attempts to fight for freedom *en masse*. If the plans were real,

---

56 Connelly to Blanc, September 16, 1840, Archives of the University of Notre Dame, quoted in Garraghan, *Jesuits of the Middle United States*, 146.

57 "Executions in the U.S. 1608–2002: The ESPY File Executions by State" (Death Penalty Information Center, n.d.), https://files.deathpenaltyinfo.org/legacy/documents/ESPYstate.pdf; "A Negro Revolt," *The Times-Picayune*, September 1, 1840; "A Revolt," *The Evening Post*, September 11, 1840; "Insurrection," *Baton-Rouge Gazette*, September 5, 1840; "Minister's Diary, St. Charles College"; "Historia Domus" (1837–1942), New Orleans Province Collection, unprocessed collection, JARC.

Ignatius likely knew of them, regardless of the extent to which he participated. Records show that enslaved communication networks along the nearby Bayou Boeuf spanned seven Louisiana parishes (counties).[58] If he did not participate, Gough may have

---

58 "Insurrection Quelled," *The Evening Post*, October 27, 1837; Acts of the State of Louisiana, March 12, 1838, 118–120; Solomon Northup and David Wilson, *Twelve Years a Slave: Narrative of Solomon Northup, a Citizen of New York, Kidnapped in Washington City in 1841, and Rescued in 1853, from a Cotton Plantation near the Red River, in Louisiana* (Auburn: Derby & Miller, 1853), 248–249; "A Negro Revolt," *The Times-Picayune*, September 1, 1840, 2; "Negro Insurrection in Lafayette," *The Times-Picayune*, September 2, 1840, 2; *New Orleans Commercial Bulletin*, September 3, 1840; "The Contemplated Negro Revolt in the Parish of Lafayette," *Daily Picayune*, September 5, 1840, 2; "A Revolt," *The Evening Post*, September 11, 1840, 2; "The Slave Revolt," *The Evening Post*, September 14, 1840; "A Negro Revolt," *Liberator*, September 18, 1840, 151; "Insurrection," *Niles' Weekly Register*, September 19, 1840; "The Insurgents," *The Times-Picayune*, September 19, 1840, 2; "Fruits of Slavery," *Liberator*, September 25, 1840; "Negroes Executed," *Daily Picayune*, September 30, 1840; "Revolt," *The Evening Post*, September 12, 1840, 2; "Insurrection," *Niles Weekly Register*, October 10, 1840; "A Negro Plot," *The Times-Picayune*, October 30, 1840, 2; "Insurrection," *Niles' National Register*, November 14, 1840, vol. 59, 176; "Summary of News," *Liberator*, November 20, 1840, 187; Albert Biever, *Diary*, New Orleans Province Collection, unprocessed collection, JARC; *The Times-Picayune*, New Orleans, February 5, 1841, 2; "Breaking up a Gang of Negroes," *The Times-Picayune*, October 30, 1846, 2; "Murder," *Liberator*, December 4, 1846, 194; Garraghan, *Jesuits of the Middle United States*, 145–146; Edward D. Reynolds, *Jesuits for the Negro* (New York: America Press, 1949); Charles S. Sydnor, "The Southerner and the Laws," *The Journal of Southern History* 6, no. 1 (1940): 3–23; David Grimsted, *American Mobbing, 1828-1861: Toward Civil War* (New York: Oxford University Press, 1998); G. P. Whittington, "Rapides Parish, Louisiana," *The Louisiana Historical Quarterly* XVI (n.d.); Harvey Wish, "American Slave Insurrections Before 1861," *The Journal of Negro History* 22, no. 3 (1937): 299–320; Herbert Aptheker, *American Negro Slave Revolts* (New York: Columbia University Press, 1943), 325–339; Joseph Cephas Carroll, *Slave Insurrections in the United States* (Boston: Chapman & Grimes, 1938); Junius P. Rodriguez, "Complicity and Deceit: Lewis Cheney's Plot and Its Bloody Consequences," in *Lethal Imagination: Violence and Brutality in American History*, ed. Michael A. Bellesiles (New York: New York University Press, 1999); Terry L. Seip, "Slaves and Free Negroes in Alexandria, 1850–1860," *Louisiana History: The Journal of the Louisiana Historical Association* 10, no. 2 (1969): 147–165; Ulrich Bonnell Phillips, *American Negro Slavery: A Survey of the Supply, Employment and Control of Negro Labor as Determined by the Plantation Regime* (New York: D. Appleton, 1918); Vernie Alton Moody, "Slavery on Louisiana Sugar Plantations" (Ph.D. diss., University of Michigan, 1924).

shared the sentiments of Northup, who voiced the risks inherent in such an uprising: "There have been times when a word from me would have placed hundreds of my fellow-bondsmen in an attitude of defiance. Without arms or ammunition, or even with them, I saw such a step would result in certain defeat, disaster and death, and always raised my voice against it."[59] Perhaps out of concern for the safety of his family, Gough found other ways to resist his enslavement, such as when he slipped away from his expected labors to seek brief respite, and damaged the Jesuits' tools and properties. Ignatius was punished for his actions by spending two Sundays in the local prison on bread and water, just as his stepson, George-Joachim (b. ca. 1836), was when he purportedly defrauded the Jesuits.[60]

The Jesuits' advocacy on Ignatius's behalf may have been motivated by their own fears. Not only may Jesuits have been reluctant to lose valuable property, they were fearful of the consequences they might suffer if Ignatius was indicted. Local planters and law enforcement had imprisoned a handful of white men they believed to be abolitionists who had incited enslaved people to rebellion. They had the men beaten, threatened them with death, and ultimately drove them out of the state. The day after Father Theodore DeLeeuw (1819–1898) went to check on Ignatius in prison, the community's superior received an anonymous letter from Lafayette, stating that the Jesuits were suspected of causing the insurrection. It declared that a volunteer contingent of about seventy-five young men would soon arrive to beat the Jesuits and then encamp themselves on the premises. The letter was apparently one of several that accused the Jesuits of having encouraged unrest, and one of several more from nativist, anti-Catholic Know-Nothings in the area who threatened the Jesuits with death or forced removal from the area. In addition, according to a later account, the Opelousas court had charged the Jesuits with supplying bondspeople with weapons and shaking hands with a Black man. Suspicion was further raised over a Jesuit having heard the confession of a relative of one of the bondspeople who led the plot. The vigilante

---

59 Northup and Wilson, *Twelve Years a Slave*, 239–240.
60 "Minister's Diary, St. Charles College."

Lafayette Volunteers and others threatened to lynch the Jesuits or drive them out of town. Fortunately for the Jesuits, their allies in Grand Coteau armed themselves and came to the Jesuits' defense. Hearing of this, the Lafayette Volunteers and other vigilante patrols stood down. Others, namely the enslaved people implicated and put to death, were not so fortunate.[61] Thus, while the Jesuits' intervention on Ignatius's behalf protected him, it was also likely an attempt to defend themselves, dissociate from targeted abolitionists, and avoid facing the same fate.

In 1842, as Pierce and Cornelia Connelly prepared to leave for Rome so Pierce could join the priesthood, the Connellys sold Sally Gough and her children to the Jesuits. The Gough family labored at Saint Charles College until the school began to falter. At some point between 1851 and 1860, the Jesuits sold the Goughs to Dr. Henry Jackson Millard (1824–1863), after most Jesuit faculty had left to focus their teaching efforts on Saint Joseph's College in Bardstown and Spring Hill College in Alabama.[62]

Inconsistent Attitudes, Common Legacy

Reliance on enslaved labor was fundamental to the operation of Jesuit schools. Moreover, students' access to these schools was defined by the color of their skin. Students of color were not permitted to attend Saint Louis University in the nineteenth century. Three students of color were dismissed from Saint Joseph College for "having been proven to be of mixed blood."[63] Sons of white enslavers and enslaved women from Louisiana

---

61 "Minister's Diary, St. Charles College"; Biever, *Diary*, 79; Reynolds, *Jesuits for the Negro*, 163–164; Connelly to Blanc letter, cited in Garraghan, *Jesuits of the Middle United States*, 145–146.

62 Pierce Connelly, "Bill of Sale of Sally and Children," September 14, 1842, New Orleans Province Collection, unprocessed collection, JARC; "Minister's Diary, St. Charles College"; "Black Baptisms Book 1," 1821–41, St. Charles Borromeo Church, Grand Coteau, Louisiana; U.S. Bureau of the Census, Seventh Census of the United States, 1850, M432, NARA, Washington, D.C.; U.S. Bureau of the Census, Eighth Census of the United States, 1860, M653, NARA, Washington, D.C.

63 "Register of Students, 1848–1861," bin 3.0110, Saint Joseph College Collection, MIS.3.007, JARC.

Sally Grayson Gough and her children joined her husband Ignatius Gough in enslavement to the Jesuits by this bill of sale from their previous enslaver, Pierce Connelly, in September 1842 (Jesuit Archives and Research Center, St. Louis, Missouri).

attended Xavier University in Cincinnati, but when Xavier had to send away its boarding students due to financial distress in 1854, Jesuit William Stack Murphy (1803–1875) wrote that while he could send white students to Saint Louis University and Saint Joseph College,

> Cincinnati located in a state (Ohio) where slavery does not exist and where blacks are better received, several Louisianans sent children of mixed blood there, that is, [they are] more or less mulatto, and almost all illegitimate or born of marriages forbidden by civil law. Bardstown and Saint Louis could not receive them without breaking the law because the laws of Kentucky and Missouri, slave states, oppose it,

and in any case all the white students would withdraw right away. Black and mixed blood finds liberty and equality only in Canada and Spanish America.[64]

Murphy's commentary exemplifies how Jesuits cited the regional laws and attitudes of the populations they sought to serve to excuse the contradictory ways members of the Society regarded and treated people of color in different regions. While willing to educate mixed-race sons of the wealthy Southern Catholic planters who supported their institutions, but only in the North, where it was safer to do so, they rejected students of color in Southern states, where they feared reactions from students and parents, benefactors, and the local community.

Jesuits' efforts to conform to the sentiments of the regions where they operated reflects Superior General Pieter Jan Beckx's decree from Rome in 1861, after the outbreak of the Civil War, that American Jesuits adopt the government and attitudes of the states where they ministered. Some proudly served as Union and Confederate chaplains. In borderlands such as Missouri, Ohio, and Kentucky following prevailing sentiments was more difficult. Murphy ordered Missouri Province Jesuits not to take sides in the conflict, though many did so anyway.[65]

---

64 Miss., 1005-II, fol. 214r, trans. Steven Hawkes-Teeples and Kelly L. Schmidt, ARSI.

65 Garraghan, *Jesuits of the Middle United States*, 147, 152–153, 156–158; Roger Fortin, *To See Great Wonders: A History of Xavier University, 1831-2006* (Scranton: University of Scranton Press, 2006), 58; John T. McGreevy, *Catholicism and American Freedom: A History* (New York: W. W. Norton, 2003), 78, 82; C. Walker Gollar, "Jesuit Education and Slavery in Kentucky, 1832 to 1868," *Register of the Kentucky Historical Society* 108, no. 3 (2010): 611–647, here 639; Letter from Francis X. Weninger, S.J., to Archbishop Purcell, n.d., Midwest Jesuit Archives (from University of Notre Dame Archives: 10807); Raymond H. Schmandt and Josephine H. Schulte, "Civil War Chaplains: A Document From A Jesuit Community," *Records of the American Catholic Historical Society of Philadelphia* 73, no. 1/2 (1962): 58–64; Sean Fabun, "Catholic Chaplains in the Civil War," *The Catholic Historical Review* 99, no. 4 (2013): 675–702; William B. Kurtz, "Priests and Nuns in the Army," in *Excommunicated from the Union: How the Civil War Created a Separate Catholic America* (New York: Fordham University Press, 2016), 68–88; James J. O'Brien, "Annals of Spring Hill College, Mobile, Ala., 1830–1914," box 00214, JARC.

American Jesuits were not all of one mind about the issue of slavery. Some objected to it, though they never associated themselves with the largely anti-Catholic, antislavery abolitionist cause.[66] Nevertheless, since the Jesuits believed in the ownership of all things in common, all Jesuits, regardless of their sentiments, were slaveowners.

Moving Forward

As evidenced by the depth of knowledge shared about enslaved people in some regions and the brief overviews given for others, the work of the Slavery, History, Memory, and Reconciliation Project continues. Jesuits were also immersed in the institution of slavery in New Orleans, Louisiana, and Mobile, Alabama, at Spring Hill College, but there is more to uncover on these fronts, and others. The project will continue to communicate its findings to the public.

In addition to supporting descendants and Jesuits in seeking to repair historical harms together, the project aims to educate Jesuits, Jesuit institutions, and the general public about their historical involvement in slaveholding, segregation, racism, and ongoing systemic issues today, and what their role should be in addressing these issues. The legacies of slavery, and the legacies descendants of the Jesuits' enslaved people have left, continue to shape communities.

Matilda Tyler (ca. 1810–1901), a woman believed to be the daughter of Proteus and Anny Queen-Hawkins, one of the families forced from Maryland in 1829, and a bondswoman of Saint Louis University, purchased her own freedom and that of her five sons between 1849 and 1859. The money for her freedom went to Saint Francis Xavier College Church, where Matilda and her family were parishioners. Matilda's resistance to her enslavement to the Jesuits was not a rejection of the Catholicism her enslavers imparted. She adhered to her faith even as her enslavers and former enslavers increasingly segregated people of

---

66 O'Brien, "Annals of Spring Hill College"; Garraghan, *Jesuits of the Middle United States*, 617.

color from white parishioners within their churches. One year after becoming free, Matilda Tyler went to the same church whose operation was funded in part by the price of her freedom and received the sacrament of confirmation. By the time her sons had become free, the Tyler family and other Black Catholics could no longer worship from the back pews of the college church but had separate Masses in a small room in the upper gallery of the same church.[67]

Matilda Tyler's story speaks to the contemporary implications of this project. What did it mean for Matilda Tyler to earn her freedom, and what does it mean for the Jesuits to use the money she gave in this way? What did Matilda's faith mean to her that she remained a member of the very church that profited from her bondage? Matilda Tyler and her family utilized the kin, faith, and community networks they had forged on the Missouri frontier to carve out meaningful lives despite their enslavement. They remained active members of Saint Francis Xavier College Church, and later Saint Elizabeth's Parish, a Jesuit parish founded specifically for Black Catholics in 1873, for generations. Saint Elizabeth's Parish closed in 1951, and many of its parishioners became part of Saint Matthew's Parish, a Jesuit-run church in the Ville neighborhood of Saint Louis.[68] Matilda

---

67 "Financial Records, 1863–1874," Doc Rec 001 0019 0013, series 19, box 85 Financial Records, SLU; Ledger of the Missouri Mission 1836–51, box 2.0147, item 5, Office of the Treasurer Collection, unprocessed collection JARC; "Missouri Mission Varia," n.d., box 2.0157, item 2, Office of the Treasurer Collection, unprocessed collection, JARC; "Confirmations, First Communions, Members Lists, 1846–1872" (St. Francis Xavier College Church), Archdiocese of St. Louis Office of Archives and Records; "Consultors and Trustees Minutes," SLU; Garraghan, *Jesuits of the Middle United States*, 561; "Work of Ours Among the Colored Folk of St. Louis," *Province Newsletters* IV (November 1922): 23; "Litterae Annuae," 1861–62, box 3.0226, folder 2, St. Louis University Collection, JARC. For more on the development of segregated worship spaces, see Schmidt, "Enslaved Faith Communities."

68 "Jesuit Chronicle: 1823–1940," JARC; Garraghan, *Jesuits of the Middle United States*, 562; Jeffrey R. Dorr, "Race in St. Louis's Catholic Church: Discourse, Structures, and Segregation, 1873–1941" (Master's thesis, Saint Louis University, 2015), 45. For more on this transition, see Schmidt, "Enslaved Faith Communities," 78–81.

Tyler and her family had become members of this parish even earlier, for in 1901, her obituary stated that funeral services would be held there. She and many other former bondspeople are buried in Calvary Cemetery in Saint Louis, frequently in unmarked graves.[69] Matilda's youngest son, Charles H. Tyler (1844–1899), in partnership with descendants of other families once enslaved by the Jesuits, was an influential leader in St. Louis's Black communities. A politician and saloonkeeper, he was a co-founder of Saint Louis's first Black baseball team and promoted other means for African American advancement in the late nineteenth century. He remained a parishioner of Saint Matthew's Parish until his death.[70]

As the project moves forward, the labor of enslaved people in the new mission territory must not be forgotten. Bondspeople were at the center of the running of the Jesuits' parishes, their missions to Native Americans and settlers in the West, as well as the development of their educational institutions, including those established in the North. This is a story that does not end in 1865. Many of the formerly enslaved remained Catholic and stayed in the same Jesuit-run communities in the regions where they had once been enslaved. How many of Matilda Tyler's descendants are still part of these communities and perhaps associated with the parishes and schools of the Society of Jesus now? How do Catholics account for the membership of descendants in parishes, schools, and other institutions that were supported in their earliest years by the unfree labor of these descendants' ancestors, institutions that Jesuits continue to

---

69 "Matilda Tyler Obituary," *St. Louis Post-Dispatch*, January 22, 1901.
70 "Death Notices," *St. Louis Globe-Democrat*, October 23, 1899; "Regular Republican Ratification Meeting!," *St. Louis Post-Dispatch*, April 3, 1885; "Said on the Street: Candidates' Chances as Discussed by the People," *St. Louis Post-Dispatch*, April 2, 1885; James E. Brunson, III, *The Early Image of Black Baseball: Race and Representation in the Popular Press, 1871–1890* (Jefferson, NC: McFarland, 2009), 160, 185–186; "Diamond Dust," *St. Louis Globe-Democrat*, May 8, 1883; "The Colored Champions Win," *St. Louis Globe-Democrat*, May 8, 1883; "Colored Colonists," *St. Louis Globe-Democrat*, April 16, 1879; "'Craps.' Description of a Peculiar Form of Gambling," *St. Louis Post-Dispatch*, February 21, 1881.

operate today? This history must be kept in mind as Jesuits, Jesuit institutions, and members of the Catholic Church seek reconciliation and begin dialogue about making amends today.

The story of the Tyler family is just one of many instances that show how the legacy of slavery and slaveholding extends into the Jesuits' parishes, missions, and schools. Catholic churches and education under the Jesuits grew increasingly segregated over the course of the nineteenth century. Today, those historically Black churches and schools often remain separate from predominantly white institutions and those that have not closed are often under-resourced. How included and supported do people of color feel in integrated, but predominantly white, Jesuit churches and schools? How can those most affected by the legacies of slavery in the neighborhoods where Jesuit institutions operate be supported? To what extent are students of Jesuit schools aware that they are the inheritors of an educational system that has been privileged through the legacy of reliance on enslaved labor? Through the Slavery, History, Memory, and Reconciliation Project, the Jesuits and their parishes, works, programs, services, and educational institutions, with descendants leading, can begin to determine what they are are obligated to do for the descendant communities that they now serve.

U.S. Catholic Religious and Slavery: Seeking Truth, Justice, and Reconciliation

JAMES FITZ, S.M.*

Introduction

For American religious men and women, actions for social justice and human transformation have become a significant aspect of their mission since the promulgation of the Vatican II constitution *Gaudium et Spes*: "The joys and the hopes, the griefs and anxieties of the people of this age, especially those who are poor or in any way afflicted, these are the joys and the hopes, the griefs and anxieties of the followers of Christ."[1] This call was reaffirmed by the post-synodal apostolic exhortation *Vita Consecrata* in 1996.[2]

In light of the call for social purpose, this article will examine a seldom-told chapter in the history of religious men and women: the nineteenth-century struggle for justice and human

---

* An earlier version of this essay was published as "U.S. Catholic Religious and Slavery: A Seldom Told Story," in the *Review for Religious* 58, no. 4 (July–August 1999): 342–363. I am grateful for the permission to reprint it in revised form with the permission of the U.S. Central and Southern Province, Society of Jesus. My interest in this topic arose partly from my friendship with the now-deceased African American Marianist, Father Paul Marshall, a leader in our religious order and in the National Black Catholic Clergy Caucus. When the article first appeared, Father Marshall was happy that the history was being acknowledged, especially by a white religious. Clearly, some important developments have happened in the years since the article was first published. Nevertheless, I believe its message still has relevance.

1 *Gaudium et Spes*, §1, https://www.vatican.va/archive/hist_councils/ii_vatican_council/documents/vat-ii_const_19651207_gaudium-et-spes_en.html.

2 For example, *Vita Consecrata*, §82, https://www.vatican.va/content/john-paul-ii/en/apost_exhortations/documents/hf_jp-ii_exh_25031996_vita-consecrata.html.

transformation, the story of slavery, and how American religious were involved in and responded to this critical issue in American social history.³ Hardly one of the glorious moments in the history of American religious life, this story can be instructive as we look at the present-day call to social transformation.

History is valuable in offering a perspective and context for understanding contemporary events and can teach multiple ways we can respond to present-day reality out of the Christian commitment and tradition. History can help us avoid being controlled by the tyranny of present opinion or practice. In the particular issue addressed by this article, American slavery, a historical viewpoint witnesses to the development of doctrine and its implications for issues facing the Church today.

History also challenges its students to remember so they will not repeat mistakes of the past. As Elie Wiesel (Jewish scholar, survivor of the Holocaust, and Nobel Prize winner) has pointed out many times, remembering is important. Humanity must remember and change so that the sins and tragedies of the past are not repeated. The study of these events may give some insight into dealing with issues and concerns of the present day. From these perspectives, is there anything that modern-day Christians, and today's Catholic religious in particular, can learn from the experience of our forebears in religious life as they dealt with a great social transformation, the abolition of slavery?

In the history of the United States, the Civil War (1861–1865) was a profound trial and test of the survival of this nation, conceived in liberty and equality. As President Abraham Lincoln said at the time, the nation was "engaged in a great civil war, testing whether that nation, or any nation so conceived and so dedicated, can long endure."⁴ This struggle split the country. Since

---

3 Only recently has the slave owning of religious men and women been widely acknowledged. See, for instance, Rachel L. Swarns, "The Nuns Who Bought and Sold Human Beings," *New York Times*, August 2, 2019, https://www.nytimes.com/2019/08/02/opinion/sunday/nuns-slavery.html.

4 Abraham Lincoln, "Gettysburg Address," November 19, 1863, http://www.abrahamlincolnonline.org/lincoln/speeches/gettysburg.htm.

the time of the war itself, historians have debated the causes of the Civil War. The different approaches to slavery in the North and the South were clearly one cause, and the abolition of slavery was a social transformation resulting from the war.

This article will examine how American Catholic religious responded to this "peculiar institution" of slavery and to its transformation. First, the approach of the U.S. Catholic Church to the slavery issue will be examined, for this is the context within which the response of American religious arose. Secondly, the involvement of American male and female religious with slaves and the ministry of religious to slaves will be examined. Third, the attitude of religious toward the institution of slavery and slaves will be considered. Lastly, some tentative conclusions will be offered as well as some discussion of religious men and women's recent efforts to atone for the past.

Besides primary source documentation, there are also significant studies on the involvement of particular religious orders with slavery, especially the Jesuits.[5] Many religious communities either have not written or are in the process of writing or rewriting histories of their foundations in this country. Once completed, these local congregational histories will be valuable in nuancing conclusions drawn from the information now available. A thorough study of the archives of religious orders and congregations throughout the country is still in process; however, enough information is available to provide an overview of the response of the American religious to slavery.

---

5   For example, R. Emmett Curran, "'Splendid Poverty': Jesuit Slaveholding in Maryland, 1805–1838," in *Catholics in the Old South: Essays on Church and Culture*, ed. Randall M. Miller and Jon L. Wakelyn (Macon, GA: Mercer University Press, 1983), 125–146, and Edward F. Beckett, S.J., "Listening to our History: Inculturation and Jesuit Slaveholding," *Studies in the Spirituality of Jesuits* 28, no. 5 (November 1996): 1–48. Significant studies compiled since this article originally appeared include Thomas Murphy, S.J., *Jesuit Slaveholding in Maryland, 1717–1838* (New York: Routledge, 2001); Kelly L. Schmidt, "Enslaved Faith Communities in the Jesuits' Missouri Mission," *U.S. Catholic Historian* 37, no. 2 (Spring 2019): 49–81; Adam Rothman and Elsa Barraza Mendoza, eds., *Facing Georgetown's History: A Reader on Slavery, Memory, and Reconciliation* (Washington, DC: Georgetown University Press, 2021).

Attitudes Toward Slavery in the U.S. Catholic Church

For most American religious of the twentieth century, the ownership of enslaved persons by their forebears in religion is disturbing. For religious formed since the Second Vatican Council (1962–1965), this aspect of their history might seem incomprehensible. The teaching of that council places slavery among the crimes against the dignity of the human person and calls the Church to work to eliminate all forms of slavery:

> The varieties of crime are numerous: . . . all offenses against human dignity, such as subhuman living conditions, arbitrary imprisonment, deportation, slavery, prostitution, the selling of women and children, degrading working conditions where people are treated as mere tools for profit rather than free and responsible persons: all these and the like are criminal; they poison civilization; and they debase the perpetrators more than the victims and militate against the honor of the creator. . . . Human institutions, both private and public, must labor to minister to the dignity and purpose of the human person. At the same time let them put up a stubborn fight against any kind of slavery, whether social or political, and safeguard the basic rights of the human person under every political system.[6]

In the Catholic Church of the early nineteenth century, no formal and absolute condemnation of slavery as an institution existed. Although recognizing abuses in the system, the Church did not see slavery as a moral evil in itself but as a result of original sin. Christians found no condemnation of slavery in the scriptures or in the writings of early church theologians: "From *Genesis* to *Philemon* one could find no condemnation of the practice. Jesus did not utter one word of censure against slavery even though it was in full existence in his day. Saint Paul, who claimed to have met the resurrected Christ, did nothing to abolish it—in fact, he did just the opposite when he said, 'Slaves, be obedient to your masters.'"[7] Although slavery per se was not con-

---

6 *Gaudium et Spes*, §27, 29.
7 Kenneth J. Zanca, ed., *American Catholics and Slavery: 1789–1866, an Anthology of Primary Documents* (Lanham, MD: University Press of America, 1994), xxxi.

demned, Pope Pius II in 1462 and Pope Urban VIII in 1639 had condemned the slave trade. Pope Benedict XIV condemned the continued enslavement of native peoples in 1741.[8]

By the end of the eighteenth century, abolition movements began in various countries and in some parts of the United States. In 1839, Pope Gregory XVI issued an apostolic letter again calling for the elimination of the African slave trade.[9] Voices opposing slavery began to arise among Catholics in European countries.[10] Catholics in the United States, however, did not take a lead in the abolitionist movement. Of the few significant Catholic voices, the most prominent came from outside the United States—the Irish leader, Daniel O'Connell. His voice did not receive a warm welcome in the United States, however.[11] Catholic leaders consistently tended to identify the abolitionists with anti-Catholic and nativist sentiments. The Know-Nothing Party platform of 1855, which combined antislavery, nativist, and anti-Catholic concerns, did nothing to win Catholic converts to the antislavery movement.[12] Catholic leaders tended to avoid the slavery issue, which divided the nation. In their 1859 provincial council meeting in Baltimore, the bishops of the United States avoided taking a stand on the issue. Although Catholic leaders admitted that human bondage was not an ideal system, they differed on the gravity of the evil and the practicality of proposals to end the system. The only element upon which they agreed was that the principles and methods of the abolitionists were a threat to the country's well-being.[13]

At the time of the Civil War, Northern church leaders generally supported the position of the Union, and Southern church

---

8   Zanca, *American Catholics and Slavery*, 37-39.
9   Madeleine Hooke Rice, *American Catholic Opinion in the Slavery Controversy* (Gloucester, MA: Peter Smith, 1964), 21.
10   John Francis Maxwell, *Slavery and the Catholic Church: The History of Catholic Teaching Concerning the Moral Legitimacy of the Institution of Slavery* (London: Barry Rose, 1975), 101–110.
11   David J. O'Brien, *Public Catholicism* (Maryknoll, NY: Orbis Books, 1996), 65. See also Rice, *American Catholic Opinion*, 80–85.
12   O'Brien, *Public Catholicism*, 53.
13   Rice, *American Catholic Opinion*, 85.

leaders generally supported the Confederacy. In 1862, Orestes Brownson, a prominent American Catholic layman and thinker, wrote that in the mind of Catholics, the preservation of the Union took precedence over slavery's abolition. As a Northerner, he wrote that it was his impression that the majority of Catholics opposed the abolitionists but were neither in favor of slavery nor opposed to gradual emancipation. At the time he supported emancipation as a political and military necessity.[14] In his manual of moral theology written in the early 1840s, Francis Patrick Kenrick, bishop of Philadelphia and later archbishop of Baltimore, regretted the institution of slavery as it was practiced in the United States but generally acquiesced in the prevailing conditions in the country. Although especially concerned about the restrictions on the education of enslaved persons and on their freedom to practice religion, he nevertheless opposed the violation of laws controlling slavery. He encouraged slaves to be obedient and masters to be just and kind. Though the original seizure of slaves was immoral, Kenrick argued that the descendants of those who originally purchased the slaves should not be held accountable.[15] Kenrick represented Catholic opinion in the United States, which generally supported the status quo. Those Catholics who saw slavery as an evil, in general, were for gradual, not forced, emancipation.

Southern Catholic leaders defended slavery, although some like Bishop Augustin Verot of St. Augustine, Florida, also pointed out that many Southern masters had abused slaves, and the war might be God's punishment for this failure. Among the abuses Verot listed were the separation of families, masters' sexual exploitation of female slaves, masters not providing religious instruction, and lack of proper clothing, food, and dwellings.[16]

---

14 See *Brownson's Quarterly Review* (October 1862) 451–487, excerpted in Zanca, *American Catholics and Slavery*, 134–139.

15 Zanca, *American Catholics and Slavery*, 200. See also Joseph D. Brokhage, *Francis Patrick Kenrick's Opinion on Slavery* (Washington, DC: Catholic University of American Press, 1955), 122–124.

16 Zanca, *American Catholics and Slavery*, 201–209. This is a sermon preached by Verot in 1861.

Like many of their fellow Americans, Catholics also suffered from a racist attitude toward the enslaved. Although Catholics recognized the slave as a human person, they did not accept enslaved persons as equals. Reflecting this belief, Orestes Brownson could write,

> We recognize in the Negro a man, and assert for him in their plentitude the *natural rights* of man, but we do not believe him the equal of the white man, and we would not give him in society with white men equality of respect to those rights derived not immediately from manhood, but mediately from political and civil society, and in this we express, we apprehend, the general sentiment of the Catholic population of this country.[17]

Religious Involvement with Enslaved Persons

In his first report to the prefect of the Congregation of the Propaganda Fide, Jesuit Father John Carroll, superior of the priests in the missions of Maryland (and later the first American bishop), sent the statistics concerning Catholics in the United States. African slaves were a significant part of the Catholic Church in Maryland, about 20% of the Catholic population.[18] Catholics owned most of these slaves. In the period before the Civil War, some American religious, like their American compatriots and fellow Catholics, owned slaves. Most early American Catholics lived in Maryland and Kentucky, states that permitted slavery. The owning of slaves was an adaptation religious made to living in America. Records document that both men and women religious owned slaves.

The Jesuits were major slaveowners. Lord Baltimore had granted them extensive lands. They owned four large estates in Maryland in Prince George's, Charles, and St. Mary's counties and two smaller plantations on the Eastern Shore. They also had two farms in eastern Pennsylvania. At first, they relied upon indentured servants, a practice they never completely abandoned. "As

---

17 Zanca, *American Catholics and Slavery*, 136.
18 Cyprian Davis, *The History of Black Catholics in the United States* (New York: Crossroad, 1990), 35.

this form of labor became increasingly difficult to secure and retain in Maryland, the Jesuit missionaries, like their secular fellow planters, turned to slave labor." The first explicit reference to enslaved persons is from 1711 (although the Jesuits probably had bondsmen and women before then). By 1765 they owned 192 enslaved persons. The Jesuits also owned slaves in the Louisiana Territory, both in St. Louis and New Orleans.[19]

Two congregations of men came to America to establish seminaries: the Sulpicians and the Vincentians (Congregation of the Mission). Because the Sulpicians were not significant landowners, they did not own a large number of enslaved persons. Individual Sulpicians in Maryland and Kentucky owned slaves.[20] At the invitation of Louis William DuBourg, apostolic administrator of the Louisiana territory, the Vincentians staffed St. Mary's Seminary in Perry County, Missouri, beginning in 1818. DuBourg provided them with slaves. The first Vincentian superior of the American mission, Father Felix DeAndreis, hesitated to accept them but did so because there were no lay brothers who could do the manual labor. In fact, DeAndreis considered the possibility of enlisting free Blacks and mulattoes into the Vincentian community but discarded the idea because he was convinced, probably rightly at the time, that if he did, no white men would enter the community.[21] The introduction of slaves was considered a necessary adaptation to the American situation. A major concern of the Vincentian superiors in Rome was that a *woman* was admitted to the kitchen and thus within the community living quarters. There was no comment about the fact that she was a slave. In 1830, the seminary had twenty-seven enslaved men and women; this appears to be the highest number at any time.[22]

---

19   Curran, "'Splendid Poverty': Jesuit Slaveholding in Maryland," 126.
20   Christopher J. Kauffman, *Tradition and Transformation in Catholic Culture: The Priests of Saint Sulpice in the United States from 1791 to the Present* (New York: Macmillan, 1988), 146. See also Stafford Poole, C.M., and Douglas J. Slawson, *Church and Slave in Perry County, Missouri, 1818–1865* (Lewiston, NY: Edwin Mellen Press, 1986), 143.
21   Poole and Slawson, *Church and Slave in Perry County, Missouri*, 144–158.
22   Poole and Slawson, *Church and Slave in Perry County, Missouri*, 162.

Of the first eight permanent communities of women religious founded within the original boundaries of the United States, six had enslaved persons: three in Maryland (the Carmelites of Port Tobacco, the Visitation Sisters of Georgetown, and the Sisters of Charity of Emmitsburg) and three in Kentucky (the Sisters of Loretto, the Sisters of Charity of Nazareth, and the Dominican Sisters of St. Catherine). The annals and traditions of these six communities refer to "Negro" or "colored servants" brought by some women as part of their dowries.[23] For example, at the Carmelite convent, where the enslaved numbered thirty by 1829, they lived 'comfortably' outside the closure and accomplished the farm work.[24] Of the first eight congregations, the Oblate Sisters of Providence (an order of African American religious in Baltimore, Maryland) and the Sisters of Our Lady of Mercy (Charleston, South Carolina) were the two congregations that did not own enslaved persons.

The other major grouping of religious during the time of slavery were those who came to the Louisiana Territory, which became part of the United States in 1803. Most of these religious were French-speaking congregations, although Spanish religious served during the time of Spanish control. In the Louisiana Territory, the Capuchins owned slaves to work their plantations, as well as the previously mentioned Jesuit ownership of slaves in the territory.[25]

Among the communities of women, French-speaking Ursulines, who came to New Orleans in 1727, had slaves provided as part of their contract with the Company of the Indies.[26] Although

---

23 Barbara Misner, *Highly Respectable and Accomplished Ladies: Catholic Women Religious in America, 1790–1850* (New York: Garland, 1988), 75.

24 Misner, *Highly Respectable and Accomplished Ladies*, 76. See also Mary Ewens, O.P., "The Role of the Nun in Nineteenth-Century America: Variations on the International Theme" (Ph.D. diss., University of Minnesota, 1971), 38.

25 Roger Baudier, *The Catholic Church in Louisiana* (New Orleans: 1939), 89, 108–109, 115–116, 131–132, 139, 202.

26 Frances Jerome Woods, C.D.P., "Congregations of Religious Women in the Old South," in *Catholics in the Old South: Essays on Church and Culture*, ed. Randall M. Miller and Jon L. Wakelyn (Macon, GA: Mercer University Press, 1983), 112.

Mother Hyacinth LeConnait, of the Daughters of the Cross, reluctantly embraced slaveholding. As local superior of a community of teaching sisters, she assured that enslaved persons received religious instruction (Archives of the Diocese of Shreveport, Louisiana).

at first reluctant to purchase enslaved persons, Mother Hyacinth LeConnait of the Daughters of the Cross (Cocoville, Louisiana) accepted the recommendation of the bishop and purchased a bondsperson.[27] The Madames (Religious) of the Sacred Heart had slaves at Grand Coteau, Louisiana, and in Missouri.[28] There is correspondence from Philippine Duchesne requesting a slave from the Vincentians.[29] The Sisters of Loretto of Bethlehem convent across the road from the Vincentians in Perry County, Missouri, also owned enslaved persons.[30]

---

27   Woods, "Congregations of Religious Women in the Old South," 113. See also Ewens, "The Role of the Nun in Nineteenth-Century America," 22.

28   Woods, "Congregations of Religious Women in the Old South," 114. See also Ewens, "The Role of the Nun in Nineteenth-Century America," 64; Davis, *History of Black Catholics*, 39.

29   Poole and Slawson, *Church and Slave in Perry County, Missouri*, 171.

30   Poole and Slawson, *Church and Slave in Perry County, Missouri*, 172.

The owning of persons led to religious purchasing and selling slaves. For the Sisters of Charity of Nazareth (Kentucky), the purchase of slaves in 1840 was an economic decision: ". . . the Council decided it was better to buy servants for the farm, etc., than pay so much for hire and then often get bad ones."[31] When the Carmelites left Charles County, Maryland, for Baltimore in 1831, the disposal of their bondsmen was one of their difficulties. According to the Carmelite centennial history, the slaves became a source of anxiety because the sisters did not have the resources to grant them their freedom, so they gave them permission to seek their own masters. The sisters received whatever price the new master gave. Older slaves were left to the care of competent persons, and the sisters provided for their necessities until their deaths.[32]

The Vincentians became involved in the sale and purchase of slaves, though they did so, at least in part, they claimed, out of concern for their bondspeople. In a letter addressed to the Vincentian general in 1840, the American provincial Father John Timon explained that the purpose of the increased buying of slaves was to bring together families. The Vincentians slowly phased out slaveholding during the 1850s and 1860s. Although personally opposed to slavery, Timon justified the decision to sell the slaves in terms of economics and politics rather than moral factors. They did not consider freeing them.[33]

The sale of the Jesuit slaves in Maryland in 1838 caused great controversy. Some Jesuits sought to free the slaves and, in the process, change the labor force running their farms from slave to free. When the Jesuits were restored in 1814, the civil corporation made a resolution to this effect in that same year; however, it was never carried out. The Jesuits became embroiled in a dispute with Ambrose Maréchal, the new archbishop of Baltimore, who had initiated claims against the Jesuit estates, arguing that they were

---

31 Misner, *Highly Respectable and Accomplished Ladies*, 82. Misner quoted from Duplicate Letter Book IV:1 in the Archives of the Sisters of Charity of Nazareth, Kentucky.
32 Misner, *Highly Respectable and Accomplished Ladies*, 77.
33 Poole and Slawson, *Church and Slave in Perry County, Missouri*, 186–189.

Bill of sale for enslaved persons, June 19, 1838, signed by Father Thomas F. Mulledy, S.J. (Archives of the Maryland Province of the Society of Jesus/Booth Family Center for Special Collections, Georgetown University Library).

meant to support the entire Church in Maryland, not just the Jesuits.[34] Any sales were delayed until the dispute could be settled.

By the 1830s, a new group of younger Jesuits was becoming uncomfortable with the estates and their status as slaveowners. By this time, however, the climate in the country had changed, and the policy of deferred emancipation became more difficult to follow.[35] Older Jesuits, mostly Europeans, supported keeping the estates. Younger Jesuits, mostly Americans, wanted to sell the estates and the slaves and concentrate on education. The older

---

34 Curran, "'Splendid Poverty': Jesuit Slaveholding in Maryland," 134–135.

35 Curran, "'Splendid Poverty': Jesuit Slaveholding in Maryland," 138.

Jesuits argued that the enslaved persons were a patrimony. Father Francis Dzierozynski wrote, "I consider the blacks under this respect only, that they are our sons, whose care and salvation has been entrusted to us by Divine Providence and are always happy under our Fathers."[36] For Dzierozynski and others, the bond between the slaves and the Jesuits should not be broken for financial reasons. They argued that selling the slaves would lead to the slaves' physical and moral ruin and would cause great scandal.[37]

In October 1836, the Jesuit superior general approved the sale of the enslaved with the condition that their religious needs must be met, families must not be separated (especially spouses), and the money must be invested for the support of Jesuits in training.[38] In June 1838, Father Thomas Mulledy, the provincial, sold the slaves to Henry Johnson of Louisiana. The main group of them was sent to Louisiana in November 1838. Mulledy was denounced to the Jesuit superior general because some families were separated, and Mulledy was subsequently replaced. The change to tenant farming ended the Jesuits' history as slaveholders. Clearly, the young Jesuits who advocated the sale of enslaved persons correctly perceived the owning of bondsmen and women as scandalous. Their manner of handling the sale clearly violated the principles of the Church concerning their sale and treatment, and they did not provide for their eventual emancipation. This, too, was a scandal.

In general, how did religious treat their slaves? In his study on American Catholics and slavery, Kenneth Zanca notes "that religious orders treated their slaves more humanely than other slave holders and generally saw to their religious education—even in the defiance of state laws. To be a 'priest's slave' or a 'nun's slave' was considered a fortunate circumstance for a slave."[39] Yet there is reason to believe that religious did not treat their slaves much differently than lay Catholics or even non-Catholic masters.

---

36 Curran, "'Splendid Poverty': Jesuit Slaveholding in Maryland," 140.
37 Curran, "'Splendid Poverty': Jesuit Slaveholding in Maryland," 141.
38 Curran, "'Splendid Poverty': Jesuit Slaveholding in Maryland," 142.
39 Zanca, *American Catholics and Slavery*, 111.

Father Thomas F. Mulledy, S.J., president of Georgetown University at the time of the 1838 sale of enslaved persons (Booth Family Center for Special Collections, Georgetown University Library).

Father Adam Marshall, the Jesuit charged with overseeing the plantations for the corporation, described the dwellings for the slaves as "almost universally unfit for human beings to live in."[40] When possible, Jesuit brothers were given charge of the farms. Father Peter Kenney, an Irish Jesuit sent by the Jesuit superior general as a special visitor to evaluate the American mission in 1820, took exception to the arbitrary treatment of the slaves by the brothers. He found general disaffection among the slaves and particular abuses (for example, whipping of pregnant women). He also found the behavior of the slaves scandalous and their practice of religion virtually nonexistent.[41] Because of the poor financial condition of the Jesuits in general in the early 1820s, the living conditions of the slaves on most of the plantations were less than adequate. However, with new management the material conditions of the slaves seemed to improve by the

---

40 Curran, "'Splendid Poverty': Jesuit Slaveholding in Maryland," 129.
41 Curran, "'Splendid Poverty': Jesuit Slaveholding in Maryland," 130.

1830s. At St. Inigoes, the most thriving of the plantations, Father Joseph Carberry instituted a system of incentives for the slaves, which led to their economic improvement. Concerning their moral and spiritual condition, despite catechesis and required attendance at Mass, Kenney found the slaves' lives to be a "moral wasteland and scandalous reproach to the Society [of Jesus]." But the slaves themselves were not always blamed: "Some Jesuits attributed the moral anarchy to the Society's own failure to discipline the slaves."[42]

Some accounts about slaves owned by religious report a general affection by the slaves for their religious owners. At St. Catherine, Kentucky, the relationship of the enslaved persons to the Dominican Sisters was one of voluntary sacrifice.[43] When the sisters wanted to build a new chapel, some of the slaves who had come to the sisters as part of a dowry voluntarily offered to do without new clothes for a year so that the money might fund the chapel. Some slaves gave their earnings toward the project. Even after emancipation, some slaves remained with the sisters until their deaths.[44] A report about the slaves owned by the Madames (Religious) of the Sacred Heart indicates that they were "happy as possible in their snug little cabins" and were converted to the Catholic faith and the "love of the Sacred Heart that was the reason for Grand Coteau's existence."[45] A historian of the earlier Jesuit mission in the United States claims that during the Revolutionary War, the slaves of the Jesuits could have abandoned the Jesuit farms when British ships raided the plantations. The priests' slaves, unlike neighboring slaves, did not abandon the plantations, and the histo-

---

42 Curran, "'Splendid Poverty': Jesuit Slaveholding in Maryland," 132.
43 Woods, "Congregations of Religious Women in the Old South," 114.
44 Misner, *Highly Respectable and Accomplished Ladies*, 84. Also reported by Woods, "Congregations of Religious Women in the Old South," 114. The two authors seem to be using a common source, a *Commemorative Booklet for American Bicentennial* (St. Catherine, KY: Dominican Sisters of St. Catherine, 1976).
45 Woods, "Congregations of Religious Women in the Old South," 114. Woods quoted from Margaret Williams, *Second Sowing: The Life of Mary Aloysia Hardey* (New York: Sheed and Ward, 1942), 103.

rian took this as a sign of the slaves' devotion to their masters.[46] There are, however, no accounts from the slaves themselves to confirm these impressions.

Ministry of Religious to Enslaved Persons

Before the Civil War, the Catholic Church in the South was small, poor, and understaffed: "Catholicism, in short, could not adequately minister to either the slave or the free blacks in the South (be they Catholic or non-Catholic), nor could Catholicism practically enforce its own teaching on the proper treatment of slaves."[47] The Church was hesitant and ambivalent in most of its efforts to work among African Americans, whether slave or free.[48] John Carroll was concerned about "a general lack of care in instructing their children and especially the Negro slaves in their religion."[49] Although local parish records indicate a high rate of baptisms among slaves throughout the antebellum period, "there is little evidence of high rates of slave identification with Catholicism in terms of attendance at Mass, marriage in the Church, or other signs of Catholic activity and devotion."[50] Despite this general lack of adequate ministry, religious provided some attention to slaves' spiritual lives.

---

46 Thomas Hughes, S.J., *History of the Society of Jesus in North America, Colonial and Federal, Volume II from 1645 till 1773* (London: Longmans, Green, and Co., 1917), 565.

47 Michael McNally, "A Minority of a Minority: The Witness of Black Women Religious in the Antebellum South," *Review for Religious* 40, no. 2 (March 1981), 261.

48 Margaret Susan Thompson, "Philemon's Dilemma: Nuns and the Black Community in Nineteenth-Century America: Some Findings," *The American Catholic Religious Life: Selected Historical Essays*, ed. with an introduction by Joseph M. White (New York: Garland, 1988), 83.

49 John Carroll, "The First American Report to Propaganda on Catholicism in the United States, March 1, 1785," *Documents of American Catholic History*, fourth ed., Volume 1 (1493–1865), ed. by John Tracy Ellis (Wilmington, DE: Michael Glazier, 1987), 149.

50 Randall M. Miller, "The Failed Mission: The Catholic Church and Black Catholics in the Old South," in *Catholics in the Old South: Essays on Church and Culture*, ed. Randall M. Miller and Jon L. Wakelyn (Macon, GA: Mercer University Press, 1983), 152.

Religious order priests provided most commonly for the slaves' attendance at Sunday and holy day Mass and the celebration of baptism and marriage. This was common among the plantations of the Jesuits, Vincentians, and Capuchins in the Louisiana Territory and on Jesuit- and Catholic-owned lands in Maryland.[51] For instance, a Jesuit mission band giving revivals on southern Maryland farms in the Jubilee Year 1851 also ministered to slaves.[52]

Some religious priests tried to protect bondspersons from abuse. In 1791, for example, the Capuchin Father Joaquin de Portillo ordered slaves to stop working on a holy day of obligation and reported the incident to the Louisiana governor because work on a holy day was a violation of the slave code in the colony.[53]

In general, religious catechized their slaves and sometimes provided basic education. Religious women catechized and educated enslaved persons, especially children. In a letter in 1856, Mother Hyacinth of the Daughters of the Cross indicates that they educated their slave named Simon.[54] There is evidence that the Visitation Sisters educated free Black girls, and this tradition may have "its origins in the instruction given to their slaves."[55] Bishop John England founded the Sisters of Our Lady of Mercy in Charleston, South Carolina, for the purpose of establishing a school for "free colored girls, and to give religious instruction to female slaves."[56] A letter of Mother Elizabeth Seton, foundress of the Daughters of Charity, evidences catechetical work among African American children. The Daughters organized classes to

---

51 Baudier, *The Catholic Church in Louisiana*, 76–77, 139, 161. A dispute arose between the Jesuits and the Capuchins over whether the Jesuits who were assigned to the Indian missions had jurisdiction and could minister to their own slaves (see Baudier, *The Catholic Church in Louisiana*, 115–116).

52 Edward F. Beckett, S.J., "Listening to our History: Inculturation and Jesuit Slaveholding," *Studies in the Spirituality of Jesuits* 28, no. 5 (November 1996), 15.

53 Baudier, *The Catholic Church in Louisiana*, 213.

54 Woods, "Congregations of Religious Women in the Old South," 113.

55 Misner, *Highly Respectable and Accomplished Ladies*, 203.

56 Misner, *Highly Respectable and Accomplished Ladies*, 204–205.

teach religion to their slaves.[57] The Ursulines in New Orleans also catechized slaves.[58]

Two religious orders of African American women were founded to educate and catechize African American children. "To work for the Christian education of colored children," four Haitian refugees founded the Oblate Sisters of Providence, "a Religious Society of virgins and widows of color." They provided education for African American children who had no other possibilities. Some children they educated may have been enslaved, although that is not always clear from the sources.[59] Supported at first by the Sulpicians in the person of Father James Joubert and later by the Redemptorists under the direction of Father Thaddeus Anwander, who was influenced by John Neumann, the sisters went about their mission under difficult circumstances. They continued a school in Baltimore that several of the sisters had started before their organization as a religious congregation in 1829.

The other religious community of African American sisters, the Sisters of the Holy Family, was founded in New Orleans for the purpose of serving and educating the poor. Before the foundation of the community, Henriette Delille, the foundress, entered into the work of teaching religion to slaves.[60] Although much of their educational work and service ministry was with poor free African Americans, they also performed catechetical work among enslaved persons.[61]

Care of slaves was also part of the outreach ministry of women religious. The Sisters of the Holy Family, prompted by

---

57 Zanca, *American Catholics and Slavery*, 143; Woods, "Congregations of Religious Women in the Old South," 112.
58 Baudier, *The Catholic Church in Louisiana*, 183.
59 Sister M. Reginald Gerdes, O.S.P., "To Educate and Evangelize: Black Catholic Schools of the Oblate Sisters of Providence (1828-1880)," *U.S. Catholic Historian* 7, nos. 2 and 3 (Spring/Summer 1988), 183–199.
60 Woods, "Congregations of Religious Women in the Old South," 115.
61 Davis, *History of Black Catholics*, 105–110; see also Woods, "Congregations of Religious Women in the Old South," 116; Baudier, *The Catholic Church in Louisiana*, 397.

the wretched condition of old, abandoned slaves, opened a home for the aged.[62] The Hotel Dieu, run by the Daughters of Charity in New Orleans, had a slave department that had special rates and "superior advantages" for members of this class.[63]

Attitude of Religious Toward the Institution of Slavery and Slaves

In general, the attitude of American religious toward slavery mirrored the attitude of American Catholics in general. Like the majority of Catholics, no male or female religious served as leaders of the abolitionist movement, but there are records of individual religious who opposed slavery. Sulpician Father Louis-Regis Deluol and Vincentian Father John Timon are two examples. In a letter to Charles Carroll's granddaughter, Deluol wrote that his feelings were most violently opposed to slavery. In the same letter, however, he indicated that he did not see slavery as opposed to divine or ecclesiastical law.[64] Timon, the Vincentian superior of the American mission, who was responsible for ending their involvement in slavery, accepted the bishopric of Buffalo, New York, because he feared he might be named coadjutor of Bardstown, Kentucky. Timon "would have intensely disliked that appointment because Negro slavery obtains in the state of Kentucky."[65] However, opposition to slavery did not, in general, lead religious to participate in efforts to abolish slavery or manumit their slaves.

Records indicate that there were religious who vocally supported slavery. Jesuit Father John Ryder of Georgetown University addressed an audience in Richmond, Virginia, in 1835. He defended slavery "as a positive benefit to the slave, while arguing that abolitionism was incompatible with Catholicism."[66]

---

62   McNally, "A Minority of a Minority," 264.
63   Woods, "Congregations of Religious Women in the Old South," 113; Baudier, *The Catholic Church in Louisiana*, 396. Baudier quoted from a booklet, "Silver Jubilee of Hotel Dieu School of Nursing" (1927).
64   Kauffman, *Tradition and Transformation in Catholic Culture*, 146.
65   Poole and Slawson, *Church and Slave in Perry County, Missouri*, 179.
66   Beckett, "Listening to our History," 45 and 45 n186.

One of the most prominent Catholic figures of the nineteenth century was Isaac Thomas Hecker, a convert, a religious, and the founder of the Paulist congregation. Hecker saw as his task the adaptation of the Catholic Church to America, "proving to Catholics that their country was not Protestant at its ideological roots, and to Protestants that Catholics were not inherently anti-democratic."[67] Like his mentor, Orestes Brownson, Hecker saw Catholicism's natural law theory as a stronger grounding for democracy than Protestantism or Lockean liberalism. Hecker's dream of America's conversion to Catholicism never materialized.[68]

At the time of the Civil War, Hecker was laying the foundations of the newly established congregation of the Paulists, but in his writings and letters, he hardly mentions the raging political issues of slavery and expansion.[69] In a sermon written in April 1861 (but which apparently was never delivered), Hecker wrote that the root of the problem between the states was the lack of a common religion.[70] In a series of articles before the war, Hecker had written that the Catholic Church was a friend of both master and slave. He contrasted the Catholic Church, which supported union and reconciliation, with the fanatic and divisive Protestant abolitionists. Hecker saw the war as a perfect example of how the Catholic Church would prevent hostility. "Slavery under the benign influence of Catholic principles and legislation, voluntarily and insensibly disappears, just as serfdom was made to give way to modern society without violence or bloodshed."[71] Hecker hoped that the Civil War would lead the country to see the value of Catholicism.[72]

On the issue of slavery itself, Hecker held views conventional for a Catholic of his day. There is evidence of his thought in cor-

---

67 Edward J. Langlois, "Isaac Hecker's Political Thought," *Hecker Studies: Essays on the Thought of Isaac Hecker*, ed. John Farina (New York: Paulist Press, 1983), 51.
68 Langlois, "Isaac Hecker's Political Thought," 66.
69 David J. O'Brien, *Isaac Hecker: An American Catholic* (New York: Paulist Press, 1992), 191.
70 Langlois, "Isaac Hecker's Political Thought," 68; see also 85 n36.
71 Quote from Hecker's sermon in Langlois, "Isaac Hecker's Political Thought," 69.
72 Langlois, "Isaac Hecker's Political Thought," 69.

respondence with Jane Sedgwick, a convert and friend in Stockbridge, Massachusetts, in the spring of 1861. Hecker's letter to Sedgwick no longer exists, but her response indicates her disagreement with his defense of servitude under certain conditions.[73] "Once the war came, Hecker told friends he had always been opposed to slavery; he even told Bishop Patrick N. Lynch of Charleston that he regarded the war as a punishment of the South for its evils."[74] One of Hecker's biographers, David O'Brien, quotes a passage from a letter of September 1861:

> The sentiment of loyal Americans whether Catholic or not is getting always and more strong and united every day against slavery and without any change of principle. We have always taken the ground that it is an evil and a disgrace which might be tolerated for a time, but ought to be gradually abolished. The Constitutional rights of the States forbade, however, any direct meddling and made it our duty to protect the institution of slavery against unjust aggression. Now, however, since slavery is so destructive of national prosperity, and the south by its rebellion has forfeited all claim to the forbearance of the north, we think the time will soon come to expel slavery from our entire country.[75]

Attitudes toward enslaved persons among religious were similar to those held by other white Catholic Americans. Although some English Protestants held the view that Negroes were incapable of baptism because they were not strictly human, Catholics did baptize slaves, especially when the slaves were their own.[76] Jesuit Father George Hunter reminded masters of their duty to treat slaves with charity: "As they are members of Jesus Christ, redeemed by His precious blood, they are to be dealt with in a charitable, Christian, paternal manner, which is at the same time a great means to bring them to do their duty to God, and therefore to gain their souls."[77]

---

73 O'Brien, *Isaac Hecker*, 192. We have no record of Hecker's response to Sedgwick's questions and arguments.
74 O'Brien, *Isaac Hecker*, 192.
75 O'Brien, *Isaac Hecker*, 192.
76 Zanca, *American Catholics and Slavery*, 113.
77 Hughes, *History of the Society of Jesus in North America*, II: 559.

Although seen as human, slaves were often treated and described in condescending and paternalistic terms. The treatment of slaves as property (i.e., moving them from one place to another) manifests the failure of religious to treat slaves as fully human. The language of religious also portrayed their condescending attitudes toward slaves. Jesuit Father Joseph Mosley, who came to Maryland at the time of the Jesuit suppression in 1773, wrote to his sister the following year: "They [enslaved persons] are naturally inclined to thieving, lying and much lechery. I believe want [poverty] makes them worse thieves and liars, and the innate heat of the climate of Africa and their natural temper of constitution gives them a bent to lechery."[78] Another Jesuit, Brother Joseph Mobberly, who managed the St. Inigoes plantation from 1806 to 1820, felt that a lack of discipline was the root of the slaves' problems. He developed a racial theory of African subservience.[79] Mobberly wrote in his diary: "The better a Negro is treated, the worse he becomes." With this attitude, there is little wonder that Mobberly was removed a month after the visit of Father Kenney in 1820.[80]

The Vincentians had difficulty with their lay brothers and their slaves: "The brothers resented the implicit identification of their work with that of slaves and were increasingly reluctant to do certain types of labor, perhaps under the influence of American attitudes."[81] Like many white laborers, the lay brothers disliked doing the work of slaves because they considered this degradation. Father Joseph Rosati, one of the Vincentian superiors, struggled with the duplicity he saw in the lay brothers who did not want slaves but refused to do the work that the bondspeople were hired or bought to do.[82]

Some religious felt compassion for the slaves, although this compassion did not always lead to action. Mother Theodore Guerin, who founded the Sisters of Providence of Saint Mary-

---

78 Zanca, *American Catholics and Slavery*, 113–114.
79 Beckett, "Listening to our History," 21.
80 Curran, "'Splendid Poverty': Jesuit Slaveholding in Maryland," 133.
81 Poole and Slawson, *Church and Slave in Perry County, Missouri*, 156.
82 Poole and Slawson, *Church and Slave in Perry County, Missouri*, 156–157.

of-the-Woods in Indiana, wrote in her journal about a trip to New Orleans:

> The most painful sight I saw in New Orleans was the selling of slaves. Every day in the streets at appointed places, Negroes and Negresses in holiday attire are exposed for this shameful traffic, like the meanest of animals at our fairs. This spectacle oppressed my heart. Lo! I said to myself, these Americans, so proud of their liberty, thus make game of the liberty of others. Poor Negroes! I would have wished to buy them all that I might say to them, 'Go! Bless Providence. You are free.' But such feelings must be concealed from the Louisianians, as this is a point on which they are very sensitive.[83]

The Vincentian Father DeAndreis also felt compassion toward the slaves. In a letter to the Vincentian community in Rome in 1819, he wrote:

> With regard to the situation of the blacks and mulattoes, these are for the most part slaves, who are condemned to eat the bread of sorrow and to bear *pondus diei et aestus* [the burden and the scorching heat, cf. Mt 20:12] and, what is worse, in their harsh condition to serve the passions of others and to be in the moral impossibility of knowing and practicing religion. They are commonly forbidden to contract marriage because of the loss that their masters would suffer as a result, something that exposes them to a thousand dangers. For the rest these natives of Africa are for the most part simple and disposed to profit by the labors that are undertaken for their salvation. They are moved at seeing a white priest interested in them since they are regarded as the offscouring and refuse of the human race. How many subjects of consolation do not these poor creatures offer me! They are instructed, they make their first communion, and then they frequent the sacraments.[84]

DeAndreis's writing flowed from personal experience. After arriving in St. Louis, Missouri, in 1818, he made the African Americans of the city an object of his special ministry. His friend and confrere, Joseph Rosati, who became the first bishop of St. Louis, rec-

---

83 Zanca, *American Catholics and Slavery*, 117.
84 Poole and Slawson, *Church and Slave in Perry County, Missouri*, 145–146.

ollected that people were astonished at seeing a scholar applying himself to this ministry with special ardor and dedication.[85]

Lessons from the Past

Several general trends can be observed from this study of American religious and slavery. Like their fellow Catholics, some American religious owned and sold enslaved persons and became entangled in their control and supervision. Although some commentators have indicated that religious in general treated their slaves better than other slave masters, there are few slave witnesses who can verify this. Religious provided sacramental ministry and education (mostly catechetical) to their slaves and to those of other Catholic masters. Religious also provided limited social services to bondspersons. The attitude of American religious toward the institution of slavery mirrored the general attitude of U.S. Catholics, who did not see slavery as intrinsically wrong. If they opposed slavery, they supported gradual, not immediate, emancipation. Although they viewed enslaved persons as human, they were often described in condescending and racist terms. Some compassion was shown, but this did not often lead to action or a desire to eliminate the institution.

As a historical account, this article could end at this point. But should more be said? Is there anything we might learn from our forebears in the faith as we grapple with social justice and social transformation issues in the world today? There are several important lessons.

A first lesson might be a challenge to more critically examine our relationship to culture. We are called to be prophetic. Our words, actions, and lives are meant to perform at least two prophetic functions: to criticize the existing sinful and unjust social consciousness and to energize the world by embodying an alternative way to live that brings hope.[86] This prophetic witness

---

85 Poole and Slawson, *Church and Slave in Perry County, Missouri*, 147.
86 For further development of the concept of religious life as acted prophecy, see my article, "Religious Life as Acted Prophecy," *Review for Religious* 41 (November–December 1982), 923-927.

can be greatly compromised when living completely apart from the culture. Conversely, when someone is so immersed in the culture that they do not see injustices, and in fact participate in them, their actions become a source of scandal.

American religious quickly adapted to the American experience of slavery. Was this an example of being too immersed in the culture to be truly prophetic? Were some religious so much outsiders (for example, unmarried French Catholic women) that criticism was muted in order not to offend? The experience of U.S. religious and slavery in the nineteenth century can challenge religious today, and indeed all Christians, to look at our present culture. Are there structures in which we are so immersed that we fail to see present injustices? Are there unjust structures that are not challenged because they might cost us personally or communally? Are we alert and attentive to the structures of culture that may need prophetic challenge and a witness to in an alternative way?

For international religious institutes, these same questions may be asked concerning new implantations in other cultures. What aspects of the new culture should be accepted as compatible with and expressive of Gospel values? What aspects are unjust and need to be opposed? As the earliest religious in America quickly adapted to the institution of slavery, are there aspects of other cultures to which religious easily adapt without critical thought? These are not easy questions, but they are important in order to be faithful to the call to prophetic witness.

Secondly, the slavery issue can also be a lesson in listening to and evaluating the message of another. Catholics, including religious, did not listen to the abolitionists because many were also anti-Catholic (but this was not true of all). Although abolitionists may have been prejudiced in their anti-Catholicism, they were prophetic in their respect for the dignity of African Americans. In our own day, the truth may be proclaimed by someone with whom we have little in common or with whom we disagree on significant issues. We need to hear the truth whether it comes from friend or foe, companion or opponent. Are we open to truth, from whatever source? Have we stopped listening to some who espouse the truth even in the midst of error?

A third lesson concerns the development of doctrine in the Catholic Church's history. In the area of social justice and transformation, there are significant examples of development. The institution of slavery, once considered a moral way to treat individuals, is now understood as immoral. Reflection over the years has helped the Church come to a new understanding of the implications of the reign of God as Jesus proclaimed it. As the early Church struggled with the issue of accepting Gentiles into the Church, so American Christians of the nineteenth century grappled with the implications of the Gospel in terms of slavery. Statements made by bishops nearly two hundred years ago have been reversed by bishops in our own day. What was once considered not intrinsically wrong is now considered a crime against human dignity. This development, therefore, can be a source of hope as we grapple with new justice issues today. As we deal with issues of right-to-life (for example, abortion and capital punishment), the dignity of women, and other contemporary issues, what appears as a small glimmer of light (even a light from outside the Church) might be the source of new insight and a new living of the reign of God in future generations. A call for change, for which there may be little interest now, may gain considerable support over time.

Efforts of Religious to Respond to the Past

Since the time of the initial writing of the article, American religious have taken steps to respond to the sin of racism. Although still a seldom told story, a number of articles and research projects have surfaced over the past two decades, specifically concerning the relationship of American religious to slavery. Though not all can be examined here, two developments will be highlighted: first, religious orders have begun recognizing and atoning for the mistakes of our ancestors in participating in the evils of slavery; and second, religious have begun to face the internalized racism that lingers from the owning of slaves which contributed to a racism that has negatively affected the cultures of religious orders.

The most prominent example of recognizing the sin of participating in slavery has been the Jesuits' response to the sale of

Joy Kang, "Write Their Names," 2021. Kang, a Georgetown University student, sketched the university's iconic Healy Hall and its surroundings, adding the names of enslaved persons the Jesuits sold in 1838 (Joy Kang).

272 enslaved members of the Georgetown University community in 1838. In 2017, the Jesuits acknowledged the sinfulness of their actions. The Jesuits apologized to the descendants of enslaved persons the Jesuits had owned and renamed two university buildings for former bondspersons, Anne Marie Becraft and Isaac Hawkins (removing the names of two Jesuits who were involved in the sale). More recently, the Jesuits and the university announced a partnership with a group known as the GU272 Descendants Association to create the Descendants Truth and Reconciliation Foundation to accelerate racial healing and justice in the United States. The Jesuits have pledged $100 million for the effort. It is the hope of religious that confronting the hard truths of the past will further conversion and reconciliation.

Women religious have made similar responses to slavery. The Georgetown Visitation Sisters, the Society of the Sacred Heart (also known as the Religious of the Sacred Heart), the Sis-

Headstone indicating the burial place of enslaved persons at the motherhouse of the Sisters of Charity of Nazareth (Kentucky): "Wm. Butler and wife and other faithful servants." The Sisters of Charity of Nazareth, among other religious communities, have acknowledged their ties to slavery (Sisters of Charity of Nazareth Archival Center).

ters of Charity of Nazareth, the Dominican Sisters of St. Catherine, and the Sisters of Loretto have all made apologies and have convened committees to address their involvement in slavery, calling for accountability and taking steps to reconcile with the descendants of the slaves they had owned.

Religious have also begun to confront the internalized racism within their orders. In 2016, the Leadership Conference of Women Religious made a commitment to "examine the root causes of injustice, particularly racism, and our own complicity as congregations." Historian Shannen Dee Williams, who addressed the national assembly that year, shared the research which informed her book, *Subversive Habits: Black Catholic Nuns in the Long African American Freedom Struggle*.[87] After the assembly, a

---

87 Shannen Dee Williams, *Subversive Habits: Black Catholic Nuns in the Long African American Freedom Struggle* (Durham, NC: Duke University Press, 2022).

number of religious orders opened their archives to her. Added to the call of the assembly, George Floyd's death in 2020 has prompted religious orders to call for a renewal of anti-racism efforts by both looking within and without their communities.

American religious men and women have been called by the Church to commit themselves to social justice and social transformation and have chosen to commit themselves to these values. Although the story of American religious involvement in and response to the institution of slavery in this country is not one of the glorious moments in the history of religious, the experience of our forebears in dealing with this issue might prove enlightening and insightful in the present-day struggle for justice.

Catholic Slaves and Slaveholders in Central Kentucky: Reconstructing a Relationship

C. WALKER GOLLAR*

LATE MARCH OF 1787, a band of Shawnee warriors on Eighteen Mile Island just above the Falls of the Ohio River (near present-day Louisville, Kentucky) fired upon a flatboat of Maryland Catholics. An ounce ball ripped through both thighs of Thomas Hill, while another bullet took the life of Hill's property, a Black man named Hall. Other white and Black voyagers stayed low while their horses were shot down one at a time. The current then took the craft out of range. Eventually, the surviving travelers made it to central Kentucky, where some bought farms on Pottinger's Creek in Nelson County. After Hill recovered from his wounds, he purchased sixty-three acres adjoining the property of another Catholic, Henry Cambron, on Cartwright's Creek, near Springfield in what would become Washington County in 1792. At Hill's home a score of Catholic families periodically gathered for prayer. Early tax receipts indicate that Hill was the largest slaveholder among these pioneers, about a quarter of whom also owned enslaved people.

Like the Hill family, numerous white lay Catholics during the late eighteenth and early nineteenth centuries left behind the exhausted tobacco fields of Maryland in pursuit of unspoiled Kentucky land. They had hoped that clergy would follow, but before such spiritual guidance could be secured, physical labor was already assured through the appropriation of enslaved Blacks. Whether or not these bondswomen and men adhered to the faith of their masters, and thus truly might be called Catholic, can only

---

* An earlier version of this essay appeared as "Catholic Slaves and Slaveholders in Kentucky," *Catholic Historical Review* 84, no. 1 (January 1998): 42–62.

be determined by piecing together what remains of their story. The reconstruction that follows demonstrates that lay Catholics not only accepted slave labor as a part of Southern culture but also essentially endorsed the institution of human bondage.[1]

Catholics as Slaveowners

The overall picture of slavery in the truly pioneering period of Kentucky largely remains obscured by the fact that neither the earliest census records nor most of the first church registers have survived, and extant records are often inconsistent. Incomplete Nelson County tithable lists reveal that 24% of the Catholics who arrived from Maryland owned enslaved people in 1786 but claim only 13% held bondswomen and men the following year.[2] Not

---

1 In his discussion of the early Catholicism in Kentucky, Benedict Webb listed the names of many of the earliest Catholic pioneers living near the waterways of Washington and Nelson County, as well as the neighboring counties noted in the chart herein. Twenty-three persons listed in the 1792 tax list of Washington County also appear in the Saint Rose Register, and/or in Webb's enumeration of the people associated with Cartwright's Creek. Five (or 21.7%) of these people owned enslaved individuals. Other Catholics appear on this tax list (e.g., Leonard Hamilton with eight enslaved people) who were not associated with the Cartwright's Creek community. Undoubtedly more Cartwright's Creek Catholics also appear on this 1792 tax list as well as on the earliest (and now lost) Saint Rose registers, but not on the surviving registers. Hill's five enslaved persons numbered only two above the average possessed by Catholic masters in this area at that time. These figures reflect almost exactly those found among the general population of Washington County. Another quarter of this early Catholic community would purchase enslaved people in due time. All statistics cited in this article were compiled by the author from the sources noted. Benedict Webb, *The Centenary of Catholicity in Kentucky* (Louisville: C. A. Rogers, 1884). Early Catholic pioneers and their enslaved people also were terrorized by some white vagabonds, as was illustrated with the case of Joseph O'Daniel. See V. F. O'Daniel, *The Father of the Church in Tennessee, or the Life, Times, and Character of the Right Reverend Richard Pius Miles, O.P., the First Bishop of Nashville* (Washington, DC: Dominicana, 1926), 39.

2 Six Catholics appeared on the 1785 Nelson County tithable lists, though none owned enslaved people at that time. Seven of twenty-nine and six of forty-seven Catholics from Maryland owned enslaved individuals according to the 1786 and 1787 Nelson County tithables, respectively. Undoubtedly, more Catholics who are hard to identify at this early stage appeared on these lists.

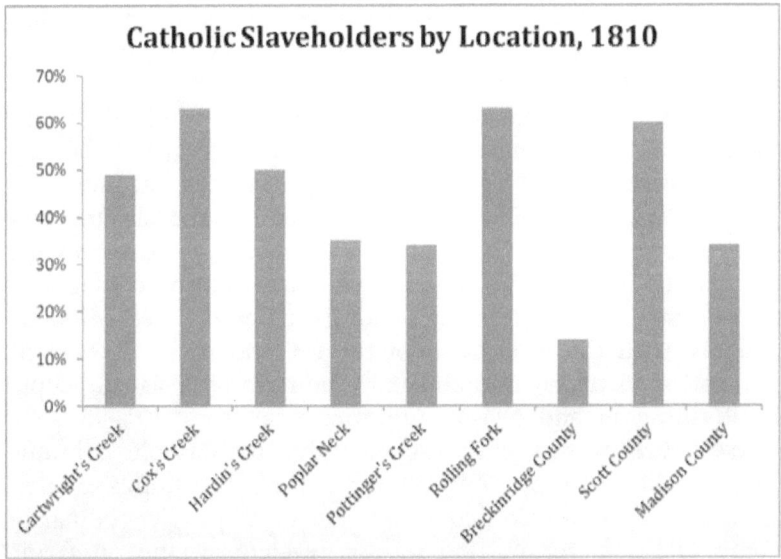

Catholics in central Kentucky had significant ties to slavery. In many communities, between one-third and one half of Catholic families owned enslaved persons (charts and images from the author).

until 1810 are more representative and consistent numbers found. By that time, according to the first surviving census records, half of the Catholic pioneers to central Kentucky owned enslaved persons, even though only one-third of the general population in this area were slaveholders at this time.[3]

When tracking individual Catholics beyond one decade, a much higher percentage emerges. For example, among the Catholic pioneers living in 1810 on Cartwright's Creek (the largest of the early Catholic communities), nearly 70% would own enslaved persons at some point in their lives. Central Ken-

---

3 The 1810 census upon which these figures, as well as the above chart, were based listed the total number of enslaved people in a given household. The earliest Catholic pioneers were identified by Webb, who also noted a handful of pioneer Catholics in Franklin County (pp. 95–96), Mason, Estill, and Bath Counties (p. 98), Hardin and Lincoln Counties (p. 112), Spencer and Bullitt Counties (p. 140), Grayson County (p. 144), Meade County (p. 147), Union County (p. 149), and Nashville, Tennessee (p. 149).

tucky Catholics and non-Catholics alike held between four and five enslaved individuals on average. Kentucky soil, more suitable for hemp and tobacco than for cotton, determined that the large plantations of the Deep South were not found in the Commonwealth (even though many Kentuckians, regardless of religious affiliation, liked to refer to their property as "plantations"). Across Washington County, at least 80% of the slaveholders owned fewer than nine people. Never higher than 4% owned twenty or more enslaved individuals. The percentage of Cartwright's Creek Catholics owning this amount corresponds roughly with the proportion of these Catholics in the overall population. Between 1810 and 1860 the ratio of enslaved people in Washington and Nelson Counties rose from 20% to 25%. These figures were slightly higher within the Catholic community. In short, more Catholics than non-Catholics owned enslaved workers. Consequently, enslaved people ordinarily comprised a larger portion of the residents living on farms owned by Catholics than they did of the population in general.[4]

The relatively close quarters on Kentucky farms sometimes bred endearment between owner and owned. House servants who not only tended their owner's private property, but often actually lived in the home and ran errands unattended by (though with the written permission of) their masters, were more likely to bond with their owners than would common field hands whose work was less rewarding and whose living condi-

---

4   Statistics involving the Cartwright's Creek settlement, as cited above and elsewhere, were based primarily on names that appeared in the register of the second church to serve this community, Saint Rose, built by the Dominicans in 1806. The surviving register (located in the Archives of the Dominican Province of St. Joseph at Providence College) records baptisms, confirmations, marriages, and burials that occurred between 1830 and 1875, but is incomplete. No records remain from the first church, Saint Ann. In addition to the persons who appeared in the Saint Rose register, more members of the Cartwright's Creek community were found in Webb, as well as in various other sources, including Washington and Nelson County wills. Census records from 1810 to 1840 simply enumerated the number of enslaved people in a given household, whereas census records from 1850 and 1860 included both free and slave schedules, with more detail as to age and sex presented for enslaved individuals.

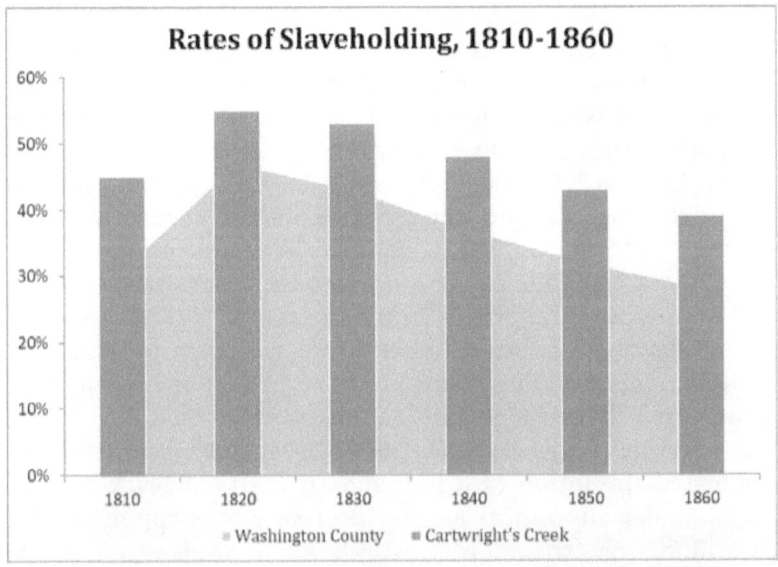

Rates of slaveholding in the Catholic settlement of Cartwright's Creek, located near Springfield in Washington County, exceeded the proportion of slave owners in the county as a whole.

tions usually less comfortable. One Black child who was raised on Cox's Creek north of Bardstown actually contracted the Celtic brogue of his Irish master.[5] And a white boy from a southern bend of Cartwright's Creek, who later became the first bishop of Peoria, Illinois, John Lancaster Spalding, fondly remembered in old age his Black nurse, Lucinda:

> What though thy face was dark . . . thy soul was fair . . .
> What though a slave, since thy pure heart did wear
> No servile yoke . . . but of immortal life was certain heir.[6]

---

5 Webb, *Centenary*, 64–65.
6 John Lancaster Spalding, "Lucinda," found in a loose collection of unpublished poems, presumably written around the beginning of the twentieth century, Archives of the Diocese of Peoria, Illinois. The family of John Lancaster Spalding was more commonly associated with the Rolling Fork settlement, which was closer to the southern bend of Cartwright's Creek than it was to Springfield.

Ann Jarboe Drady had become so attached to her enslaved man, Jacob, that she successfully employed legal means to thwart her husband's plan to sell him.[7] And in consequence of a provision in the will of Nancy Lancaster, all of her enslaved people were freed after caring for nine years for Lancaster's crippled Black child, Charles.[8] Occasionally such faithful service was so rewarded. For example, the townspeople of Springfield purchased Louis Sansbury's freedom after his heroic efforts during the cholera epidemic in 1833. In 1861 Sansbury was buried at the Dominican Church of Saint Rose. Once in a great while before slavery's abolition, other free Blacks also appeared on Catholic registers.[9] For example, of the 1,642 persons buried at Saint Rose between 1830 and 1865, six were free Blacks. Two of the marriages registered at Saint Rose between 1830 and 1848 celebrated the union of a free and an enslaved Black person. Never under any other category do free Blacks appear on the Saint Rose register.

---

7   Washington County Circuit Court record book, February 1801.

8   Washington County, Kentucky Wills, F 110, Last Will and Testament of Jeremiah Lancaster, Sr. (d. 1834), written August 8, 1833; Washington County, Kentucky Wills, G 114–115, Last Will and Testament of Nancy Lancaster (d. ca. 1839), written May 27, 1839; and "Anderson, Indiana [news]paper" cited by Nathaniel E. Green, *The Silent Believers: Background Information on the Religious Experience of the American Black Catholic, with Emphasis on the Archdiocese of Louisville, Kentucky* (Louisville, KY: West End Catholic Council, 1972), 63.

9   Sansbury repeated his heroic efforts during the 1854 cholera epidemic. Orval W. Baylor, *Early Times in Washington County, Kentucky* (Cynthiana, KY: Hobson Press, 1942), 100–102. Some records imply that Sansbury prior to his liberation may have been as mobile as William Hayden, one of Kentucky's more famous, though rather atypical enslaved persons. Washington County Court Order Book F (1843–1852), October 22, 1850; Order Book G (1852–60), December 15, 1853 and February 20, 1854; Will Book K, 556; William Hayden, *Narrative of William Hayden, Containing a Faithful Account of his Travels for a Number of Years, Whilst a Slave in the South* (Cincinnati: 1846). For other emancipations, see Washington County Court Orders, 1843, Emancipations; Washington County Will Book G, 362; Michael L. Cook and Bettie Anne Cook, eds., *Pioneer History of Washington County, Kentucky, As Compiled from Newspaper Articles by Orval W. Baylor and Others* (Owensboro, KY: McDowell Publications, 1980), 157–158; *Washington County, Kentucky, Bicentennial History, 1792–1992* (Paducah, KY: Turner Publishing, 1991), 236.

Enslaved Catholics' Religious Commitments

One day before a Dominican priest from Saint Rose arrived to celebrate afternoon Mass at Francis S. Anderson's farm near Thompkinsville, Anderson decided to spend the morning in the fields but instructed his enslaved boy to come and get him as soon as the priest had arrived. In due time the boy ran out and exclaimed, "The candles are lit and they're going at it!" Benedict Webb, while recounting a visit with Levi Smith, more specifically pointed to slave involvement in household prayer:

> At an early hour of the evening Mr. Smith invited me into the room adjoining the one in which we were sitting, where the members of the family were assembled for night prayers. The greater number of these were my entertainer's colored slaves. Having prostrated ourselves on our knees, I was surprised to hear the prayers given out, not by the master of the house, but by one of his female slaves. The voice of the woman, who appeared to be about forty years old, was so pathetic and well balanced, so true in its enunciation of the words of the petitions, and so evidently a reflex of the emotions of a heart that had at the time no place in it for anything beyond the act in which she was engaged, that I caught myself wondering where she could have acquired gifts and graces which, under like circumstances, I have not unfrequently seen disregarded by better educated people of the white race. Without hurry, and with proper modulation and emphasis, she uttered the petitions set down in the formularies, and, with equal truth to their sentiment, she was answered by the rest. When we arose from our knees that night, I felt that I would like to ask that christian woman's blessing.

Not the presence of enslaved people but the precedence of a female bondswoman had impressed Webb. Other enslaved individuals also were acclaimed as model Christians, including Uncle Harry of missionary priest Stephen Theodore Badin and Uncle Abraham of Charley Boone.[10] A Nelson County enslaved man,

---

10 Story on Anderson courtesy of his great-granddaughter, Linda Anderson, Librarian, Kentucky Historical Society, Frankfort, Kentucky; Webb, *Centenary*, 78n–79n; on Uncle Harry, Martin John Spalding, *Sketches of the Early Catholic Missions of Kentucky: from their Commencement in 1787, to the*

Harry Smith, claimed that his mother, Eliza, had "lived and died a true Catholic, a devoted christian."[11]

Between 1830 and 1849 more enslaved Catholics were baptized than their number warranted. In other words, during this time 31% of all baptisms performed at Saint Rose, by way of example, were administered upon enslaved Blacks, even though according to the relevant censuses, enslaved persons constituted only 25% of the population living at that time on Catholic property. Enslaved and free people served as sponsors for slave baptisms, though enslaved Catholics did not sponsor white people.[12] One dying woman was refused baptism by her Baptist master since full immersion seemed too risky for such an ill person. Then the enslaved woman dreamt that a singularly dressed man offered to make her a Christian without immersion. A few days later Dominican priest Edward Fenwick called upon the house and not only baptized the woman but, in due time, also baptized the master who duly was affected by the accurate forecast of the dream.[13] On such rare occasions, other enslaved adults likewise were welcomed into the Church.

Throughout the 1830s and 1840s, the number of enslaved Catholics confirmed and married at Saint Rose was only slightly less than their relative proportion of the Catholic population, as well as their comparative participation in baptisms would have suggested. Thus, whereas enslaved people constituted 25% of the

---

Jubilee of 1826–7 (Louisville: B. J. Webb and Brother, 1844), 116–117; and on Uncle Abraham, Saint Rose Death Register, October 16, 1847, p. 156. Webb recorded that the Black and white children on Pottinger's Creek enthusiastically anticipated visits from Father Robert Byrne. See Webb, *Centenary*, 36n.

11 Harry Smith, *Fifty Years of Slavery in the United States of America* (Grand Rapids, MI: West Michigan Printing, 1891; reprinted by the Clarke Historical Library), 9.

12 In neither the Saint Rose nor the Saint Joseph Cathedral register appears record of an enslaved person sponsoring a white person. Nathaniel E. Green "from talking to older living Catholics" learned that "black slaves could not be sponsors of other black slaves." Such recollections did not reflect the actual practice. Green, himself, cited in full a typical baptismal record that showed an enslaved person sponsoring another enslaved person. Green, *Silent Believers*, 36.

13 Webb, *Centenary*, 90–91.

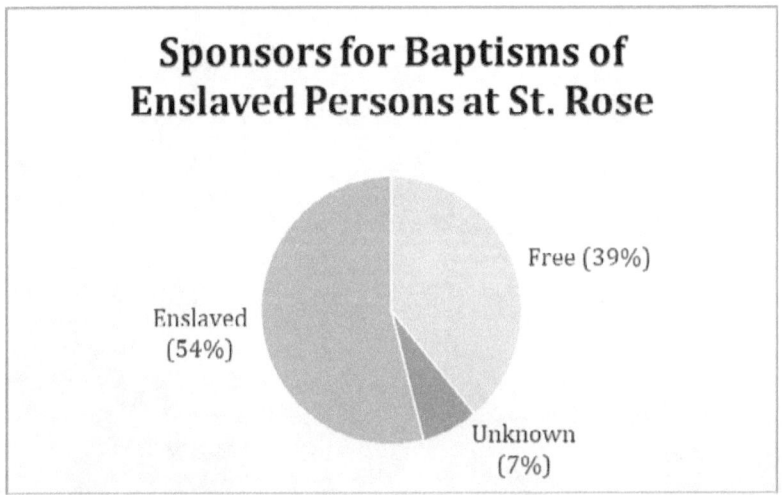

The church registers of Saint Rose indicate that enslaved persons often chose other bondspeople to serve as baptismal sponsors, suggesting some agency in their religious practice.

population of individuals living on Catholic farms near Cartwright's Creek and were involved in 31% of Saint Rose baptisms during this time, only 22% of the confirmations and 17% of the marriages involved enslaved people in this period. But the number of slave burials was slightly higher than their proportion of the population and about the same as the baptismal record would have implied: 30% of those interred at Saint Rose during this time were enslaved. These overall figures confirm only in part historian Randall Miller's observation that the relatively easy act of baptizing enslaved people generally was not matched by an equally high rate of slave participation in other sacramental activity. Instead, figures from the Saint Rose register show that enslaved Catholics rather steadily went to church.[14]

Fathers Stephen T. Badin and Charles Nerinckx both had insisted that enslaved people not only be given access to the

---

14 Randall Miller, "Slaves and Southern Catholicism," in *Masters and Slaves in the House of the Lord: Race and Religion in the American South, 1740–1870*, ed. John B. Boles (Lexington: University of Kentucky Press, 1988), 131.

An early picture of Saint Rose Church in Springfield, Kentucky. The church registers record numerous sacraments for bondspersons.

sacraments, especially that of Christian marriage, but also that they be taught the rudiments of faith.[15] Presumably most churches, certainly including Saint Joseph's Cathedral in Nelson County and Saint Pius in Scott County, conducted catechism classes specially designed for enslaved persons. Yet on the very day a Catholic school for Black and white children was to be opened in Bardstown in 1808, it burned to the ground. One can only speculate on how it caught (or was set) afire. Regardless, this mishap averted the overt opposition that Bishop John England of Charleston, South Carolina, faced twenty-seven years later after he had opened a school to teach free Black children. After white people had rioted in protest, England was forced to close the school. Four years later, John Forsyth, the secretary of state under Andrew Jackson, criticized Pope Gregory XVI's 1839 con-

---

15 Diary of Father Charles Nerinckx, 16, Archives of the Sisters of Loretto; Spalding, *Sketches of the Early Catholic Missions of Kentucky*, 67; Joseph Herman Schauinger, *Stephen T. Badin, Priest in the Wilderness* (Milwaukee: Bruce, 1956), 25.

demnation of the slave trade. Yet in a series of eighteen letters published in the Charleston *United States Catholic Miscellany*, England argued that the pope's statement did not apply to domestic slavery. Moreover, England showed how the Church consistently had accepted the peculiar institution. But England failed to recognize that most Church statements concerning servitude largely sought to ameliorate slave conditions.[16] Such was the case in an article from the Cincinnati *Catholic Telegraph*, which immediately predated England's exposition. Reprinted in the Bardstown *Catholic Advocate*, this Cincinnati piece encouraged Catholics to give their "servants . . . the same opportunity for the practice of their religion" that masters might enjoy. This constituted an obligation of "serious and solemn importance," which could be realized by following these guidelines:

> When the servants are advanced in age, they should be permitted to attend church on every Sunday and such other days as the fulfillment of their other duties may require; and when they are young, no occasion should be omitted to inspire them with a love for virtue and heartfelt and enduring fidelity for the church.

Without evading work, enslaved persons were encouraged to develop religious commitment.[17]

After a series of local retreats late in 1837, the *Catholic Advocate* noted that the attendance of servants was "particularly regular and edifying."[18] And in November 1839, during a retreat at Saint Thomas just outside of Bardstown, a "deep impression on all present" reportedly was made by the participating servants.[19] During church services, enslaved Catholics generally sat apart from their masters, sometimes behind and occasionally in the

---

16   See Peter Clarke, *A Free Church in a Free Society: The Ecclesiology of John England, Bishop of Charleston, 1820–42: A Nineteenth Century Missionary Bishop in the Southern United States* (Hartsville, SC: Center for John England Studies, 1982).

17   *Catholic Advocate*, April 6, 1839.

18   *Catholic Advocate*, October 7, 1837; *Catholic Advocate*, November 17, 1838. On catechism classes, see *Catholic Advocate*, August 3, 1839, and Webb, *Centenary*, 97.

19   *Catholic Advocate*, November 9, 1839.

loft, or "Nigger Heaven," as it was called. But segregation managed Kentucky Catholic churches at this time, as, for example, women sat apart from men and children from their parents. Thus Daniel Rudd, the editor of the *American Catholic Tribune*, claimed that while attending the Bardstown Cathedral as an enslaved boy, he was not discriminated against except concerning the order in which he received the sacraments.[20] Frank Evans, another enslaved Catholic, maintained that during twenty-two years in Marion County he received the sacraments frequently.[21] Historian Stephen J. Ochs has pointed out that religious instruction in colonial Louisiana and Maryland depended on the often lacking zeal of lay masters. Thus, Ochs concluded that the postbellum work of the Mill Hill Fathers was "the most organized effort of the Catholic Church to evangelize Afro-Americans in the United States."[22] Yet registers from antebellum central Kentucky indicate certain determined effort and success, at least in bringing Blacks to the altar. Moreover, enslaved workers helped to build many of the Catholic structures throughout central Kentucky, including, as legend has it, the giant columns and breastwork on the first cathedral.

Endorsement of Slavery

About the only Kentuckian with any Catholic connection who seemed bothered by slavery was Irish-born E. J. "Patrick" Doyle. Raised a Catholic, Doyle had studied at Saint Joseph's College in Bardstown, but as the *Catholic Advocate* later claimed, "his mind was a perfect blank regarding all religious knowledge, and so the dear youth threw himself with spontaneous conviction as

---

20 *Catholic Telegraph*, quoted in *Catholic Advocate*, April 6, 1839; Joseph H. Lackner, "Dan A. Rudd, Editor of the *American Catholic Tribune*, From Bardstown to Cincinnati," *Catholic Historical Review* 80, no. 2 (April 1994), 267. Racial discrimination in Catholic churches remained the rule after emancipation, even before the 1904 Kentucky Day Law institutionalized segregation across the state.

21 Cited in Cyprian Davis, *The History of Black Catholics in the United States* (New York: Crossroad, 1991), 46.

22 Stephen J. Ochs, *Desegregating the Altar: The Josephites and the Struggle for Black Priests, 1871–1960* (Baton Rouge: Louisiana State University Press, 1990), 9.

well as affection into the sympathetic arms of the Presbyterians." After Doyle had become a fervent opponent of the Catholic Church, his next logical step, at least according to many Catholics, would be to join the fanatical abolitionists. These extremists, at least in the mind of the *Catholic Advocate*, falsely had charged slaveholders with harsh treatment of their enslaved workers.[23]

Catholics in Kentucky certainly dared not to challenge the legal institution of slavery and thus fuel the anti-Catholic sentiment which, throughout the 1830s, '40s, and '50s, had accused Catholics of maintaining supreme allegiance to a foreign pope. In response to these charges, Catholics in the South argued that they were fully American and clearly showed their respect for American ways by, among other things, owning people. But such accommodation alone does not explain why Catholics owned *more* enslaved people than non-Catholics. Neither does it account for the fact that, unlike their Christian and American brethren (the Kentucky Baptists, Methodists, and Presbyterians), Catholics never split over the issue of slavery. In short, had Catholics merely represented American society, they would have entertained divergent opinions on slavery as did various groups across the border state of Kentucky. But Bluegrass Catholics almost unanimously endorsed the peculiar institution.

Beyond any particular issue, Catholics envisioned themselves as the safeguard of social order. Catholics viewed abolitionists, on the other hand, as the most recent personification of the Protestant reverence for personal whim. Thus, the *Catholic Advocate* quoted loudly from the New Orleans *Louisiana Advertiser*, which claimed

> that in slave-holding states, a greater degree of social equality, religious liberality, and of truly republican feeling exist, than in non-slaving states, and that in proportion as a state is infected with the verus [sic] of abolition, in a like ratio is it noted for bigotry and narrow selfishness.[24]

When Doyle, indeed, did become an avid abolitionist and later led an insurrection of enslaved Kentuckians in the summer of

---

23 *Catholic Advocate*, March 23, 1836.
24 *Catholic Advocate*, January 5, 1839.

1848, Catholics blamed this behavior on his Presbyterian connection.[25] On the verge of the Civil War, the new diocesan paper, *The Guardian*, specifically attributed "The True Cause of Our Calamity" to Protestantism. With an "unbridled license of private Scriptural interpretation," Northern Protestants had proven slavery a sin while Southern Protestants had proclaimed it lawful. Thus, all of Protestantism, *The Guardian* concluded, "has succeeded in arraying section after section, and stirring up those bitter feelings which render all cordial union of these States next to an impossibility." The misguided and misguiding abolitionists especially deserved blame for arousing hostilities.[26] In effect, Protestant abolitionism, not slavery, stood out as the sin according to Kentucky Catholics, or at least in the minds of those who published their views. Completely absent from the Kentucky Catholic papers not only was any antislavery sentiment, but also any theological justification for slavery or, for that matter, any discussion whatsoever of the issue beyond the direct refutation of abolitionism.

Common Catholic opinion was articulated by one writer who argued that Protestant abolitionists failed to see that "as a class, the slaves appear as happy and contented as any; and the Patriarchal government under which they exist, seems the only one suited to their natures."[27] When the Colonization Society for the North Side of Washington County was formed late in 1833, not a single Catholic joined the roster. The Nelson County branch of this organization met at the Bardstown Presbyterian Church and the Bardstown Baptist Meeting House. But the *Bardstown Herald* never noted that any meeting occurred at a Catholic institution and never mentioned any Catholic participation.[28]

---

25   *Catholic Advocate*, August 26, 1848. Also see *Catholic Advocate*, September 9, 1848, and Marion Lucas, *A History of Blacks in Kentucky, Volume 1: From Slavery to Segregation, 1760–1891* (Frankfort, KY: Kentucky Historical Society, 1992), 73.
26   Louisville *Guardian*, February 23, 1863.
27   *Catholic Advocate*, February 18, 1837.
28   See Cook and Cook, *Pioneer History of Washington County, Kentucky*, 26; *Bardstown Herald*, January 21, June 30, 1832, August 12, 1852, and February 10, 1853.

Many Catholics believed that if emancipated, enslaved people simply would wander aimlessly and become a burden on society. One group of enslaved people living on the southern bend of Cartwright's Creek, when told by their master that Lincoln had set them free, merely responded, "But Missus Spalding, where are we to go?"[29] A few enslaved workers apparently prayed that they not be freed, fearful for their own safety yet undoubtedly also beseeching God in this manner because their masters had told them to do so.[30] Such attitudes indicated for some Catholics that the institution of slavery certainly was not the sin that the abolitionists claimed it was. Some evil may exist, but this was manifested primarily in the international slave trade, or on plantations of the Deep South, which did not depend on, as the *Catholic Advocate* described it, the "mild and gentle" form of slavery found in Kentucky.[31] A former professor at Saint Joseph's and the future archbishop of Baltimore, Francis Patrick Kenrick, while coadjutor to Philadelphia, wrote in the late 1830s a popular manual for moral theology that included reflections on slavery. In this work, Kenrick encouraged masters to "show themselves gentle and even-handed ... [and to] lighten the condition of their slaves with humanity and with zeal for their salvation."[32] In Kentucky, this admonition was realized, by way of example, in the

---

29 The author heard this story from his own oral family history, and also has heard virtually the same refrain from other genealogists. In his short story, "Two Gentlemen of Kentucky," James Lane Allen may have best captured such undying attachment of an enslaved person to master. See James Lane Allen, *Flute and Violin, and Other Kentucky Tales* (New York: Harper and Brothers, 1896), 97–134.

30 Green, *Silent Believers*, 44.

31 *Catholic Advocate*, March 10, 1849. The *Catholic Advocate* periodically noted the atrocities of the slave trade. For example, see December 15, 1838, February 13, 1841, March 13, and 20, 1844, April 8, 1845, and November 6, 1847. Andrew Jackson and local politician, Charles A. Wickliffe, were vilified as "slave traders." See *Bardstown Herald*, August 23, 1828 and July 20, 1831. The *Catholic Advocate* also contained news which depicted a harsher form of slavery in the South. For example, see December 24, 1836, December 30, 1837, April 9, 1839, March 24, May 5, July 10, and August 14, 1841. One writer also claimed that conditions of servitude in England were worse than those of slavery in the United States (August 7, 1847).

32 Quoted in Davis, *Black Catholics*, 49.

life of William Johnson, Esq., who was eulogized as having, among other virtues, kindness to his "servants."[33] Kentucky Catholics generally did not refer to their Black people as "slaves."

Enslaved Catholics' Family Ties

Father Badin early on grew concerned over what he had perceived as the harsh treatment of some servants, and in particular, over the virtual disregard of masters toward Black family ties.[34] Of the enslaved children baptized either at Saint Rose or at Saint Joseph's Cathedral prior to 1840, only 24% came from households that included both parents. More common was the pattern illustrated in the March 24, 1833, baptism of Mary. Her father, Cornelius, was owned by Thomas Medley, while she and her mother were owned by the widow Yates.[35] Like Mary's case, 36% of these baptisms noted that the parents did not live on the same farm. Another 40% fail to name the father of the child.[36] The relatively

---

33 *Catholic Advocate*, November 10, 1838.
34 Badin to Bishop John Carroll, August 4, 1796, Priestland (Washington County, Kentucky), translation by Edward Barnes, S.C.N., Archives of the Archdiocese of Baltimore; Carroll to Badin, August 2, 1794, in *Catholic Telegraph*, May 7, 1853; Webb, *Centenary*, 176.
35 Saint Rose Baptismal Register, March 24, 1833, p. 44.
36 Through the 1840s the number of parents living together decreased to 18%. During this time, 17% of the Washington County slave households with children (persons under ten years of age) included no parental figure (a male or female enslaved person at least twelve years older than the oldest enslaved child). Thirty-six percent included a mother figure (an enslaved woman at least twelve years older than the oldest child) but no father figure (an enslaved man at least twelve years older than the oldest child). An additional 2% included a father figure but no mother figure. In short, only 45% of slave households included possible parents of children residing therein. The 1850 census was the first to record the exact age and sex of enslaved people, and thus the first which provided the information upon which the above observations could be made. Throughout the 1850s, the number of slave households with two parental figures increased about the same amount as did the number of households with no parental figures. Whether or not these possible parents actually had conceived the children in the household cannot be determined. Undoubtedly, many had not. Webb noted that in frontier Kentucky "a boy of twelve years . . . was not infrequently found to be just as available at the plow as a youth of twenty." Indicating that enslaved

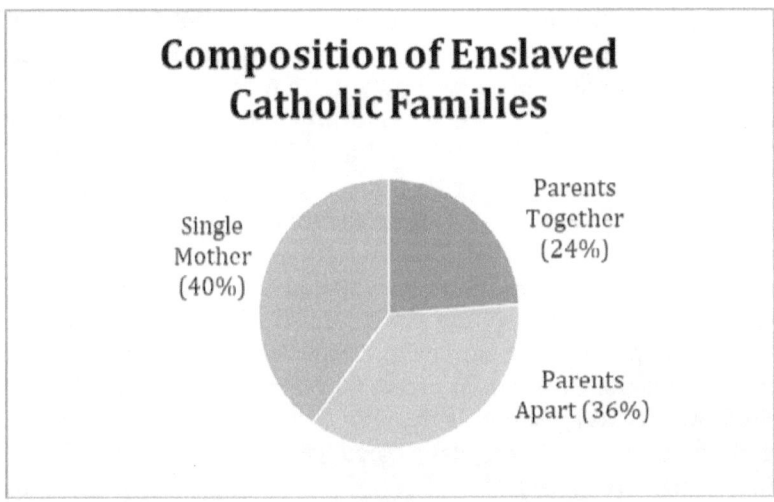

Composition of Enslaved Catholic Families

Single Mother (40%)
Parents Together (24%)
Parents Apart (36%)

Baptismal registers suggest the composition of enslaved families, often with parents living apart on separate farms or, most often, with no mention of the father.

small slave households in Kentucky determined that married couples generally would not be owned by the same person and thus were less likely to live together. Of the eighty slave marriages recorded from 1830 to 1848 at Saint Rose, only seven involved persons owned by the same master. Burial records for free people regularly noted family ties but gave no such indication for enslaved Catholics. More typical was one casual remark which simply noted the internment of "A black child belonging to somebody."[37]

---

children generally went to the fields earlier in age than white children did, Webb underscored the uniqueness of Margaret Mills Abell who was as exacting of service with her children as she was with her enslaved workers. In light of these realities, historian John Blassingame fixed the end of childhood for enslaved people at around ten years of age, when a child generally started working in the fields. Webb, *Centenary*, 106; John W. Blassingame, *The Slave Community: Plantation Life in the Antebellum South* (New York: Oxford University Press, 1972), 184–185.

37   Saint Rose Register, March 29, 1843, p. 137. By way of exception to the general pattern, Elisha Metcalf purchased the wife of one of his enslaved men so that, as was later reported, "the father could have her society at home on the plantation." Smith, *Fifty Years*, 9.

Catholics made careful arrangements for the disposition of their human property even though, at least as one master had suggested, an enslaved person may not have been as desirable in Kentucky as was a good horse.[38] On July 8, 1801, Thomas Hill for "natural love & affection" sold to his children five people: Grace, Jerry, and their sons, David, John, and Daniel. On January 4, 1803, Hill sold to his son Clement a woman named Mary and her child.[39] The vast majority of Cartwright's Creek Catholics willed that their enslaved property be handed down to descendants. Other Catholics ordered that all or some of their enslaved people be sold at public auction, and a couple of these owners determined that their human property be offered only to Catholics.[40] Two owners freed some of their enslaved people in their wills, and one bachelor, Peter Adams, arranged that all of his enslaved individuals be freed. But in this case, either unwilling to acknowledge that Adams truly wished to emancipate his workers or, more likely, reluctant to let go of a potentially lucrative inheritance, Adams' siblings contested the will, suggesting that Adams' enslaved people had coerced him into including the note on liberation. The court eventually proved the authenticity of the will, and Adams' enslaved people were freed. But during the four years of deliberation, the oldest man, Thomas, passed away.[41]

---

38 Will of Joseph Carrico, written May 27, 1833 and probated August 26, 1833, Washington County Will Book E, p. 211.

39 Washington County Deed Book, reprinted in *Lebanon and Marion County, Kentucky* (publication of Marion County Historical Society) 4, no. 3 (Spring 1995). Clement Hill already owed his life to the Black man named Hall who had been shot by the band of warriors back in March of 1787. Hall had fallen dead atop, and thus, effectively protected, then eleven-year-old, Clement, whose eventual offspring numbers in the thousands.

40 Similar preference for a Catholic buyer was expressed in advertisements which appeared in the *Catholic Advocate*, July 27, 1839, December 6, 1839, and August 19, 1848.

41 Will of Peter Adams, written July 25, 1846 and probated December 15, 1856, Washington County Will Book J, p. 456; Bond Concerning Inventory of Adams estate, November 15, 1852, Washington County Court Orders; Deposition of Dr. John H. Polin, dated December 10, 1852; Bond Contesting the Will, December 20, 1852; Order concerning decision of Marion County Circuit Court, November term, 1856. Fifty-eight wills from Cartwright's Creek Catholics were identified, forty-five of which mentioned enslaved people. Forty-two specified that the enslaved property be handed down to heirs.

> **FOR SALE,**
> **LIKELY NEGRO GIRL,**
> *(for ready cash.)*
>
> WILL be offered at Public auction at the house of Rich'd Head, Bardstown, on the first day of April next—A likely negro girl, about 18 years old, of fair character, healthy and strong, a good honest house servant, one that is acquainted with house business, and can work very well on a farm if required.— She is the property of Joseph Adams deceased.
> JOHN HAGAN, *Administrator.*

"For Sale" notice, *Bardstown Repository*, March 23, 1815. Notices regarding enslaved persons for sale or wanted runaways were frequently found in central Kentucky newspapers.

The *Catholic Advocate* and the *Bardstown Herald* periodically posted for sale, along with "OATS" and "WHEAT," "LIKELY NEGROES."[42] Enslaved people were sold outside as well as within the local Catholic community with little regard for Black family ties. At least two Bardstown Catholics, Joseph Price and William Mattingly, traded enslaved people for profit downriver.[43]

---

42 *Catholic Advocate*, September 29, 1838. On one occasion, an advertisement announced that the enslaved people were "country born" (*Bardstown Herald*, January 5, 1831). This paper included notice of events from various denominations, though certainly was partial to Catholicism. From its inception in 1825 to 1828, the *Bardstown Herald* went under the title, *The Western Herald*.

43 See *Bardstown Herald*, March 2, 1831, and July 7, 1853. Historian J. Wintston Coleman identified as a Lexington slave trader, John Mattingly, a man who more than likely was Catholic. See Coleman, *Slavery Times in Kentucky* (Chapel Hill, NC: University of North Carolina Press, 1940), 155, 166–167. For record of one slave sale by a Catholic, see Bill of Sale of Jerry of Clement Parsons to Henry Purdy, June 4, 1822, Mss q564, Cincinnati Historical Society.

Only one of the thirteen slave auctions advertised in the *Catholic Advocate* insisted that an enslaved family not be separated any further. The woman to be sold already did not live in the same home but only in the same city as her husband.[44]

An enslaved person's family became more of a concern if that person ran away. A Lexington man announced in the Nelson County paper that his man, Bill, had fled hoping to make his way to Bardstown "as his wife was taken to the neighborhood of that place a short time ago."[45] Two other masters suspected that their runaway, Paul, would not stray far from his native county "as his family are there [and] we think he would leave it very reluctantly."[46] And after "a bright mulatto boy" named Tom disappeared on Saturday night, March 25, 1837, his owner suspected that he may have gone to Hart County, where he had been raised.[47] Many other owners, in the same fashion, rightly figured that their enslaved people ran not for freedom but for family.[48] In 1853, the *Bardstown Herald* claimed that through the Underground Railroad enslaved people had been "constantly carried away to Canada."[49] Still, fugitives were said overwhelmingly to have found life in the North less desirable than earlier servitude in Kentucky.[50] Undoubtedly such testimonies had been reported, if not totally fabricated, in order to discourage escape. However, disappointment with freedom in the North, indeed, may have been caused by the increased breakup of the family which freedom would have brought. Of the estimated 400,000 enslaved persons who did make it to Canada, about half returned to the states after emancipation, assuredly due, in large part, to family ties left behind.

---

44   *Catholic Advocate*, January 26, 1839.
45   *Bardstown Herald*, September 29, 1832.
46   *Bardstown Herald*, February 17, 1836.
47   *Catholic Advocate*, April 1, 1837.
48   Between 1836 and 1839, seven notices of slave runaways appear in the *Catholic Advocate*. No such notices appear after this time. In the fragments of the *Bardstown Herald* which survive between 1828 and 1855, runaway notices appear at a slightly higher rate, and continue all the way up to 1855. Most of these notices were submitted by Catholic owners.
49   *Bardstown Herald*, September 24, 1853.
50   *Bardstown Herald*, October 8, 1853.

Catholic Owners' Treatment of Enslaved Persons

White children were taught to fear runaways, for as one such boy later wrote, the fugitive might "keep us in a cave and cut off a limb . . . and cook it whenever they became hungry, keeping us alive as long as possible."[51] Patrollers, such as Catholic Captain Leonard Hamilton from southern Washington County, were appointed to round up runaways and, in fact, often made a game out of this commission.[52] Historian J. Winston Coleman has explained that "Negro hunting, Negro catching, Negro watching, and Negro whipping constituted the favorite sport of many youthful whites."[53] Once apprehended, runaways generally were severely beaten and then sold south to the town that was commonly called "Nigger Hell," that is, New Orleans.[54]

Judge Elisha Metcalf of Saint Michael's Church in northern Nelson County, as a matter of course, had all his human property baptized and, just as routinely, beaten. "It was no uncommon thing," Metcalf's bondsman, Harry Smith recalled, "for Massa to have forty or fifty slaves [not all of whom were his] tied and whipped a day for . . . trifling affairs."[55] Announcements of runaways often included note of distinguishing scars and physical handicaps which may have testified merely to the harshness of slave life, if not also to the savagery of some Catholic owners. At least one Catholic, James M. Wheatly, was actually ordered by the court to care for his neglected elderly slave, Emily.[56]

Local newspapers periodically depicted enslaved people as ignorant yet volatile. Thus, threat of insurrection such as that led by Nat Turner was met by a strong show of force from the white community even though the persons who dared to run away gen-

---

51   Cook and Cook, *Pioneer History of Washington County, Kentucky*, 326.
52   Washington County Court Orders, 1822, Miscellaneous Papers.
53   Coleman, *Slavery Times*, 97.
54   Smith, *Fifty Years*, 15.
55   According to Smith, neighbors regularly paid Metcalf twenty-five cents per enslaved person to administer a beating, thus making him a "whipping master." See Smith, *Fifty Years*, 12.
56   County Attorney vs. James M. Wheatly, March 28, 1855, Washington County Court Orders.

erally proceeded both alone and as quietly as possible.⁵⁷ Every now and then, with an especially so-called unruly bondsman or woman, a "whipping master" experienced with flogging persons was employed. Edward McLean had thrashed Maria of Richard Beall several times before showing up again on July 17, 1830. This time she was ready for him. When McLean approached, Maria unveiled a knife and managed to stab him twice. He died later that day and was subsequently buried at Saint Rose. A Catholic jury convicted Maria of murder, and Judge C. C. Kelly sentenced her to be hanged on September 28. But before the order could be carried out, Governor Thomas Metcalfe intervened. In a most unusual decision, Metcalfe judged that Maria's action was not altogether unjustifiable and thus granted her a free and full pardon.⁵⁸

As the slave or free status of the mother determined the status of her children, the appearance of light-colored enslaved persons most likely indicated somewhere in the lineage a Black mother and a white father, or in other words, sexual exploitation of master upon slave. On the verge of the Civil War, nearly a quarter of the enslaved people recorded in the Washington County census were designated mulatto. When a so-called "Catholic Gentleman" offered in the *Catholic Advocate* "a fair price" for an enslaved woman "for his own services," he may have been looking for what was called a "fancy girl."⁵⁹ Historian Marion Lucas has described these women as "attractive, young, often genteel, usually mulatto females who were purchased to be mistresses or prostitutes."⁶⁰

---

57   *Catholic Advocate*, April 29, December 30, 1837, November 9, 1839, April 24, 1841, August 14, 21, and 30, 1841, May 6, 1843, April 20, 1844; *Bardstown Herald*, January 21, 1832.

58   Pardon of Maria (a woman of color), December 4, 1830, Executive Journal, Governor Thomas Metcalfe, Kentucky State Archives; Miscellaneous Papers, 1830, Washington County Court Order Book. Also, Cook and Cook, *Pioneer History of Washington County, Kentucky*, 137–138.

59   *Catholic Advocate*, September 29, 1838.

60   Marion Lucas added, "Numerous Kentucky slaves spoke of beautiful slave girls on their farms who had been taken as mistresses by their owners, a fact which the number of mulattos seemed to confirm." Lucas, *History of Blacks*, 86. One of the more tragic cases of sexual exploitation of an enslaved woman has been chronicled by Melton A. McLaurin in the case of *Celia, A Slave* (Dresden, TN: Avon Books, 1991).

Some of the most revolting accounts of slave auctions detail the humiliations suffered by these women.[61] At least one Catholic bishop, Augustin Verot of Saint Augustine, Florida, who actually considered the institution of slavery to be sanctioned by God, nonetheless denounced this abuse of slave women.[62] But, in general, the practice caused no commotion as long as it remained a private affair.[63]

Rebecca Lovell's house of ill fame in Springfield several times had been prosecuted for prostitution because young male Blacks were said to have frequented the place.[64] Thus when Ralph, one of Richard Spalding's slave boys, wished to marry Ellen, a girl who Spalding recently had purchased, Spalding suggested that the boy's youth ought not to be a deterrent but rather might be viewed as an asset. Marrying young, Spalding had surmised, Ralph would "have none of the responsibility of her family on him," yet would have found a means to curb his sexual passion and, in the process, place one of Spalding's women "beyond the reach of temptation." Spalding mocked Ralph's desire to delay the marriage so that he might, as Spalding had presumed, "establish himself in business somewhere, where he can provide for a family before [he] takes a wife to himself." Finally, Spalding explained that the past arrangement to hire Ralph out in service to the Bardstown cathedral need not change, for Spalding saw no reason why Ralph would have to live, at least in the beginning, with his new wife in order to satisfy conjugal duties.[65] In essence, Spalding advocated slave marriage, not as a means to cultivate the slave family, but rather as a vehicle by which sexual

---

61 For example, see Coleman, *Slavery Times*, 115ff.
62 Davis, *Black Catholics*, 54.
63 When discussing Richard M. Johnson's relationship with his slave mistress in Scott County, William H. Townsend argued that the ignominy of the marriage had more to do with the openness and not the nature of the affair. See William H. Townsend, *Lincoln and the Bluegrass: Slavery and Civil War in Kentucky* (Lexington: University of Kentucky Press, 1955), 75–80.
64 "Rebecca Lovell's House of Ill Fame," 1835, Washington County Court Orders.
65 Richard Marcus Spalding to Benedict Joseph Spalding, December 24, 1846, "Evergreen Bend" (on Cartwright's Creek just north of Lebanon), Benedict Joseph Spalding Papers (BJS) 2/44, Archives of the University of Notre Dame.

passion could be allayed. Though Spalding seemed genuinely concerned in this fashion, at least about the sexual promiscuity of his enslaved people, down Spalding's own family tree, oddly enough, have been passed rumors that Richard Spalding had fathered both slave and free children.[66] At about the same time that young Ralph was contemplating wedlock, the *Catholic Advocate* responded to some of the awful realities of slave life by calling for the legal recognition of slave marriages.[67]

An Enduring Faith?

Because many Blacks had received the Catholic rites of baptism, Eucharist, confirmation, marriage, and Christian burial, they might be called enslaved Catholics. But these bondswomen and men certainly were not honored in this world as children of God. At best, Catholicism may have given enslaved people the spiritual strength to endure the regular insults which came from their masters. One Black spiritual whose devotion to the mother of Jesus may indicate some Catholic connection also may express the aspiration of enslaved people who had been associated with Catholic masters:

> I want some valiant soldier here . . . To help me bear de cross
> Done wid driber's dribin' . . .
> Done wid massa's hollerin' . . .
> Done wid missus' scoldin' . . .
> I want some valiant soldier here . . . To help me bear de cross
> O hail, Mary, hail! O hail, Mary, hail! O hail, Mary hail!
> To help me bear de cross.[68]

Once the cross of slavery had been lifted, most Black people found little use for Catholicism. No record confirms this fact more clearly than does the burial register of Saint Rose. Each year from 1830 to 1865, at least 25% of the people laid to rest had been enslaved. But from 1866 to 1875, barely 5% of the burials were of Blacks, or "negroes" and not "servants" as they formerly

---

66 The present writer is the great-great-grandson of Richard Spalding.
67 *Catholic Advocate*, March 10, 1849.
68 William Francis Allen, et al., *Slave Songs of the United States* (New York: A. Simpson and Co., 1867), 45.

were called. Many other Church records prove this mass exodus from Catholicism. Archbishop Martin John Spalding spoke of the "golden opportunity to reap a harvest of souls" after emancipation. And in 1870, Spalding's nephew, Father John Lancaster Spalding, boldly argued for the spiritual rights of formerly enslaved persons, claiming that both before and after the Civil War, Black people rightly enjoyed free access to the sacraments.[69] Yet unfortunately, as some historians have pointed out, the Catholic Church failed miserably in its mission to formerly enslaved individuals.[70]

Some Blacks did stay with the Church, as is indicated by two present-day predominantly Black congregations: Holy Rosary in Springfield and Saint Monica in Bardstown. Other nearby churches also include a significant Black population. These include Saint Charles and Saint Augustine in Marion County, and Saint Mary in Boyle County. Nevertheless, the story about Catholic lay people in frontier Kentucky indicates that the Church had disappointed Blacks long before the Civil War.

Though masters gave enslaved people religious affiliation, they took away more immediate bonds, such as the family, and thus earned but perfunctory commitment from the Black population. Enslaved Blacks may have been equal before the eyes of God but certainly not before the eyes of white human beings. Perhaps the more hierarchical worldview promoted in the Catholic Church that tended to stress authority and respect from above, readily and without shame fixed enslaved Blacks at the bottom of the ladder. Less structured Christian churches more easily may have felt the inconsistent human ethic promoted by

---

69 "Has the Negro a Soul?" *Catholic Advocate*, July 16, 1870.

70 Randall M. Miller, "The Failed Mission: The Catholic Church and Black Catholics in the Old South," in *Catholics in the Old South: Essays on Church and Culture*, Randall Miller and Jon Wakelyn, eds. (Macon, GA: Mercer University Press), 149–170; and Ochs, *Desegregating the Altar*, 9–48. In his article, Miller failed to recognize the Catholic population of central Kentucky among his five admittedly small regional divisions of Catholics in the South. But he did write about the relatively obscure other Catholic enclave in Western Kentucky of French and German Catholic settlers. See Miller, "The Failed Mission," 151.

slavery. Meanwhile Catholic lay people not only accommodated to American ways that included slavery but virtually in unison promoted the peculiar institution. Thus, in the end, many so-called Catholic servants, baptized yet beaten, may have intoned the words of the slave girl, Harriet Jacobs, when she sang,

> Ole Satan' church is here below.
> Up to God's free church I hope to go.
> Cry amen, cry amen, cry amen to God![71]

---

71 Linda Brent (Harriet Jacobs), *Incidents in the Life of a Slave Girl* (Boston: 1861), reprinted in Henry Louis Gates, Jr., ed., *The Classic Slave Narratives* (New York: New American Library, 1987), 400.

American Reaction to Gregory XVI's Condemnation of the Slave Trade

JOHN F. QUINN*

IN DECEMBER 1839, Pope Gregory XVI issued *In Supremo Apostolatus*, an apostolic letter that condemned the slave trade in no uncertain terms. He published the statement at the prompting of the British government, which had been campaigning for years to bring it to an end. The British believed that a papal letter might persuade Spain and Portugal to enforce the laws against slave trafficking in their domains, but it had little impact on either country. Instead, Gregory's pronouncement set off a debate both within and without the Catholic community in the United States. During the 1840s and '50s, it twice surfaced during presidential campaigns, was hotly debated by supporters of the Irish Repeal[1] movement, and was hailed by the abolitionist leader Wendell Phillips. Even the Catholic bishops, who were very wary about making political pronouncements, were drawn into the fray. Indeed, as the Church's ranks swelled through immigration from Ireland and to a lesser extent from German states and made it America's largest religion, arguments raged over what it really taught about slavery.[2] All the

---

* An earlier version of this essay appeared as "'Three Cheers for the Abolitionist Pope!': American Reaction to Gregory XVI's Condemnation of the Slave Trade, 1840–1860," *Catholic Historical Review* 90, no. 1 (January 2004): 67–93. The author wishes to express thanks to Philip Gleason, Edmund Wehrle, Jr., John McGreevy, Joseph Capizzi, Kevin McGrath, O.P., Bradley Lewis, George Antone, and William T. Quinn for their comments and to Sister Eugena Poulin, R.S.M., Alexander Calenda, and Robert Evans for their help with translations. Funding for this research was obtained from the National Endowment for the Humanities and Salve Regina University.

1 Repealers wanted to undo the Act of Union of 1801, which joined Ireland closely to Great Britain. Repeal would have allowed the Irish to have their own legislature in Dublin again.

2 By 1850 there were 1.6 million Catholics in America, which was almost ten percent of the total population. See Jay P. Dolan, *The American Catholic Experience* (New York: Doubleday, 1985), 160–161.

way up until the Civil War, abolitionists repeatedly put forward Gregory's letter when trying to make the case that the Catholic Church opposed slavery and defenders of slavery tried to interpret it in a narrow fashion so as to minimize its significance.

Enlisting the Pope

In the 1830s, the British government was on a crusade to suppress the African slave trade.[3] The British and the Americans had both outlawed the practice in 1807, and France had followed suit in 1818.[4] At the Congress of Vienna in 1815, the British had persuaded the other powers to sign a declaration against the slave trade, but it was vague and nonbinding.[5] They then negotiated separate treaties with Spain and Portugal in an effort to suppress it. By 1838 Lord Palmerston, the British foreign secretary, was growing impatient. Slaves were still being shipped by the thousands from Africa to Cuba and Brazil.[6] Consequently, he looked to the United States and to the papacy for help. He contacted the American ambassador to the Court of St. James, Andrew Stevenson, to see if the United States might be interested in sponsoring a worldwide conference on the slave trade. Stevenson, a Virginia slaveholder, was not enthusiastic, but he duly passed on the proposal to the U.S. Secretary of State, John Forsyth, a Georgian, who was deeply suspicious of anything that smacked of abolition.[7] Although opposed at least in theory to the slave trade, Forsyth was not about to devote American resources to such a project.

Palmerston had more reason for optimism with regard to the papacy. In 1815 Pope Pius VII had issued a brief condemning the slave trade in response to an appeal from the British foreign secre-

---

3 David R. Murray, *Odious Commerce: Britain, Spain and the Abolition of the Cuban Slave Trade* (New York: Cambridge University Press, 1980), x–xi; Linda Colley, *Britons: The Forging of a Nation, 1707–1837* (New Haven, CT: Yale University Press, 1992), 350–360.
4 Hugh Thomas, *The Slave Trade* (New York: Simon & Schuster, 1997), 625.
5 Murray, *Odious Commerce*, 50–56.
6 Roughly 10,000 slaves were brought into Cuba illegally in 1838. See Murray, *Odious Commerce*, 112.
7 Andrew Stevenson to John Forsyth, February 29, 1840, Stevenson Family Papers, container 43, Library of Congress, Washington, D.C.

Pope Gregory XVI, author of the antislavery bull *In Supremo Apostolatus* (from *Il trionfo della Santa Sede e della Chiesa*, 1832).

tary, Lord Castlereagh.[8] In July 1839, Thomas Aubin, the British consul at Florence, wrote to the pope's secretary of state, Cardinal Luigi Lambruschini, asking for a declaration from the Holy See. Aubin noted that the British had been working for years to suppress the trade. While most European countries had willingly cooperated with them, the British had had trouble with certain countries which were "in spiritual communion with the Holy See."[9] Aubin was sure that a public declaration on this subject by the pope would be "most advantageous to the cause of humanity and would render a great honor to the Roman government."[10]

---

8   Castlereagh was looking for a statement from the pope to support the declaration made against the slave trade by the Congress of Vienna. See John Francis Maxwell, *Slavery and the Catholic Church* (Chichester: Barry Rose, 1975), 73; Francois Renault, "Aux origines de la lettre apostolique de Gregoire XVI *In Supremo* (1839)," *Memoire Spiritaine* 2 (November 1995): 145–146.

9   Thomas Aubin to Most Rev. Luigi Lambruschini, July 13, 1839, Pos. 40, fasc. 15, Archivio Segreto Vaticano, Congregation for Extraordinary Ecclesiastical Affairs: Inghilterra (hereafter, ASV, CEEA).

10   Aubin to Lambruschini, July 13, 1839, ASV, CEEA.

When Gregory learned of Aubin's letter, he decided to put the matter before the cardinals who served in the Congregation for Extraordinary Ecclesiastical Affairs.[11] Before being elected pope in 1831, Gregory had served for six years as prefect of Propaganda Fide, the curial congregation that oversaw Catholic missions all over the world. Keenly interested in evangelizing Africa, Asia, and Latin America, Gregory was very much aware of the hardships that these peoples were enduring. No doubt the slave trade was of great concern to him.[12]

To assist the other cardinals in their deliberations, Lambruschini drew up a lengthy memorandum on the subject. In his report, he sharply criticized the British government for its long record of hostility toward the Holy See. Considering these tensions, he declared that it would be neither "convenient" nor "useful" for the pope to make any allusion to the British if he were to issue a letter.[13]

Lambruschini also noted that there were many defenders of slavery and the slave trade in the Church who could offer a host of reasons to justify them. Among other points, they would make reference to Abraham and Jacob and other patriarchs owning slaves; to St. Paul's counsel to slaves to obey their masters; and to the Council of Gangra (330) and other councils which appeared to affirm the legitimacy of slavery and the slave trade. None of these claims impressed him much: "All of these arguments tending to excuse or justify slavery and the trafficking of Negroes have their responses, and have been refuted by expert writers and theologians."[14]

---

11   Pope Pius VI had set up this office in 1793 to deal with the exceptional issues raised by the French Revolution. After the Revolution, the congregation advised the pope on foreign relations. See Charles G. Herbermann, ed., et al., *Catholic Encyclopedia* (New York: Robert Appleton, 1912), XIII: 145–146.

12   Gregory also wanted to staff mission territories with native priests and bishops. See Peter Guilday, *The Life and Times of John England, First Bishop of Charleston*, 2 vols. (New York: The America Press, 1927), II: 282; Owen Chadwick, *A History of the Popes, 1830–1914* (Oxford: Clarendon Press, 1998), 46–49.

13   "Inghilterra," Pos. 40, fasc. 15, p. 2, ASV, CEEA; Claude Prudhomme, "La papaute face a l'esclavage: quelle condamnation?" *Memoire Spiritaine* (Premier semestre 1999): 144.

14   "Inghilterra," Pos. 40, fasc. 15, p. 4, ASV, CEEA; Renault, "Aux origins," 147.

Lambruschini felt that the time was propitious for the pope to issue a new statement. Arguing that Pope Gregory should draw on the writings of his predecessors, he provided the pope and cardinals with copies of the relevant papal pronouncements and Holy Office statements dating back to the 1400s. He also took up the sensitive matter of whom the pope should address. At the time, neither Spain nor Portugal nor any of the Latin American republics had diplomatic relations with the Holy See.[15] If a letter were directed to the rulers of these states, there was a good chance it would never be published. He noted that a letter could be sent to the bishops of these nations, but he feared such a move would antagonize the political leaders.[16]

When the cardinals met with the pope, they agreed that he should issue a public declaration on the slave trade: it would not be directed to any person or nation in particular, and no reference would be made to Great Britain's role in it. A letter was promptly drafted by one of the cardinals and edited by the pope. In the final version, Gregory noted that due to the Church's influence, "there were no slaves allowed amongst the great majority of the Christian nations" in the Middle Ages. Subsequently, however, Christians, motivated by sheer greed, began to traffic in Indians and Negroes. This trade had been repeatedly condemned by the Holy See. He listed five of his predecessors who had forbidden it: Pius II (1462), Paul III (1537), Urban VIII (1639), Benedict XIV (1741), and Pius VII (1815).[17] As the practice was still widespread among Christians, he felt obligated to add his voice to those of the earlier popes and "vehemently admonish . . . that none henceforth dare to subject to slavery, unjustly persecute, or despoil of their goods, Indians, negroes or other classes of men." Lay Catholics were informed that they would face excommunication if they disobeyed, and clergy, too, were

---

15 All of these countries were controlled by liberal, anticlerical regimes. Since 1834, the Spanish government had been battling the Carlists, who were ardently conservative and Catholic.

16 "Inghilterra," Pos. 40, fasc. 15, pp. 7–8, ASV, CEEA.

17 For an account of these popes' statements, see Joel Panzer, *The Popes and Slavery* (New York: Alba House, 1996), 7–43. David Brion Davis argues that these papal statements were politically motivated. See *The Problem of Slavery in Western Culture* (Ithaca, NY: Cornell University Press, 1966), 99–101.

sternly warned not to oppose this teaching. The letter was published on December 3, which was the feast of St. Francis Xavier, the Jesuit missionary who spent years evangelizing the people of India and Japan.[18]

Although principally concerned with the slave trade, the letter had enough antislavery language in it that it could easily be seen as an attack on the institution of slavery as well. On the other hand, since Gregory said nothing about the need to free the slaves, it could be viewed as simply a condemnation of the slave trade.[19] Furthermore, the pope's decision to issue a public declaration provoked speculation about his intended audience. Those who were interested in American slavery seized on it and claimed that the pope had the United States in mind.

---

18 An English language version of the letter appears in the *United States Catholic Miscellany*, March 14, 1840 (hereafter, *USCM*).

19 There is still no consensus today among scholars about his intent. Hugh Thomas argues that Gregory followed a "pure abolitionist line" (*The Slave Trade*, 666). For a similar view, see Panzer, *The Popes and Slavery*, 44–48, and Claudia Carlen, I.H.M., *Papal Pronouncements: A Guide, 1740–1978* (Ann Arbor, MI: Pierian Press, 1990), 27. Robert Emmett Curran says that he "explicitly condemned the slave trade and seemed to condemn by implication . . . slavery itself." See "Rome, the American Church, and Slavery," in *Building the Church in America: Studies in Honor of Monsignor Robert F. Trisco on the Occasion of his Seventieth Birthday*, ed. Joseph C. Link and Raymond J. Kupke (Washington, DC: Catholic University of America Press, 1999), 30. Curran's view is shared by this writer and by Cyprian Davis, O.S.B, in *The History of Black Catholics in the United States* (New York: Crossroad, 1990), 39–40, and Leslie Woodcock Tentler, *American Catholics: A History* (New Haven: Yale University Press, 2020), 119–120. James Hennessey, S.J., claims that the pope "condemned the slave trade, but not slavery itself." See *American Catholics: A History of the Roman Catholic Community in the United States* (New York: Oxford University Press, 1981), 145. This is also the conclusion of John Tracy Ellis, *American Catholicism*, 2nd ed. (Chicago: University of Chicago Press, 1969), 89; John T. McGreevy, *Catholicism and American Freedom: A History* (New York: W.W. Norton, 2003), 50, 52; and John T. Noonan, *A Church that Can and Cannot Change: The Development of Catholic Moral Theology* (Notre Dame, IN: University of Notre Dame Press, 2005), 104–108. Finally, the legal scholar John Maxwell contends that Gregory did not intend to ban the slave trade outright but only wanted to bring an end to "unjust slave trading" (*Slavery and the Catholic Church*, 74).

Spreading the Word

British officials were very pleased with the statement and hoped that it would have an effect on Spain and Portugal since they were at least nominally Catholic. However, getting the letter published in those countries proved quite difficult.[20] Aubin arranged to have copies of it published in Turin and in the German city of Lübeck.[21] At the end of December, the London *Times* printed the letter in full.[22]

In early January, Irish abolitionists took note of it as well. James Haughton, a Unitarian antislavery activist, wrote to Daniel O'Connell of the "noble-minded bull of his Holiness the Pope on the subject of slavery."[23] While O'Connell was best known for helping to secure Catholic Emancipation in 1829, he had also played a pivotal role in Parliament's decision to eliminate slavery in the West Indies in 1833.[24] Indeed, he had been a thoroughgoing abolitionist since 1824 and often gave speeches on the subject.[25] Haughton felt that this would be an opportune time for O'Connell to send the Irish in America one of his "powerful appeals" on slavery.

O'Connell was interested enough in the pope's letter that he went to the trouble of copying it down word for word at this time.[26] However, he did not accede to Haughton's request. At the

---

20   The letter appeared in the *Gaceta de Madrid* in 1840, but the British were unable to get it published in Cuba because of opposition from the island's ruler, the captain-general. See Thomas, *The Slave Trade*, 666.

21   Serge Daget, "A Model of the French Abolitionist Movement and its Variations," in *Anti-Slavery, Religion, and Reform: Essays in Memory of Roger Anstey*, ed. Christine Bolt and Seymour Drescher (Folkestone, UK: W. Dawson, 1980), 73.

22   [London] *Times*, December 31, 1839.

23   James Haughton to Daniel O'Connell, January 11, 1840, in *The Correspondence of Daniel O'Connell*, 8 vols. (New York: Barnes & Noble, 1972–1980), VI: 2673.

24   Itzhak Gross, "The Abolition of Negro Slavery and British Parliamentary Politics, 1832–1833," *Historical Journal* 23 (1980), 63–85.

25   Douglas C. Riach, "Daniel O'Connell and American Anti-Slavery," *Irish Historical Studies* 20, no. 77 (March 1976), 5.

26   There is a handwritten copy of the letter dating from February 1840 in the O'Connell Papers, P 12/5/171, Archives Department, University College Dublin, Dublin, Ireland.

moment, he was simply too enmeshed in the workings of Parliament to devote any time to the antislavery campaign.[27] Instead another Irish Catholic, Doctor R. R. Madden,[28] made it his mission to publicize the pope's letter. A British-appointed judge on the Mixed Commission in Havana, Madden had gone to the United States in November 1839 to serve as an expert witness in the *Amistad* trial.[29] He had argued persuasively that the forty slaves involved in the mutiny had been kidnapped in Africa and shipped to Cuba. His testimony helped the enslaved persons gain their freedom and made him a hero among American abolitionists.[30]

Madden for his part was not impressed by what he had seen in America. This had been his third visit to the United States in a span of five years. From his American travels he had concluded that Northern whites "detest the people of colour . . . with a degree of rancorous animosity that is almost incredible."[31] On the subject of race, he had learned to his "surprise and sorrow" that the Irish immigrants were just as bigoted as everyone else: "They are not only indifferent and apathetic on the subject of the emancipation of the slaves, but they are even strenuously opposed to the efforts of those who labour in behalf of this cause of justice and humanity."[32]

With the pope having spoken out so forcefully, Madden felt that this was the time for abolitionists to make clear that slavery was contrary to the Catholic tradition. In January 1840, he addressed a meeting of the Hibernian Anti-Slavery Society (HASS)

---

27 Oliver MacDonagh, *The Emancipist: Daniel O'Connell, 1830–1847* (London: Weidenfeld & Nicolson, 1989), 183–185.

28 Richard Robert Madden (1798–1886) was trained as a surgeon but gave up his practice in 1833 to work for abolition. See David R. Murray, "Richard Robert Madden: His Career as a Slavery Abolitionist," *Studies: An Irish Quarterly Review* 61 (Spring 1972), 41.

29 The Mixed Commission was comprised of English and Spanish judges and was empowered to prosecute anyone involved in illegal slave trading. For Madden's work in Cuba, see Murray, *Odious Commerce*, 121–124.

30 Howard Jones, *Mutiny on the Amistad* (New York: Oxford University Press, 1988), 99–110.

31 T.M. Madden, ed., *The Memoirs—chiefly autobiographical—from 1798 to 1886 of Richard Robert Madden* (London: Ward & Downey, 1891), 88.

32 *Dublin Weekly Register*, February 1, 1840.

in Dublin on the subject of Christianity and slavery. He made the bold claim that Gregory was only the latest in a long line of Christian figures to denounce slavery. He noted that a number of Church Fathers had condemned it, including St. Cyprian and Tertullian. In the medieval period, he found a number of saints such as Raymond of Peñafort who had dedicated their lives to ransoming slaves. He also pointed to holy men such as saints Francis Xavier and Peter Claver who had spent their lives ministering to slaves. He concluded by noting that the *Catechism of the Council of Trent* (1570) explicitly condemned slavery in its discussion of the Seventh Commandment.

Having presented his case to a very sympathetic audience, Madden next tried to enlist the Catholic bishops of Ireland. As the bishops were preparing to assemble for their annual meeting in Dublin in February, Madden wrote to ask them to put slavery on their agenda.[33] He hoped the bishops would use the occasion of *In Supremo* to produce an antislavery manifesto of their own. To assist them, he sent a summary of the presentation that he had given to the HASS on the history of Catholic opposition to slavery. He was convinced that a strong statement from the Irish hierarchy would help make "our countrymen in America acquainted with the obligation which this Bull so forcibly points out." As it turned out, the Irish bishops spent all three days of their meeting locked in a bitter debate over the school system that the British government was erecting.[34] Consequently, they had no time to attend to Madden's request or any other matter.[35]

Americans Take Note

Like Ireland's bishops, the Catholic hierarchy in America had a major meeting scheduled in 1840. Since 1829, the bishops had

---

33   R. R. Madden to the Archbishops and Bishops of Ireland, [February 1840], printed in the *Irish Catholic Directory* (1841), 367–368.

34   Emmet Larkin, "The Quarrel among the Roman Catholic Hierarchy over the National System of Education in Ireland, 1838–1841," in *The Celtic Cross*, ed. Ray B. Browne, et al. (Lafayette, IN: Purdue University Studies, 1964), 121–146.

35   No other topic was broached at the meeting. See Minute Books, Dublin Diocesan Archives, Dublin, Ireland.

been meeting every third or fourth year in Baltimore for a weeklong provincial council. They were holding their Fourth Provincial Council in May and would have to find a way of dealing with the difficult issues raised in Gregory's letter. The Irish-born bishop of Cincinnati, John B. Purcell, hailed the letter in his newspaper, the *Catholic Telegraph*. Describing the pope as "the right sort of abolitionist," Father Edward Purcell, the editor and the bishop's younger brother, declared that the letter makes

> us hug ourselves in the comfortable feeling that we live not in a slave-holding state. Following in the footsteps of his venerable predecessors, the father of the faithful shews that all his children, no matter for their complexion, are equally objects of his affectionate solicitude; and that no pretext of necessity or convenience, can justify in the sight of God, or screen from his righteous displeasure, the odious traffic in human flesh.[36]

For the Southern bishops, however, the letter was much more problematic. Bishop Benedict Fenwick of Boston sensed the difficulties ahead. Writing to Archbishop Samuel Eccleston of Baltimore, Fenwick remarked, "The Pope's Bull . . . will place our southern bishops in no very pleasant situation."[37] The leading figure among the Southern bishops—and indeed the whole body—was John England of Charleston, South Carolina. Born in Ireland, England had come to Charleston in 1820 to serve as its first bishop. An enthusiast for all things American, England hoped that he and his fellow Catholics would readily gain acceptance from the Protestant majority.[38] As the leading Catholic figure in a rabidly proslavery state, England was determined that his coreligionists not be tarred with the abolitionist label. In 1835 England himself had been rumored to be an abolitionist sympathizer

---

36 [Cincinnati] *Catholic Telegraph*, March 18, 1840. For Purcell's antislavery leanings, see McGreevy, *Catholicism and American Freedom*, 82–85.

37 Most Rev. Benedict Fenwick to Most Rev. Samuel Eccleston, March 11, 1840, Archives of the Archdiocese of Boston, Boston, Massachusetts.

38 Guilday, *John England*, II: 71–72, 374; R. Frank Saunders, Jr., and George A. Rogers, "Bishop John England of Charleston: Catholic Spokesman and Southern Intellectual, 1820–1842," *Journal of the Early Republic* 13, no. 3 (Fall 1993), 301–322.

because he had established schools for free Black children. Fearing violence, he had closed the schools and issued a statement disavowing any connection with abolitionism.[39]

Once again facing the possibility of having his church associated with abolitionism, England decided to act quickly and address *In Supremo* head on. In March 1840, he printed the full text of Gregory's letter in Latin and in English in his newspaper, the *U.S. Catholic Miscellany*. In the same issue, England penned an editorial praising the pope for condemning the slave trade: "The gross misconduct of Spain and Portugal . . . in carrying on this traffic is palpably cruel and demoralizing. More than a quarter of a century has passed away since our Union has lifted her voice and armed her fleets for its suppression." He then added that "the document is far from censuring those, who without their own choice, have been placed under the necessity of managing their property with a delicacy, a responsibility and a perplexity, to which they who vilify us are strangers."[40]

At the provincial council two months later, England played a much more prominent role in the proceedings than did the primate and host, Archbishop Eccleston. England preached for an hour and a half at the opening Mass on the progress that the Church had made in America over the previous fifty years.[41] Midway through the week, a memorial Mass was offered for a deceased bishop and was followed by a public session. At the start of this session, the pope's letter was read but then the bishops devoted the rest of their time to the question of their priests' behavior. They were seeking the best means to encourage their clergy to lead more edifying lives. Evidently, *In Supremo* was only

---

39 Adam L. Tate, *Catholics' Lost Cause: South Carolina Catholics and the American South, 1828–1861* (Notre Dame, IN: University of Notre Dame Press, 2018), 176–185; Joseph Kelly, "Charleston's Bishop John England and American Slavery," *New Hibernia Review* 5, no. 4 (Winter 2001), 53–56; Guilday, *John England*, II: 151–156.

40 *USCM*, March 14, 1840. See also Suzanne Krebsbach, "Rome's Response to Slavery in the United States," *Catholic Historical Review* 105, no. 2 (Spring 2019): 331–332.

41 Bishop's Journal, May 17, 1840, Archives of the Archdiocese of Boston; *USCM*, May 23, 1840.

John England, bishop of Charleston, South Carolina, argued that *In Supremo Apostolatus* did not apply to domestic slavery as practiced in the U.S. (Diocese of Charleston, South Carolina).

read in Latin and was not discussed at all.[42] The *U.S. Catholic Miscellany* had a correspondent attending the council, and all he could report was that "a decree of the Pope . . . was read."[43]

By week's end, England had delivered five major addresses. At the final Mass on Sunday, May 24, he preached for an hour and a half on the four marks of the Church. As the council concluded, England had reason to be pleased. The bishops had produced statements on mixed marriages, the temperance movement, and several other questions and had dealt discreetly with *In Supremo*.[44] A potentially volatile issue had been handled skillfully and put to rest—or so it must have seemed.

---

42 Joseph E. Capizzi, "For What Shall We Repent? Reflections on the American Bishops, Their Teaching, and Slavery in the United States, 1839–1861," *Theological Studies* 65, no. 4 (December 2004), 783.

43 USCM, May 30, 1840.

44 Peter Guilday, *A History of the Councils of Baltimore, 1791–1884* (New York: Macmillan, 1932), 123–126.

Thwarting Tippecanoe

In the summer of 1840, the Democrats found themselves in an unfamiliar position: they seemed to be headed toward a crushing defeat in November. They had controlled the presidency since 1828, when Andrew Jackson had routed John Quincy Adams. Jackson had retired after two terms and had been succeeded by his vice-president, Martin Van Buren. Short in stature and balding, Van Buren had no military experience and little in the way of charisma. Furthermore, a severe depression had hit the country in May 1837—just two months after Van Buren assumed office—and showed no signs of abating.[45]

Worse yet, the Whigs had settled on William Henry Harrison, a retired general who had fought the Indian leader Tecumseh at Tippecanoe and had battled the British in the War of 1812. Well aware that the Whigs were a "catch-all" party, embracing Southern slaveholders and antislavery Northerners and people with conflicting views on banking and tariffs, Harrison and his associates carefully refrained from taking strong stands on these questions and instead promised to restore prosperity and bring an end to corruption.[46] Whig strategists employed catchy slogans for the general and his running mate such as "Tippecanoe and Tyler, Too" and referred to the president as "Martin Van Ruin."[47]

To defeat the Whigs, the Democrats decided that they had to focus on the issues. At their convention in Baltimore, the delegates produced a nine-point statement that stressed the party's commitment to states' rights and its steadfast opposition to any efforts by abolitionists "to interfere with questions of slavery."[48]

---

45 Michael F. Holt, *The Rise and Fall of the American Whig Party* (New York: Oxford University Press, 1999), 61–70; Daniel Walker Howe, *What Hath God Wrought: The Transformation of America, 1815–1848* (New York: Oxford University Press, 2007), 502–508.

46 Holt, *The Rise and Fall*, 104–110; Arthur M. Schlesinger, Jr., ed., *History of American Presidential Elections*, 4 vols. (New York: McGraw-Hill, 1971), I: 665–684.

47 Senator John Tyler was Harrison's running mate. Howe, *What Hath God Wrought*, 571–588.

48 "The Democratic Platform of 1840," in Schlesinger, *History*, I: 691.

In August, Democratic leaders decided to make a concerted effort to inform Southerners about the Whigs' views on slavery. Twelve Democratic members of Congress sent a letter "To the People of the Slaveholding States" warning them that a "fanatical sect" of abolitionists was growing ever more brazen and that Harrison had "expressed no opinions on the subject on which the South can rely."[49] A few days later, Secretary of State Forsyth followed up with a letter to his fellow Georgians. While the congressmen's letter stressed the danger that the South faced from crazed Northerners, Forsyth pointed out that considerable pressure was also being applied from overseas:

> The Government of Great Britain . . . has lately been employing itself as the volunteer or selected agent of the Pope, in presenting an apostolic letter on slavery to some of the Spanish American States—a letter which it is not at all improbable was prepared under influences proceeding from the British Isles.

He went on to note that the British had allowed slaves to flee to Canada, had enlisted Africans in their army, and had sent commissioners to Cuba to police the slave trade. He also alluded to the World Anti-Slavery Convention which had been held in London in June, noting that "the brutal O'Connell was quite at home" at it.[50] He concluded his address on an almost apocalyptic note: "The shadows of the troubles in store for us, at home and abroad, are darkening and stealing upon us. . . . What measures of precaution are required? The gravest thought and most anxious deliberation are demanded, to meet the dangers which sooner or later will come."[51] Along with his address, Forsyth attached the pope's letter and a report on the Whig convention indicating the role abolitionists played in securing Harrison's nomination.

---

49 *Baltimore-American*, September 5, 1840; *Globe*, August 25, 1840.

50 For the World Anti-Slavery Convention, see Henry Mayer, *All on Fire: William Lloyd Garrison and the Abolition of Slavery* (New York: St. Martin's Press, 1998), 288-293; Riach, "Daniel O'Connell," 6–7.

51 Quoted in the *Globe*, September 19, 1840; *Niles National Register*, September 26, 1840.

Letters to Forsyth

When Bishop England read Forsyth's address, he was incensed at Forsyth for misrepresenting the pope's letter so seriously. Furthermore, it appeared to him that Forsyth was trying to stir up anti-Catholic sentiment in the South by tying the pope to abolition. Earlier in the campaign, England, who had Democratic sympathies, had defended the Democrats from accusations of anti-Catholicism.[52] When Whig editors dredged up charges against Van Buren saying that he had discriminated against Catholics in the early 1830s, England demonstrated that the allegation was groundless. His intervention had earned him praise from Democratic newspapers like *The Globe* and opprobrium from the *Niles National Register* and other Whig journals.[53] Now just two months later he felt obligated to rebut Forsyth, the Democrats' senior statesman.

England was not the only Catholic to take offense at Forsyth's remarks. In October, a retired Whig congressman, William Brent,[54] expressed his concerns to England:

> I cannot but think that you must disapprove of the unjustifiable attack made upon the Pope by Mr. Forsyth. . . . [I]t shows the prejudiced feelings of the administration against our Religion and had I no other reasons for opposing Mr. Van Buren's re-election, I most certainly, would do it, for the unpardonable attack . . . upon the Head of my Church.[55]

Although Brent did not realize it, England had already begun replying to Forsyth in late September. After reading Forsyth's address, England wrote an open letter to him and printed it in the *U.S. Catholic Miscellany*. He challenged Forsyth's contention that the papal letter had been written at the request of the British and asked

---

52 For England's Democratic loyalties, see Saunders and Rogers, "Bishop John England," 314–315; Guilday, *John England*, II: 523–526.

53 See, e.g, *Globe*, September 1, 1840; *Niles National Register*, September 26, 1840.

54 Brent represented Louisiana from 1823–1829. See *Notable Names in American History* (Clifton, NJ: T. J. White, 1973), 71–74.

55 William L. Brent to Most Rev. John England, October 21, 1840, England Papers, box 4, Charleston Diocesan Archives, Charleston, South Carolina.

John Forsyth, U.S. Secretary of State, sparred with Bishop England over the meaning of In *Supremo Apostolatus*, interpreting the pope's apostolic letter as in favor of abolitionism (Library of Congress).

him to provide evidence for his claim. England's main concern, however, was to disprove Forsyth's charge that the letter dealt with slavery. He explained that the pope's warning about "reduc[ing] into slavery Indians, negroes, or other classes of men" referred to the slave trade. The pope could not have had American slaves in mind because they had been born into slavery and had never experienced liberty. At the end of his long letter, England still had more to say about the pope's declaration, and so he promised a second installment: "In my next, sir, I shall give additional reasons to show that our holy father, Pope Gregory XVI, is not the associate of abolitionists, and that the Catholics of the south should not be rendered objects of suspicion to their fellow citizens."[56]

The following week, England published another detailed letter to Forsyth, offering two more reasons to show that Gregory's letter concerned only the slave trade. First, he pointed out that the letter was "formally read and accepted" by the bishops at

---

56 *USCM*, September 29, 1840.

their provincial council. Noting that seven of the thirteen bishops were from slaveholding states, he declared that none of them took it to censure "domestic slavery." He then recounted a discussion that he had with Pope Gregory when he visited him in Rome in 1836.[57] During their conversation, Gregory remarked: "Though the southern states of your union have had domestic slavery as an heir-loom, . . . they are not engaged in the *Negro traffic*."[58]

By this point, England was confident that he had demonstrated the true meaning of Gregory's letter. However, because he saw the question of slavery "as one of great moment at the present time, and likely to become much more troublesome before many years shall elapse," he decided to furnish Forsyth—and the rest of the nation—with a comprehensive history of the Church's teaching on slavery.

In the weeks following, England examined the treatment of slavery in the Old and New Testaments. He contended that slavery was widespread in ancient Israel and was not explicitly condemned by Jesus or St. Paul and then moved on to the patristic age, where he focused on heretical groups such as the Gnostics and the Manichees. Within these movements were many abolitionist militants who urged slaves "to desert their owners."[59]

As the weeks passed, the election came and went and Harrison and the Whigs prevailed. The Democrats were only able to win seven states as opposed to nineteen for the Whigs. Most of the South, including Forsyth's Georgia, had opted for Harrison. These developments did not deter Bishop England from his project. In January 1841, an editor of the *U.S. Catholic Miscellany* explained that England sought "to exhibit the perfect compatibility of the Domestic Slavery, as it now exists in our southern states, with the principles and practices of the Christian religion."[60]

---

57 Pope Gregory had appointed England his legate to Haiti in 1833 and directed him to negotiate a concordat with the Haitian president. See Guilday, *John England*, II: 270-313; Tate, *Catholics' Lost Cause*, 178–179.
58 *USCM*, October 4, 1840. Emphasis in original.
59 *USCM*, October 28, 1840.
60 *USCM*, January 2, 1841.

Over the next four months, England produced nine more lengthy, pedantic letters on the subject, filled with Latin, Italian, and Greek quotations. By April, he had completed eighteen letters and had taken his history of Europe up to 1000 A.D. Although only half-finished, he was forced to put aside his work at this point because of a trip he was taking to Ireland. As it turned out, he returned to America ill and died in April 1842.[61]

Although the project was incomplete, England's key points came through clearly. He had shown that slavery was commonplace throughout the first millennium and had argued that the Church had at least tolerated the practice. He noted legislation enacted at various synods describing the circumstances under which slaves could be ordained as priests and the penalties assessed on owners who allowed their slaves to work on the Sabbath. At the same time, he claimed that Church leaders were always working to improve the lot of the slaves and safeguard their rights. He contended that the Church took the exact same position in his own age.

Their limitations notwithstanding, England's letters constituted a powerful apologia for slavery.[62] It is no wonder that on the day following England's death, the editors of one of Charleston's leading newspapers declared: "Of the South, he was a true friend and an able champion, fearlessly throwing the weight of his character, influence and intellect, in favor of her much misunderstood and much reviled institutions."[63]

"Cling by the Abolitionists"

As Bishop England was finishing off his last letter to Forsyth, Irish abolitionists were again talking about their need to draft an antislavery address to the Irish who had settled in America.

---

61 Guilday, *John England*, II: 530–540.
62 Madeleine Hooke Rice, *American Catholic Opinion in the Slavery Controversy* (New York: Columbia University Press, 1944), 66–70; George W. Potter, *To the Golden Door: The Story of the Irish in Ireland and America* (Boston: Little, Brown, 1960), 382–384.
63 *Charleston Courier*, April 12, 1842.

Daniel O'Connell, the "Irish Liberator," supported both Irish Repeal and slavery's abolition in the U.S., though he attracted few Irish Americans to his position on slavery (Library of Congress).

O'Connell had been asked on a number of occasions to draw up such a letter.[64] While he had promised to write one, the press of other business forced him to keep putting it off. In the summer of 1841, O'Connell was as busy as ever, preparing for a general parliamentary election. Consequently, two of the leading members of the HASS, James Haughton and R. D. Webb, took it upon themselves to write the long-awaited letter. The Irish Address was brief and its language was very clear and pointed.

Assuring the Irish emigrants that they "possess great power, both moral and political, in America," Haughton and Webb urged

---

64 In addition to Haughton, two American abolitionists, Elizur Wright and James G. Birney, had contacted O'Connell in 1838 and 1840, respectively. See Elizur Wright to O'Connell, October 20, 1838, in Maurice R. O'Connell, ed., et al., *Correspondence of Daniel O'Connell*, 8 vols. (Dublin: Blackwater Press, 1972–1980), VI: 1837–1840, Letter 2566, pp. 193–194; Dwight Dumond, ed., *The Letters of James Gillespie Birney, 1831–1857*, 2 vols. (New York: Appleton-Century, 1938), II: 683.

them to "treat the colored people as your equals, as brethren. By all your memories of Ireland, continue to love liberty—hate slavery—CLING BY THE ABOLITIONISTS—and in America, you will do honor to the name of Ireland."[65] While they described slavery at one point as a "sin against God and man," they mostly focused on natural rights and the need for America to live up to the principles expressed in the Declaration of Independence. They made no reference to Catholicism or to Pope Gregory's letter.

O'Connell was happy to sign the letter as were Dr. Madden and Father Theobald Mathew, the temperance reformer. O'Connell also put his nationwide network of Repeal wardens to work gathering supporters.[66] By December 1841, 60,000 Irishmen had signed on. The letter was carried to America by Charles Lenox Remond, a Black abolitionist who had been lecturing and raising money in Ireland for several months.[67] Remond presented it to his friend and mentor William Lloyd Garrison upon his arrival. Garrison was ecstatic; this was just the sort of message that he ardently wanted the Irish immigrants to hear. The Irish in Boston were solidly backing the Democratic Party and were proving to be strongly opposed to the city's small Black community.[68] In hopes of changing some minds, Garrison decided to hold a mass meeting in Boston to publicize the address.[69]

---

65 *The Liberator*, March 25, 1842.

66 There are several letters from Repeal wardens regarding their efforts to obtain signatures. One warden from Kells wrote to say that he had obtained 500 signatures in his town: "Everybody here is willing to abolish slavery but the vile faction that allways kept this country and every other country in bondage. For instance, I called two I believe Orangemen and when they saw the great man's name [O'Connell] that was first to that Petition they walked away and would not sign." Repeal Warden to T. M. Ray, November 28, 1841, Loyal National Repeal Association Papers, Ms. 13, 623, National Library of Ireland, Dublin.

67 For Remond's Irish tour, see C. Peter Ripley, *The Black Abolitionist Papers*, 5 vols. (Chapel Hill: University of North Carolina Press, 1985) I: 7–8, 97–103.

68 Thomas H. O'Connor, *The Boston Irish: A Political History* (Boston: Northeastern University Press, 1995), 81–84.

69 Gilbert Osofsky, "Abolitionists, Irish Immigrants, and the Dilemmas of Romantic Nationalism," *American Historical Review* 80, no. 4 (October 1975), 898–899.

On January 28, 1842, 5,000 people, including perhaps 1,500 Irish immigrants, crowded into Faneuil Hall.[70] At the meeting, the speakers tried their hardest to woo their Irish listeners. Garrison, a strong supporter of O'Connell and Repeal, went out of his way to identify himself with Ireland:

> England, in true slaveholding style, says that Ireland cannot take care of herself, and therefore *she* will take care of the Emerald Isle. . . . But Ireland has about made up her mind, that she will no longer be the vassal of England, to be subjected to famine, oppression and misrule.[71]

He then proceeded to read the Irish Address to his listeners.

Garrison was followed by Wendell Phillips, a young well-heeled Bostonian. Since Phillips had just spent the better part of two years in Italy, it was fitting that he would be the one to speak about the Catholic religion.[72] While in Rome, he had been astounded by the Church's color-blindness:

> African lips may join in the chants of the Church, unrebuked even under the proud dome of St. Peter's; and I have seen the colored man in the sacred dress pass with priest and student beneath the frowning portals of the Propaganda College at Rome, with none to sneer at his complexion.[73]

Phillips may have been referring to George Paddington, a young Black priest who was then studying in Rome.[74]

---

70   Faneuil Hall had a capacity of 5,000. For estimates on the Irish presence, see *Liberator*, February 18 and April 1, 1842; Osofsky, "Abolitionists, Irish Immigrants," 899.
71   *Liberator*, February 4, 1842.
72   Phillips' wife, Ann, was ill so they took a European tour at the direction of her doctors. See James Brewer Stewart, *Wendell Phillips: Liberty's Hero* (Baton Rouge: Louisiana State University Press, 1986), 76–82; Oscar Sherwin, *Prophet of Liberty: The Life and Times of Wendell Phillips* (New York: Bookman Associates, 1958), 109–119.
73   *Liberator*, February 4, 1842.
74   Paddington, who was born in Dublin, was ordained in 1836 by Bishop England and served in Haiti. In 1840 he came to Rome to study. In a letter to a Black Catholic layman, Pierre Toussaint, he tells of putting on the Roman ecclesiastical attire for the first time. Paddington to Toussaint,

He finished his remarks by noting that

> a long line of Popes, from Leo to Gregory, have denounced the sin of making merchandize of men—that the voice of Rome was the first to be heard against the slave trade—and that the bull of Gregory XVI forbidding every true Catholic to touch the accursed thing, is yet hardly a year old.[75]

Garrison was certain that he and Phillips and Remond had connected with their Irish audience. Soon after the meeting, he wrote to R. D. Webb and told him it had made "a great impression on the public mind."[76] As time passed, however, Garrison became increasingly pessimistic. Bishop John Hughes of New York City led the opposition. He said that the letter was possibly a forgery and that even if it were shown to be authentic, it would be "the duty of every naturalized Irishman to resist and repudiate the address with indignation . . . because . . . [it] . . . emanated from a foreign source."[77] The leading Irish-American newspapers followed Hughes's lead. The editors of the *Boston Pilot* and the *St. Louis Reporter* noted that Dr. Madden's name appeared well above those of O'Connell and Father Mathew, so perhaps Madden—a paid employee of the British government—was the real author.[78] Hughes had also complained that the address singled out Irish Americans as a group distinct from other Americans. He wanted to be thought of as an American first and foremost. This point would be echoed by various Irish American newspapers and Repeal Associations.[79]

December 20, 1840, Pierre Toussaint Papers, New York Public Library. See also Davis, *The History of Black Catholics*, 93–94.

75 *Liberator*, February 4, 1842; Manisha Sinha, *The Slave's Cause: A History of Abolition* (New Haven, CT: Yale University Press, 2016), 360–361.

76 William Lloyd Garrison to R. D. Webb, February 27, 1842, quoted in Osofsky, "Abolitionists, Irish Immigrants," 900.

77 *Liberator*, March 25, 1842. For Bishop Hughes's claim that the letter was forged, see Angela F. Murphy, *American Slavery, Irish Freedom: Abolition, Immigrant Citizenship, and the Transatlantic Movement for Irish Repeal* (Baton Rouge: Louisiana State University Press, 2010), 82–84.

78 *Liberator*, March 25 and April 15, 1842.

79 Rice, *American Catholic Opinion*, 81–84; Riach, "Daniel O'Connell," 10–12.

Having received so much criticism for an address that he had not written, O'Connell said little about American slavery for the rest of the year. And on the rare occasions when he did speak out on the subject, he coupled his statements with denunciations of Garrison's heterodox religious opinions.[80] O'Connell was focusing more and more on his Repeal campaign. Wendell Phillips feared that O'Connell's "noble lips" had been "clogged with gold" from Repeal societies in Charleston and other Southern cities.[81]

In the fall of 1842, O'Connell dramatically announced that 1843 would be the "Repeal Year," and from this point on the movement gained momentum both in Ireland and the United States.[82] In March 1843, Repealers began staging massive rallies throughout Ireland. In the United States, new Repeal Associations sprang up throughout the country from Syracuse to New Orleans and Natchez. Each association collected dues and forwarded monies to Dublin as their contributions to the "Repeal Rent." Thomas Mooney, an Irish Repeal agent in New York City, could barely contain himself: "There is no language I can use [that] would convey an adequate idea of the feeling that is growing up in this country on behalf of Repeal."[83]

In May, as plans were being laid for even larger rallies, the slavery issue surfaced once again. At a Repeal meeting in Dublin, a letter from the Pennsylvania Anti-Slavery Society was read that criticized Irish Americans for their stance on slavery. Much of the meeting was then given over to a speech by O'Connell denouncing American slavery.[84]

In July the Cincinnati Repealers decided to respond to the points raised by the Pennsylvania abolitionists. Along with a $113 contribution for the Repeal Rent, the Repealers enclosed a

---

80   Garrison had criticized clerical authority and had questioned the observance of the Sabbath on Sunday. For these pronouncements, O'Connell branded him a "religious maniac." See Riach, "Daniel O'Connell," 12.
81   Riach, "Daniel O'Connell," 15; Stewart, *Wendell Phillips*, 111.
82   See Lawrence McCaffrey, *Daniel O'Connell and the Repeal Year* (Lexington: University of Kentucky Press, 1967).
83   Thomas Mooney to Editor, *The Nation*, March 11, 1843.
84   *The Nation*, May 15, 1843; Potter, *To the Golden Door*, 398–399.

detailed letter explaining their views. While noting that they lived in a free state and considered slavery "an evil of the highest magnitude," they claimed that there was no easy way to eradicate it because American slaves had been reduced to a "state of degradation." Freeing them immediately, as abolitionists desired, would have disastrous consequences. The Repealers were sharply critical of the abolitionists, remarking that the "Roman Catholic Church has no bitterer enemies" in America. They closed their letter by noting that slavery is "sanctioned by professed Christian ministers of almost every persuasion."[85]

In August, an indignant O'Connell listened as his son John read the Cincinnati statement at a Repeal meeting.[86] Seeing it as a full-fledged apologia for slavery, O'Connell declared that a reply would be drafted. At the time, however, he and his associates were planning to hold their largest Repeal meeting ever in October outside of Dublin. On the eve of the great rally, Repealers learned that the British prime minister, Robert Peel, had banned it, and O'Connell, always law-abiding, acquiesced. With his Repeal campaign stalled, O'Connell decided to devote his energies to answering the Cincinnati address.

On October 10, O'Connell presented a lengthy and emotional reply at a regular Repeal meeting. He began by declaring his "utter amazement at the perversion of mind and depravity of heart which your address evinces. . . . It was not in Ireland you learned this cruelty." He then offered a point-by-point refutation of each of their claims. To the assertion that slaves were hopelessly degraded, O'Connell attributed their condition to their lack of education and not to any natural inferiority of their race. To show what Blacks could achieve if provided with educational opportunities, he referred to two Black priests studying in Rome who have "distinguished themselves in their scientific and theological course." To the charge that many abolitionists were anti-Catholic, O'Connell agreed that there were many "wicked and calumniating enemies of Catholicity and of the

---

85 *Freeman's Journal*, August 31, 1843; Sinha, *The Slave's Cause*, 361.
86 For O'Connell's pained expression, see Samuel May, Jr., to Garrison, August 26, 1843, printed in *Liberator*, October 6, 1843.

Irish," but argued that the best way to disarm them was to take the side of the slave.

O'Connell was particularly troubled by the report that most Catholic priests were proslavery. He said he simply could not believe it. He then reminded them of Pope Gregory's teaching:

> [E]very Catholic knows how distinctly slave holding, and especially slave trading, is condemned by the Catholic church. That most eminent man, his Holiness the present pope, has by an allocution, published throughout the world, condemned all dealing and traffic in slaves. . . . Yet, it subsists in a more abominable form than his Holiness could possibly describe in the traffic which still exists in the sale of slaves from one state of America to another. . . . If you be Catholics, you should devote your time and best exertions to working out the pious intentions of his Holiness.[87]

In his account of Pope Gregory's letter, O'Connell was replying not only to the Cincinnati Repealers but to Bishop England as well. For even if it were true that the pope was concerned with the slave trade and not slavery, O'Connell believed that the letter still applied to the United States because vast numbers of slaves were being bred in the Upper South and shipped to the Deep South.

O'Connell concluded his address with a call to the Cincinnati Repealers to "come out of the councils of the slaveowners, and at all events to free yourselves from participating in their guilt."

To reinforce his point about Pope Gregory's teaching, he enclosed a copy of *In Supremo* with his letter.[88]

"Three Cheers!"

While still chafing from O'Connell's criticisms, Garrison nonetheless decided to hold another rally in Faneuil Hall to pub-

---

87 *The Nation*, October 14, 1843.
88 For accounts of O'Connell's exchange with the Cincinnati Repealers, see Murphy, *American Slavery*, 150–173; Maurice R. O'Connell, *Daniel O'Connell: The Man and his Politics* (Dublin: Irish Academic Press, 1990), 127–130; Theodore W. Allen, *The Invention of the White Race* (London: Verso, 1994), 174–176.

licize his address.⁸⁹ Billing it as a "Grand Meeting on Irish Repeal and American Slavery," the organizers attracted a considerable number of Irish men and women.⁹⁰ At the meeting Garrison praised O'Connell and the Repeal movement and then proceeded to read the address.

Garrison was followed by Wendell Phillips, who hailed O'Connell for having "a heart large enough for all climes and colors, for the Irish peasant and Negro slave." Aware that the Cincinnati Repealers had charged abolitionists with harboring anti-Catholic views, Phillips was determined to set the record straight. Hailing Pope Gregory for his letter, Phillips read portions of it to his listeners. Declaring that it was "the first papal bull ever read in Faneuil Hall, in this city of the Puritans," he then asked,

> [W]here is the sect among all the hundreds of our country, which can point to such an explicit testimony upon slavery and the slave trade, emanating from its head and leader in the present day? *Not one*. . . . Prejudice against Catholics among abolitionists! I propose three cheers for the abolitionist Pope Gregory XVI—and may they ring out gloriously from these arches of Liberty's home!⁹¹

While three long cheers were given for Gregory, the tenor of the meeting changed dramatically when the next speaker, John C. Tucker, vice-president of the Boston Repeal Association, arose. An Irish Catholic immigrant, Tucker claimed to be opposed to slavery, but declared that he was an American and did not want to be controlled by O'Connell or the pope. When he finished his remarks, he was warmly applauded by the Irish in the crowd. A second Irish speaker, D. W. O'Brien, echoed Tucker's comments and was also well received.

After four hours, the meeting broke up with little resolved. The abolitionists were quite discouraged. Noting that only one Irishman

---

89 Garrison sent O'Connell an anguished letter asking him why he had gone out of his way to "attack me personally in the most contemptuous manner." Garrison to O'Connell, December 8, 1843, printed in *Liberator*, December 8, 1843.

90 *Liberator*, November 17, 1843.

91 *Liberator*, November 24, 1843. Emphasis in original.

in the audience had spoken up on behalf of abolition, a writer for the *Liberator* concluded that "the Irish only care about Repeal."⁹²

Bishop England's "Celebrated Letters"

While this Faneuil Hall rally had proved even more of a failure than the previous one, Catholic defenders of slavery nonetheless felt that they needed to respond. In December 1843, the editors of the *U.S. Catholic Miscellany* took up the issue once again. To demonstrate that Pope Gregory condemned only the slave trade, they summarized the historical arguments put forth by the late Bishop England. In addition, they quoted Bishop Francis P. Kenrick of Philadelphia, who had recently published a three-volume guide to moral theology intended for seminarians.⁹³ In his chapter on slavery, Kenrick acknowledged that it was regrettable that there were so many slaves in the United States and that "it has been necessary to pass laws prohibiting their education, and in some places greatly restricting their exercise of religion. Nevertheless since such is the state of things, nothing should be attempted against the laws."⁹⁴

William George Read, a wealthy Catholic lawyer and close friend of the late Bishop England, decided that more needed to be done.⁹⁵ Consequently, he collected England's eighteen letters to Forsyth and had them published in a bound volume. In the

---

92 *Liberator*, November 24, 1843. For the abolitionism and Repeal meeting, see Murphy, *American Slavery*, 162–165; John F. Quinn, "Expecting the Impossible? Abolitionist Appeals to the Irish in Antebellum America," *The New England Quarterly* 82, no. 4 (December 2009): 705.

93 See Joseph Brokhage, "Francis Patrick Kenrick's Opinion on Slavery" (Ph.D. dissertation, Catholic University of America, 1955); Hugh J. Nolan, *The Most Reverend Francis Patrick Kenrick, Third Bishop of Philadelphia, 1830–1851* (Philadelphia: American Catholic Historical Society, 1949), 241–242.

94 *USCM*, December 9, 1843. For Kenrick's contention that slavery must be maintained for the sake of the common good, see Brokhage, "Francis Patrick Kenrick's Opinion," 149–164; Capizzi, "For What Shall We Repent?," 781 n54, 789.

95 Read, a Harvard graduate and convert to Catholicism, was sought after as a lecturer for Catholic organizations. See William George Read Papers, Ms. 1400, Maryland Historical Society, Baltimore, Maryland.

preface, he explained that O'Connell's "late most unwarrantable attempt to impart the semblance of religious authority, to his incendiary appeals concerning slavery" left him no choice but to publish England's letters. Otherwise, he feared that many American Catholics might adopt O'Connell's "theological errors."[96] By March 1844, the *Letters to Forsyth* was in print.[97]

O'Connell's Last Days

It is not clear that O'Connell took any notice of Read's book. At this time, he was concerned much more with his own affairs. In February 1844, he and seven other Repealers had been convicted of seditious conspiracy and sentenced to a year in prison.[98] With his health failing and the Repeal movement sputtering, O'Connell had little time for American matters.

Occasionally, he would condemn the annexation of slaveholding Texas. And there were times when he would go on at length about slavery.[99] When Frederick Douglass visited Dublin and took part in a Repeal meeting in September 1845, he listened spellbound as O'Connell spoke for over an hour on the wickedness of American slavery.[100] Still, O'Connell made no further efforts to enlist the Irish in America into the antislavery movement.

In the fall of 1845, Ireland was beset by a partial famine. Half of the potato crop was destroyed by a fungus. As the famine

---

96 William George Read, ed., *Letters of the Late Bishop John England to the Honorable John Forsyth on the Subject of Domestic Slavery* (Baltimore: J. Murphy, 1844), iii.

97 Favorable notices on the book appeared in the *USCM*, March 16, 1844, and in the Baltimore archdiocesan paper, the *U.S. Catholic Magazine* 3 (March 1844), 203.

98 O'Connell and his associates were released after serving three months because the judgment was overturned on appeal. See MacDonagh, *The Emancipist*, 250–251.

99 See Osofsky, "Abolitionists, Irish Immigrants," 903–905.

100 See Tom Chaffin, *Giant's Causeway: Frederick Douglass's Irish Odyssey and the Making of an American Visionary* (Charlottesville: University of Virginia Press, 2014), 60–64; John F. Quinn, "'Safe in Old Ireland': Frederick Douglass's Tour, 1845–1846," *The Historian* 64, nos. 3/4 (Spring & Summer 2002), 540–541.

worsened in 1846, O'Connell marshalled all of his remaining energies on behalf of the Irish peasants. In the winter of 1846, O'Connell's doctors directed him to go to a warm and sunny part of the Continent. O'Connell agreed and set off on a pilgrimage to Rome to meet the new pope, Pius IX. (Gregory XVI had died in the summer of 1846.) The trip proved too taxing for him, however, and he died en route in May 1847.

With the deaths of O'Connell and Pope Gregory XVI, the Catholic Church had lost its two most prominent antislavery figures. By this time, Catholic defenders of slavery had likewise lost two of their key spokesmen: Bishop England had died in 1842, and William George Read had died in 1846.[101]

While the major protagonists were gone, the skirmishing continued. In 1846, Ignatius Reynolds, who had succeeded John England as bishop of Charleston in 1844, decided that England's scholarly writings should be assembled and published in five bound volumes.[102] Three years later, 1,200 copies of *The Works of the Right Reverend John England* appeared in print. In his preface, Reynolds praised England for his erudition and eloquence and for his skill at "accommodating himself to the circumstances, and spirit of the age, in which we live."[103] He added that the *Works* were one of the first substantial Catholic contributions to American intellectual life. Because of Reynolds' efforts, readers had yet another opportunity to see England's letters to Forsyth. If they had missed them when they appeared in the *U.S. Catholic Miscellany* in 1840-1841 or when Read reprinted them in 1844, they could find them in their entirety in Volume III of the *Works*.

Free Men, Frémont, and Francis

In the fall of 1856 Pope Gregory's letter appeared one last time in the United States. In the presidential race, the newly-

---

101 For Read's obituary, see *U.S. Catholic Magazine* 5 (May 1846), 287–288.

102 For Reynolds' appeal for subscriptions, see *U.S. Catholic Magazine* 6 (December 1847), 670–671; Guilday, *John England*, II: 409–411.

103 Ignatius Reynolds, ed., *The Works of the Rt. Rev. John England* (Baltimore: John Murphy, 1849), v.

formed Republican Party nominated John C. Frémont, a popular young explorer with little political experience. He was pitted against James Buchanan, a bland Pennsylvania Democrat, and Millard Fillmore, the former president who was the candidate of the nativist Know-Nothing Party. At their convention in June, the Republicans condemned slavery in the territories. With Kansans literally at war over slavery, the Republicans placed the blame for the bloodshed squarely on Senator Stephen Douglas and his fellow Democrats. Douglas's Kansas-Nebraska Act of 1854 directed the settlers of the territories to decide for themselves whether to allow slavery. Sensing that "Bleeding Kansas" might cost the Democrats the election, enthusiastic Republican delegates left the convention eager to campaign, with "Free Speech, Free Soil, Frémont" as their rallying cry.[104]

Democrats fought back assailing Frémont as a fanatical abolitionist whose election would threaten the Union.[105] While Frémont sought to avoid the slavery issue as much as possible, his supporters at the New York *Independent*, a leading antislavery newspaper, decided to focus on it in an effort to draw Irish Catholic voters to the Republican ticket.[106] In August they printed the pope's letter on their front page side by side with an article lamenting that the

> leaders of the Roman Catholics of this country have generally adopted the policy of the late Bishop England ... in limiting the application of [Gregory's letter] to the slavery and slave traffic of Africa ... and have practically regarded American slavery as a thing which even the Pope must not venture to pass judgment upon.

To demonstrate that at least a few Catholics were heeding the pope's directives, they recounted a conversation between a "gen-

---

104 Schlesinger, *History*, II: 1023–1024.
105 Schlesinger, *History*, II: 1066–1077, 1088–1094.
106 The *Independent* was founded by Congregationalists in 1848 and had a circulation of 30,000 by 1856. Henry Ward Beecher was one of its contributing editors, and Lewis Tappan was a key financial supporter. See Debby Applegate, *The Most Famous Man in America: The Biography of Henry Ward Beecher* (New York: Doubleday, 2006), 231–236.

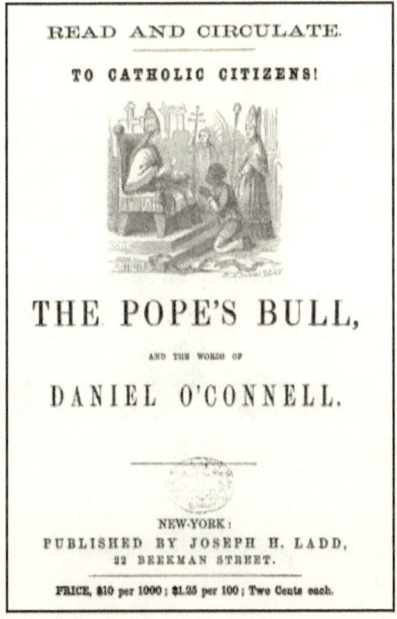

The title page of *The Pope's Bull and the Words of Daniel O'Connell* (1856), a reprint of *In Supremo Apostolatus* and a selection of O'Connell's antislavery comments. The Republican Party printed the pamphlet to promote their presidential candidate John C. Frémont.

tleman" and "Francis," his Irish Catholic employee. When asked about the election, Francis declared himself for Frémont because "no true Catholic can vote to support slavery. . . . [W]e have a Bull of the Pope against it, and no conscientious Catholic will go against [it]. . . . [T]hose that are sincere in their religion, will have to vote for Frémont."[107]

In September the Republican Party printed 40,000 pamphlets comprised of the pope's letter, excerpts from O'Connell's reply to the Cincinnati Repealers and the *Independent*'s dialogue between Francis and his employer. The *Independent*'s editors predicted that the publication would play an influential role in the election: "No Romanist, in view of this allocution from the Papal Chair,

---

107 *Independent*, August 28, 1856.

can conscientiously cast a vote which shall aid to make Kansas a slave state; and the tract should be freely circulated in every Roman Catholic district."[108]

The pamphlets drew some notice. One Catholic from Buffalo, who was not sure he could trust a Protestant journal like the *Independent*, wrote to the Catholic publisher Orestes Brownson to ask if it were true that the pope had "abolished the slave trade?"[109] The editor of the *Boston Pilot* was concerned enough about the stir raised by the *Independent* that he ran a front-page article entitled, "The Catholic Church and the Question of Slavery."[110] Although unattributed, the article was an excerpt from Bishop Kenrick's moral theology textbook.[111] In many respects, Kenrick's defense of slavery was more useful to journalists than England's letters to Forsyth. Whereas England dealt with many obscure matters from the patristic era and offered no conclusion, Kenrick presented a clear, succinct case for the legitimacy of slavery in all its forms.[112]

In the end, these antislavery appeals made no headway with Catholic voters.[113] Even without Catholic support, Frémont still ran strongly in the North, capturing 55% of the vote and winning

---

108   *The Pope's Bull and the Words of Daniel O'Connell* (New York: Joseph H. Ladd, 1856), 7; *Independent*, September 11, 1856.

109   Daniel Magone, Jr., to Orestes Brownson, September 9, 1856, I-3-m, University of Notre Dame Archives, Notre Dame, Indiana.

110   *Boston Pilot*, September 20, 1856, cited in Patrick W. Carey, "Political Atheism: *Dred Scott*, Roger Brooke Taney, and Orestes A. Brownson," *Catholic Historical Review* 88, no. 2 (April 2002), 210.

111   Thomas H. O'Connor, *Fitzpatrick's Boston, 1846–1866: John Bernard Fitzpatrick, Third Bishop of Boston* (Boston: Northeastern University Press, 1984), 176–177.

112   For example, while noting that the international slave trade was forbidden—and quoting Pope Gregory to that effect—Kenrick said that Catholic masters could auction off their slaves, but it would be preferable if they sought Catholic buyers. Masters were likewise free to beat their slaves if they were disobedient. See John Joseph Lardner, "Kenrick's Moral Theology: Its Adaptation to American Conditions" (S.T.L. thesis, Catholic University of America, 1921), 64–70; Brokhage, "Francis Patrick Kenrick's Opinion," 71, 96; Nolan, *The Most Reverend Francis Patrick Kenrick*, 241.

113   Schlesinger, *History*, II: 1029–1030.

eleven of sixteen states, including New York. He picked up less than 1% of the vote in the South, however.[114] By winning all of the South, his home state of Pennsylvania and four other Northern states, Buchanan was able to gain a majority in the Electoral College.[115]

Just days after Buchanan was sworn into office, the nation was jolted by the Supreme Court's decision in *Dred Scott v. Sandford*. Scott, a slave who lived in Missouri, sought his freedom on the grounds that his owner had taken him at various times into free states. Writing for the majority, the eighty-year-old Chief Justice, Roger B. Taney, rejected Scott's petition, noting that he was not an American citizen and therefore had no standing to file suit in a federal court. The majority added that no Black person—whether slave or free—could hold U.S. citizenship.[116]

When Orestes Brownson learned of the decision, he immediately gave vent to his displeasure in his journal, *Brownson's Quarterly Review*. While he accepted portions of the ruling, he strongly disagreed with the Court's judgment that Blacks could not be citizens.[117] He was even more upset that such a decision should have emanated from Taney:

> Mr. Chief Justice Taney is a Catholic, and knows that from 1482[118] the popes have condemned on pain of excommunication, the reduction of African negroes to slavery. . . . We regret that in giving the opinion of the court the learned judge did not recollect what he is taught by his religion, namely the unity of the race, that all men by the natural law are equal, and that negroes are men, and therefore as to their rights must be regarded as standing on the same footing with white men.[119]

---

114   Frémont was not even on the ballot in most of the southern states. See Schlesinger, *History*, II: 1094.
115   David Potter and Don E. Fehrenbacher, *The Impending Crisis, 1848–1861* (New York: Harper & Row, 1976), 260–266; James M. McPherson, *Battle Cry of Freedom* (New York: Oxford University Press, 1988), 155–162.
116   McPherson, *Battle Cry of Freedom*, 170–178.
117   Carey, "Political Atheism," 213.
118   Presumably, Brownson was referring to Pope Pius II's letter of 1462.
119   "The Slavery Question Once More," in *The Works of Orestes A. Brownson*, 20 vols. (Detroit: T. Nourse, 1882–1887), XVII: 91–92.

Most Catholic editors disagreed with Brownson and were angered by his attacks on Taney and the Supreme Court. For example, James McMaster, editor of the *New York Freeman's Journal*, sharply rebuked Brownson: "The ground of right and justice which sustains our own laws is that the slaveholder has a claim to the service of his slave recognized by the law of God, and the law of the land." He cautioned readers that Brownson's interpretation should not be seen as "the Catholic view of the Slavery Question."[120]

Conclusion

Time and again for almost two decades, abolitionists inside and outside the Catholic Church struggled to publicize the teachings of Pope Gregory XVI and his predecessors. *In Supremo* was the document to which they repeatedly referred when trying to show that America's largest religion was on their side. Despite the assistance of such influential figures as Daniel O'Connell and Orestes Brownson, the abolitionists made little headway. While the pope and his leading advisers sympathized with the antislavery movement, they were not about to intervene. During the remainder of his reign, Pope Gregory offered no further statements on the subject and made no effort to clarify what he meant in his 1839 letter. As Robert Emmett Curran notes, popes in the mid-nineteenth century operated in a reactive mode. They would respond to queries and petitions but would rarely act on their own initiative. The papacy was still recovering from the damage that it had suffered during the French Revolution and the Napoleonic Wars. Only with Vatican Council I (1869-1870) would the Holy See begin to take a more assertive role in governing the Church.[121]

Along with reticent friends in Rome, abolitionists faced determined opposition from most American Catholics. Among

---

120 *New York Freeman's Journal*, April 11, 1857, cited in Carey, "Political Atheism," 219.

121 Curran, "Rome, the American Church, and Slavery," 41, 48–49; Krebsbach notes that Rome considered issuing a letter on slavery in the 1850s but was preoccupied with the fate of the Papal States. See Krebsbach, "Rome's Response," 340–343.

the bishops, they had to contend with England and Kenrick, who were skilled at mining the proslavery aspects of the Church's tradition, and with Hughes, who was skilled in the ways of American politics. With such strong adversaries and with no open supporters in the hierarchy, antislavery Catholics were at a distinct disadvantage.

Catholic newspapers were similarly unsympathetic. During these years, not a single Catholic editor was unequivocally antislavery.[122] The Catholic papers would print neither the text of the Irish Address nor O'Connell's letter to the Cincinnati Repealers. When discussing slavery, they depicted abolitionists as anti-Catholic bigots and warned that abolition would have terribly disruptive consequences.[123]

Would it have made much difference if the Catholic clergy and press had been more critical of slavery? Perhaps not. The majority of Catholics were unskilled, impoverished Irish immigrants who were trying to gain acceptance in America. They saw free Blacks as their primary competitors for jobs as laborers and dockworkers.[124] By the 1830s, tensions between the two communities were periodically triggering violence.[125] Even if Irish Catholics had been on better terms with Blacks, they still would have been loath to align themselves with Garrison and other abolitionists who were denouncing the Constitution and calling on the Northern states to secede.[126] As Gilbert Osofsky notes, the "much abused Irish immigrant could not afford the

---

122 One editor who occasionally voiced misgivings about slavery was Patrick Donahoe of the *Boston Pilot*. See O'Connor, *Fitzpatrick's Boston*, 168–170; Rice, *American Catholic Opinion*, 78–80. The Cincinnati *Catholic Telegraph* would eventually express antislavery views but not prior to the Civil War.

123 Rice, *American Catholic Opinion*, 72–85; Potter, *To the Golden Door*, 374–384.

124 In fact, free Blacks were not numerous enough to present any real economic challenge to the Irish. See Kerby A. Miller, "Green over Black: The Origins of Irish American Racism" (M.A. thesis, University of California, Berkeley, 1969), 36–48.

125 Noel Ignatiev, *How the Irish Became White* (New York: Routledge, 1995), 99–136.

126 For Garrison's disunionism, see Mayer, *All on Fire*, 300–329.

luxury of political radicalism."[127] Even if all Irish Catholics in America had been familiar with the words of the "abolitionist pope," most would no doubt have argued that *In Supremo* did not apply to them.

---

127 Osofsky, "Abolitionists, Irish Immigrants," 905.

An Antislavery Archbishop: John B. Purcell and the Slavery Controversy among Border State Catholics

DAVID J. ENDRES*

Introduction

Historians who study the U.S. Catholic response to slavery have primarily focused on a few prominent Northern ecclesiastical and intellectual leaders who exhibited a consistently conservative approach: desiring reconciliation between North and South, critical of abolitionism, and wary of emancipation.[1] Though such sentiment was dominant, other voices did emerge that would challenge this approach.[2] Archbishop John Baptist

---

* An earlier version of this essay was published as "Rectifying the Fatal Contrast: Archbishop John Purcell and the Slavery Controversy among Catholics in Civil War Cincinnati," *Ohio Valley History* 2, no. 2 (Fall 2002): 23–33.

1 Studies that focus on Northern Catholic opinion include Walter G. Sharrow, "Northern Catholic Intellectuals and the Coming of the Civil War," *New York Historical Society Quarterly* 58 (1974): 34–56; Charles P. Connor, "The Northern Catholic Position on Slavery and the Civil War: Archbishop Hughes as a Test Case," *Records of the American Catholic Historical Society of Philadelphia* 96 (1985): 35–48; William B. Kurtz, *Excommunicated from the Union: How the Civil War Created a Separate Catholic America* (New York: Fordham University Press, 2016); William Kurtz, "'This Most Unholy and Destructive War': Catholic Intellectuals and the Limits of Catholic Patriotism," in *So Conceived and So Dedicated: Intellectual Life in the Civil War-Era North*, ed. Lorien Foote and Kanisorn Wongsrichanalai (New York: Fordham University Press, 2015), 217–235.

2 Among the antislavery voices in the U.S. Church was layman and convert Orestes Brownson, Bishop Martin Henni of Milwaukee, Wisconsin, and Bishop Josue Young of Erie, Pennsylvania. See Kurtz, *Excommunicated from the Union*, 94–107. According to John McGreevy, besides Purcell, Brownson was the only other "prominent Catholic" to support immediate emancipation by 1862. See John T. McGreevy, *Catholicism and American Freedom: A History* (New York: W.W. Norton, 2003), 67.

Purcell (1800–1883) of Cincinnati, Ohio, was among these minority voices, the first U.S. Catholic bishop to show public support for the emancipation of enslaved persons. Through his teaching and the influence of his diocesan newspaper, the *Catholic Telegraph*, Purcell attempted to convince his people of the inconsistency of slavery's existence in a free nation while striking at the racial, religious, and political discord that shaped the loyalties of Catholics in antebellum America. Purcell's contribution to the intellectual and moral conversation of the period has largely been overlooked, often mentioned only in passing as an example of divergent Northern Catholic opinion.[3]

The United States in the mid-nineteenth century was in the midst of a great struggle, weakened by sectional conflict and torn over slavery's practical and moral repercussions. For many, slavery was not simply a question of human dignity or personal liberty. The debate brought to the fore the difficult questions of states' rights and the proper relationship of labor to economic gain. Americans of every locality and viewpoint entered into the debate concerning the country and its future. Many, especially in the South, wished to preserve the nation as it was, a country of local liberty in which the institution of slavery could be both maintained and expanded. For abolitionist Northerners, however, slavery symbolized all that prevented the country from achieving political, social, and moral purity. As a language common to the North and South, religious belief was central to the debate and often meshed with political and ethnic ideologies to lend strength to the slavery controversy.

Religion could affirm the practices of either the slaveholder or the abolitionist. As President Abraham Lincoln stated of the North

---

3 For brief analysis of Purcell's antislaveryism, see, for instance, McGreevy, *Catholicism and American Freedom*, 82–85; M. Edmund Hussey, "John Baptist Purcell: First Archbishop of Cincinnati," in *Patterns of Episcopal Leadership*, ed. Gerald P. Fogarty (New York: Macmillan, 1989), 97–100; William Kurtz, "'This Most Unholy and Destructive War,'" 225–226. For a somewhat longer treatment comparing Purcell to Louisville's Bishop Martin John Spalding, see Carl C. Creason, "United, Yet Divided: An Analysis of Bishops Martin John Spalding and John Baptist Purcell during the Civil War Era," *American Catholic Studies* 124, no. 2 (Spring 2013): 49–69.

and South in his second inaugural address: "Both read the same Bible and pray to the same God, and each invokes His aid against the other."[4] Consequently, religious schism often preceded political separation as religious groups became polarized over slavery. The Presbyterians and Baptists attempted to preserve institutional unity until the outbreak of the war, while the Methodist Church split into two factions in 1845 when some refused to agree to a slaveholder as bishop. Even when attempts to preserve unity appeared successful, internal division often existed. In 1837 the Presbyterian Church divided into New and Old Schools; the former became increasingly antislavery and found its greatest strength among New Englanders, while the latter was composed of conservative members, mainly Southerners.[5]

Amid sectional conflict and religious disunion, the Catholic Church in the North and throughout the border regions attempted to bridge these divisions, identifying with neither the abolitionists nor proslavery apologists, both of which it considered radicals.[6] Marked by conservatism, the Catholic Church spoke in favor of moderation and compromise, not rash action. Most Catholic bishops rallied for unity and reconciliation, hoping to act as witnesses to peace and calm in a troubled nation.[7]

One episcopal voice pierced through the silence: Archbishop John B. Purcell of Cincinnati. As the first U.S. Catholic bishop to

---

4 Ray P. Basler, ed., *The Collected Works of Abraham Lincoln* (New Brunswick, NJ: Rutgers University Press, 1959), VIII: 333.

5 John R. McKivigan and Mitchell Snay, eds., *Religion and the Antebellum Debate over Slavery* (Athens: University of Georgia Press, 1998), 16–17; Eugene Genovese, "Religion in the Collapse of the American Union," in *Religion and the American Civil War*, ed. Randall Miller, Harry Stout, and Charles Wilson (New York: Oxford University Press, 1998), 78–79.

6 Some Catholic bishops in the South did side with the interests of slavery and slaveholders. See Gracjan Kraszewski, "Devout Catholics, Devoted Confederates: The Evolution of Southern Catholic Bishops from Reluctant Secessionists to Ardent Confederates," *Catholic Historical Review* 106, no. 1 (Winter 2020): 77–106, and his larger work, *Catholic Confederates: Faith and Duty in the Civil War South* (Kent, OH: Kent State University Press, 2020).

7 Kurtz, *Excommunicated from the Union*, 30–33; on the "muted voice" of Catholics, see Mark A. Noll, *The Civil War as a Theological Crisis* (Chapel Hill: University of North Carolina Press, 2006), 129–132.

publicly support the immediate emancipation[8] of the enslaved, Purcell faced considerable opposition. Clergy and laymen throughout the country, his fellow American bishops, and religious and secular publications discouraged his meddling in what many considered a political matter unrelated to religion. Even when opposition was not overt, Purcell had to contend with an ambivalent immigrant Church, largely disinterested in the slavery question from the standpoint of morality yet aware of the potential for its demise to affect the economic balance of life in both the North and South.

Beginning with mild protestations against slavery, Purcell eventually became an outspoken proponent of the war and emancipation. Purcell worked to temper antiwar sentiment, help transform racist ideologies, and convince his flock of emancipation's moral and practical necessity. Though seen as unsuccessful, Purcell helped ease tensions, curb discrimination, and bring attention to the ethical and social ramifications of the slavery question. As one of the few who bonded their Catholic faith with antislaveryism, Purcell heralded emancipation as consistent with Christ's example and integral to the Church's mission of bringing unity, hope, and salvation.

Early Experiences of Slavery

In 1818, at age eighteen, Purcell immigrated from Ireland to Maryland's eastern shore, where he served briefly as a tutor, probably teaching youngsters Latin and Greek. Here, he would have likely had his first experiences of hereditary, race-based slavery. Two years later, in 1820, he was invited to teach at Mount St. Mary's College in Emmitsburg, Maryland, and simultaneously commenced studies for the priesthood. In addition to employing free Blacks and white laborers, the school held more than a dozen enslaved persons during Purcell's time as a student.[9]

---

8 The "immediate emancipation" distinction is important since some U.S. bishops were moving in the direction of "gradual emancipation" or at least, antislavery. None, however, including Purcell, embraced the abolitionist label, owing to the strong connection between anti-Catholicism and abolitionism.

9 Thomas R. Ulshafer, P.S.S., "Slavery and the Early Sulpician Community in Maryland," *U.S. Catholic Historian* 37, no. 2 (Spring 2019): 19.

He remained at the school for only three years before being tapped to finish his studies in France, but after ordination, he returned to the school as a professor, becoming president in the autumn of 1829.

Whatever his views on slavery, Purcell became a *de facto* enslaver in assuming Mount St. Mary's presidency. The bondspersons transferred to him by deed included six men, most likely agricultural laborers working the college's land, and ten women, serving as domestics at the school.[10] Their degree of interaction with Purcell and whether and how he managed them is unknown. Still, a letter to the college's vice president, Father Francis Jamison, shows Purcell's unease with slavery: "I am particularly anxious that something decisive be done regarding our Negroes." He wrote that two of the bondsmen, Dan and Louis, had "gone off" (possibly as runaways), to which he said he could only respond: "God's peace be with them!" Purcell wrote that he considered releasing three others—Abraham, Nace, and Peter—because he could "easily procure white men" to work in their place.[11] Apparently, Father Jamison disagreed. The only manumission recorded during Purcell's presidency was for Abraham, released nearly two years after the letter to Jamison.[12]

Purcell was not successful in replacing the college's enslaved persons with white laborers; the last of the college's enslaved persons were not emancipated until 1858.[13] But this was not Pur-

---

10 Transfer of Property, John F. McGerry to John B. Purcell and Francis B. Jamison, December 9, 1829, recorded January 9, 1830, Frederick County, Maryland Land Records, Deed Book JS-33, pages 62–64. The names of the bondspeople were recorded as Abraham, Nace, Barney, Peter, Daniel, Lewis, Mary, Henrietta, Prudence, Catherine, Rachael, Mary, Elizabeth, Ann Maria, Cecelia, and Monica.

11 Father John B. Purcell to Father Francis Jamison, September 10, 1830, RG-14: Manuscript Collection, Rhoads Memorial Archives, Mount St. Mary's University, Emmitsburg, Maryland.

12 Abraham Lea (Lee?), age thirty-eight, was manumitted by Purcell. See Manumission of Abraham Lea, May 29, 1832, Frederick County, Maryland Land Records, Deed Book JS-40, pages 246–247.

13 Daniel C. Nusbaum, "Mount St. Mary's and the American Civil War," *Analecta: Selected Studies in the History of Mount St. Mary's College and Seminary* 1, no. 5 (2004): 3.

cell's doing since he was informed during the summer of 1833 of his appointment as bishop of the Diocese of Cincinnati. In relinquishing his role as president and preparing to move west, he transferred his bondspeople to his successor. Yet, Purcell's time in Maryland, which included four years as a slaveowner, may have contributed to his negative assessment of slavery.[14]

"The Fatal Contrast"

The trajectory of Purcell's thoughts on slavery is not always clear from the extant sources, but there are snippets of evidence that suggest he was appalled by the "peculiar institution." In 1838, Purcell publicly voiced his distaste for slavery yet seemed unwilling to assert these views to his fellow American Catholics or to become associated with the antislavery movement. At a speech given in his native town of Mallow, County Cork, Ireland, Purcell spoke of the inconsistency between the U.S. Declaration of Independence and slavery—borrowing the sentiments of the antislavery leader and the father of the Irish repeal movement, Daniel O'Connell.[15] Purcell later termed this inconsistency "the fatal contrast," acknowledging his belief that the United States could not tolerate the institution of slavery if it were to be faithful to its ideals. At the time of his 1838 speech, however, Purcell blamed the "virus" of slavery not on Americans as much as the English who had established it during the colonial period. As an Irish-American bishop, Purcell found it safer to be anti-English than to level charges at his fellow citizens. The *Catholic Telegraph*, the official newspaper of the Diocese of Cincinnati, reported Pur-

---

14 From joint to sole ownership: John B. Purcell to Francis B. Jamison, October 10, 1833, recorded October 11, 1833, Frederick County, Maryland Land Records, Deed Book JS-44, pages 192–195.

15 On O'Connell's charge of American hypocrisy for tolerating slavery, see Angela F. Murphy, *American Slavery, Irish Freedom: Abolition, Immigrant Citizenship, and the Transatlantic Movement for Irish Repeal* (Baton Rouge: Louisiana State University Press, 2010), 30–32. Fifteen years after his death, O'Connell's antislavery appeals were reprinted in the *Catholic Telegraph*. See Angela F. Murphy, "'Though Dead He Yet Speaketh': Abolitionist Memories of Daniel O'Connell in the United States," *American Journal of Irish Studies* 10 (2013): 22–24.

Archbishop John B. Purcell became among the most significant antislavery voices in the U.S. Catholic Church (Archives of the Archdiocese of Cincinnati).

cell's speech but quickly added that the bishop understood there were "a great many political improvements, however desirable, that a government could not from prudential motives introduce as soon as it wished."[16]

In a letter to a European bishop, Purcell reported that one of the significant advantages of the Diocese of Cincinnati was "the absence of Negroes, none of whom is held in slavery in this state."[17] That same year, in commenting on Pope Gregory XVI's condemnation of the slave trade, Purcell's *Catholic Telegraph* affirmed that the people of Ohio should be grateful to live in a state without slavery. Purcell's opinion surely became known among the hierarchy, as Bishop Peter Kenrick of St. Louis, Mis-

---

16   *Catholic Telegraph*, October 11, 1838.
17   Bishop John B. Purcell to Archbishop Vincent Edward Milde, ca. 1840, II-4-g, University of Notre Dame Archives, Notre Dame, Indiana (hereafter UNDA).

souri, reminded him that his courageous stance was less so in Cincinnati than in the South—where one could be lynched for antislavery preaching.[18]

Race, Religion, and Politics on the Border

The climate and makeup of Purcell's diocese and the position of Catholic bishops throughout the country encouraged silence on the slavery issue. The Diocese of Cincinnati, which had included only sixteen churches and less than 7,000 Catholics when Purcell arrived in 1833, swelled with German and Irish immigrants during the next three decades. In recognition of its increased population, Cincinnati became an archdiocese in 1850, and Purcell was elevated to archbishop. Ten years later, in 1860, the Archdiocese of Cincinnati, spanning approximately the southern two-thirds of Ohio, claimed 150,000 Catholics. Nearly 55,000 of the Catholics in the archdiocese lived in Cincinnati, accounting for thirty-five percent of the city's population.[19]

As the number of Catholics in Ohio increased, Purcell's role as spokesman for the Church in the West intensified. In 1837, as a young bishop, he participated in a weeklong public debate on the Catholic religion with Reverend Alexander Campbell, the founder of the Disciples of Christ. In reporting the debate, Cincinnati's secular press expressed its agreement that Purcell had helped to encourage toleration of Catholics and correct various falsehoods held about the faith. The debate was closely followed and caused Purcell to become better known to Catholics and non-Catholics throughout the country.[20]

---

18 *Catholic Telegraph*, March 14, 1840; Bishop Peter R. Kenrick to Bishop John B. Purcell, February 17, 1843, II-4-h, UNDA.

19 Anthony H. Deye, "Archbishop John Baptist Purcell and the Civil War" (M.A. thesis, University of Cincinnati, 1944), 4–5; Bridget Ford, *Bonds of Union: Religion, Race, and Politics in a Civil War Borderland* (Chapel Hill: University of North Carolina Press, 2016), 14–22.

20 Alexander Campbell and John B. Purcell, *A Debate on the Roman Catholic Religion* (St. Louis, MO: Christian Board of Publication, 1837); Margaret DePalma, *Dialogue on the Frontier: Catholic and Protestant Relations, 1793–1883* (Kent, OH: Kent State University Press, 2004), 89–97.

In the decades leading up to the Civil War, nativist sentiment was widespread in the border region, including Cincinnati. Catholics and the foreign-born were often denied employment and participation in community affairs because it was believed that they sought to undermine American ideals through their allegiance to a foreign power, the pope. The Reverend Lyman Beecher, president of the Lane Theological Seminary in Cincinnati, warned fellow Protestants in 1834 of the "Popish plot" to take over the region in his tract, *A Plea for the West*. Fears such as this gave rise to the American Party, popularly called the Know Nothings, which sought to bar Catholics from political involvement and delay naturalization for immigrants.[21] The anti-Catholic hysteria peaked in Cincinnati in 1853 when the visit of Archbishop Gaetano Bedini resulted in rioting. Over five hundred protesters attempted to march to the episcopal residence where Bedini was staying. Police, however, blocked the route, and sixty-five individuals were arrested.[22]

Occupying the lower socioeconomic classes of society and subject to discrimination, the Irish and German Catholics generally identified with the Democratic Party, a natural affiliation given the Republican Party's support for prohibition, abolition, and nativism. The Catholic immigrant considered all three detestable assaults upon his way of life.[23] Abolitionists were often nativists, and the union of these ideals was not incidental. The Know Nothing literature of the era asserted that the Catholic Church and slavery were both "founded and supported on the basis of ignorance and tyranny" and that the two were natural co-workers in their opposition to "freedom and republican institutions."[24] Following the

---

21 Ford, *Bonds of Union*, 17–21, 23–27. See Tyler Anbinder's *Nativism and Slavery: The Northern Know Nothings and the Politics of the 1850s* (New York: Oxford University Press, 1992) for information on the rise and fall of the Know Nothing Party and its connection to slavery.

22 David J. Endres, "Know-Nothings, Nationhood, and the Nuncio: Reassessing the Visit of Archbishop Bedini," *U.S. Catholic Historian* 21, no. 4 (Fall 2003): 1–16.

23 Frank L. Klement, "Catholics as Copperheads During the Civil War," *Catholic Historical Review* 80, no. 1 (January 1994): 36.

24 Quoted in James J. Hennesey, *American Catholics: A History of the Roman Catholic Community in the United States* (New York: Oxford University Press, 1981), 145.

demise of the Know Nothing Party, the Republican Party received many former Know Nothings into its ranks, and this close association of abolitionism and nativism resulted in solid support for the Democratic Party among Catholic immigrants.[25]

Chief among the immigrants' fears was the abolitionist goal of emancipating the slaves. Cincinnati's ethnic population believed emancipation would result in a mass exodus of formerly enslaved people from the South, arriving to claim their jobs. In 1841, tension between the city's immigrants and Blacks resulted in three days of mob violence in which both Irishmen and African Americans were killed. During the summer of that year, a multitude of rumors, including the reported sexual advances of two African American men toward a "very respectable lady," fueled the tension. The *Catholic Telegraph*, as might have been expected, blamed the nativist white population for the rioting, absolved the city's African Americans, and admitted that there may have been "two or three Irishmen" among the troublemakers.[26] However sporadic, these incidents of violence were indicative of the overarching prejudice and fear on the part of the Irish that the Blacks would surpass them economically.[27]

There was less conflict between Germans and Blacks in Cincinnati, and a number of Germans were abolitionists, though few German Catholics were among them. By the 1850s, a greater

---

[25] See Eric Foner, *Free Soil, Free Labor, Free Men: The Ideology of the Republican Party Before the Civil War* (New York: Oxford University Press, 1995), 226–260, for a discussion of the link between the Republican Party and nativism. Foner argues that Republicans viewed nativism as a political liability and tried to disassociate the party from anti-immigrant policies while at the same time courting the votes of former Know Nothings. Catholics recognized that cultural nativism lingered in the Republican Party even after political nativism had been disavowed.

[26] Anthony H. Deye, "Archbishop John Baptist Purcell of Cincinnati, pre-Civil War years" (Ph.D. dissertation, University of Notre Dame, 1949), 255; *Catholic Telegraph*, September 11, 1841. On the 1841 riot, see Nikki Taylor, *Frontiers of Freedom: Cincinnati's Black Community, 1802–1868* (Athens: Ohio University Press, 2005), 117–126.

[27] For a war-time example of economically-motivated violence against Blacks, see Taylor, *Frontiers of Freedom*, 197–198.

Cincinnati riverfront engraving, ca. 1850, showing the Ohio River—across which lay the slaveholding state of Kentucky (Cincinnati Map Collection).

proportion of Cincinnati Germans opposed slavery's westward expansion than were in favor. Some German radicals in Cincinnati called for the repeal of the 1850 Fugitive Slave Law and an end to slavery throughout the country.[28] Despite the presence of abolitionist Germans in Cincinnati, the Germans and African Americans also clashed, though they did so less forcefully due to the economic advantage of the Germans over the Irish. The Cincinnati Irish lived closer to the Blacks, had lower rates of literacy and capital ownership than other groups, and were competitors for the same low-paying jobs.[29]

---

28 Bruce Levine, "Community Divided: German Immigrants, Social Class, and Political Conflict in Antebellum Cincinnati," in *Ethnic Diversity and Civic Identity: Patterns of Conflict and Cohesion in Cincinnati Since 1820*, ed. Henry Shapiro and Jonathan Sarna (Urbana: University of Illinois Press, 1992), 70, 76–81.

29 Wendell P. Dabney, *Cincinnati's Colored Citizens: Historical, Sociological and Biographical* (Cincinnati: Dabney Publishing, 1926), 40, 49; Nancy Bertaux, "Economic Change and Occupational Decline," in *Race and the City: Work, Community, and Protest in Cincinnati, 1820–1970*, ed. Henry Louis Taylor, Jr. (Urbana: University of Illinois Press, 1993), 140; Taylor, *Frontiers of Freedom*, 23–25.

Cincinnati maintained close social and economic ties with its southern and western neighbors, leading the city to identify with the Lower Midwest/Upland South region. This broad borderland included southern Ohio, Indiana, and Illinois, as well as parts of Kentucky, Tennessee, and Missouri.[30] In many of these areas, freed Blacks were not accepted. Instead, the population sought to keep the nation "as it is" with African Americans "where they are." The fear that Blacks would take jobs the immigrant population typically held only increased in the years leading up to the Civil War as African Americans trickled north across the Ohio River and began to compete with foreign-born laborers.[31] The *Cincinnati Enquirer* warned its readers of the perils to come: "Hundreds of thousands, if not millions, of slaves . . . will come North and West and will either be competitors with our White mechanics and laborers, degrading them by their competition, or they will have to be supported as paupers and criminals at the public expense."[32] For immigrant laborers in Cincinnati, the potential loss of jobs to African Americans was a concern that did not loom somewhere in the future but was real prior to emancipation.

Calming the Storm of Secession

At the same time Cincinnati Catholics feared emancipation for economic reasons, Catholic bishops worried that slavery could destroy the Church's unity. The Holy See in 1839, through Pope Gregory XVI's letter, *In Supremo Apostolatus*, asked Catholics throughout the world to refrain from engaging in the slave trade:

---

30   For the role of sectionalism, see Matthew Salafia, *Slavery's Borderland: Freedom and Bondage Along the Ohio River* (Philadelphia: University of Pennsylvania Press, 2013); Christopher Phillips, *The Rivers Ran Backward: The Civil War on the Middle Border and the Making of American Regionalism* (New York: Oxford University Press, 2016); Matthew Stanley, *The Loyal West: Civil War and Reunion in Middle America* (Urbana: University of Illinois Press, 2017); John R. McKivigan, "The Battle for the Border State Soul: The Slavery Debate in the Churches of the Border Region," *Ohio Valley History* 12, no. 2 (October 2012): 48–71.

31   Frank L. Klement, "Sound and Fury: Civil War Dissent in the Cincinnati Area," *Cincinnati Historical Society Bulletin* 35, no. 2 (1977): 99–114; Phillips, *Rivers Ran Backward*, 268–274.

32   Quoted in Lyle Koehler, *Cincinnati's Black Peoples: A Chronology and Bibliography, 1787–1982* (Cincinnati: University of Cincinnati, 1986), 56–57.

"We warn and adjure earnestly . . . that no one in the future . . . exercise that inhuman traffic by which the Blacks, as if they were not men but rather animals [are] bought, sold, and devoted sometimes to the hardest labor."[33] The pope had thus unquestionably written against the trade, but it was much debated whether he disapproved of all forms of slavery.

Despite this papal admonition, the U.S. bishops became associated with maintaining the status quo regarding slavery. A few bishops, like John England of Charleston, South Carolina, wrote that the pope's letter should not be interpreted as a condemnation of slavery in the United States.[34] For the most part, the bishops agreed that abolitionists were fanatics, yet at the same time, only a few Southern prelates overtly defended the peculiar institution. Even the bishops most loyal to the South recognized the abuses of slavery, believed that African Americans were human beings with souls, and advocated their natural right to maintain their families.[35] Bishop England, though a slavery supporter, opened a school for Black children in his diocese, closing it only in response to intense local opposition.[36] Most bishops, especially in the North and the border regions, occupied a middle ground that valued peace over justice, as evidenced by the First Plenary Council of Baltimore (1852), in which the bishops were silent on the issue. Church historian Peter Guilday wrote that the council helped solidify the role of the Church in America:

> Catholics realized more acutely than ever the real meaning of the Church's place in American life, and non-Catholics appreciated the fact that there was a body of American spiritual leaders who meant to bring to the disturbed condition of the times the one asset the country needed: peace and calm.[37]

---

33   Pope Gregory XVI, *In Supremo Apostolatus* (1839), https://www.papalencyclicals.net/greg16/g16sup.htm.

34   Kenneth J. Zanca, *American Catholics and Slavery, 1789–1866: An Anthology of Primary Documents* (Lanham, MD: University Press of America, 1994), 128–129.

35   Zanca, *American Catholics and Slavery*, 110–111.

36   Hennesey, *American Catholics*, 146.

37   Peter Guilday, *A History of the Councils of Baltimore, 1791–1884* (New York: Arno Press, 1969), 169–170.

The Church's conservatism was not only expressed by the Church hierarchy, who feared the ruin of their own ecclesiastical institution, but was echoed by Catholics of every locality who worried that their states, communities, and families could be ripped apart by the slavery question.

The bishops of the Cincinnati Province, composed of neighboring dioceses in Michigan, Ohio, Kentucky, and Indiana, met in Cincinnati twice during the years preceding the war. At each meeting, the bishops issued a pastoral letter instructing the clergy and laity of their dioceses. When the local ordinaries convened the First Provincial Council of Cincinnati in 1855, the bishops followed the precedent set at the First Plenary Council of Baltimore in 1852 and refrained from taking up the slavery issue. Instead, the bishops advised their people to "fervently pray to God that He would bless and preserve the Union."[38] At the Second Provincial Council of Cincinnati held three years later, the bishops made no mention of slavery, seeking to distance the Church from what they perceived to be a political discussion.[39]

In Cincinnati, the *Catholic Telegraph* mirrored the opinion of the Church hierarchy and the local citizenry by maintaining its desire for peace and unity. In an editorial on "Union and Catholicity," the editor—likely Archbishop Purcell's brother, Father Edward Purcell[40]—wrote that the Church could not be blamed for America's disunion because "the Catholic Church has never lent any strength to the excitement. She has said both to North and South be just, be moderate, patient, charitable. If the Union falls to pieces, now it will not be through her influence

---

38 *Pastoral Letter of the First Provincial Council of Cincinnati to the Clergy and Laity* (Cincinnati: John P. Walsh, 1855), 12.

39 *Pastoral Letter of the Second Provincial Council of Cincinnati to the Clergy and Laity* (Cincinnati: John P. Walsh, 1858).

40 On the question of the authorship of the *Catholic Telegraph*'s editorials, see Satish Joseph, "'Long Live the Republic!' Father Edward Purcell and the Slavery Controversy: 1861–1865," *American Catholic Studies* 116, no. 4 (Winter 2005): 33. While Archbishop Purcell could have authored some editorials, most were likely authored by Father Edward, though "the views expressed by Father Purcell were probably the views of the archbishop."

Father Edward Purcell, editor of Cincinnati's *Catholic Telegraph* and brother to Archbishop John B. Purcell, echoed his brother's antislavery sentiments (Archives of the Archdiocese of Cincinnati).

but through her want of influence."[41] Though committed to patience and peace, the Church's desire for calm could not quiet the impending storm that Southern secession and rebellion would bring.

This storm of politics, religion, economics, and race that swirled around Purcell forced him to reconsider his response. Though not deaf to the influence of his people and fellow bishops, Purcell's opinions on slavery and emancipation were shaped by those closest to him. His chief advisors were his brother, Edward Purcell, and Sylvester Rosecrans, who was named auxiliary bishop of Cincinnati in March 1862. Both men held positions of influence in the diocese and, through the *Catholic Telegraph*, were responsible for the expression of local Catholic opinion during the war years. Edward Purcell was editor of the official newspaper of the Diocese of Cincinnati for almost forty years,

---

41 *Catholic Telegraph*, December 1, 1860.

beginning in 1840, and acted as the financial manager of the archdiocese and pastor of the cathedral.[42] Sylvester Rosecrans, the younger brother of Union General William Starke Rosecrans, was the newspaper's co-editor until he was named auxiliary bishop.[43] Both favored the Union and emancipation, and the opinions expressed in the *Catholic Telegraph* never strayed far from Purcell's sentiments.

At the time of Lincoln's election in 1860 and the beginning of Southern secession, Archbishop Purcell, the *Catholic Telegraph*, and the Catholics of Cincinnati were generally united in their belief that compromise should be used as a means of preserving the Union. Politically, Catholics were an essential source of support for the Democratic Party and were accused of tainting the electoral process by voting consistently with those who shared their religious and ethnic affiliations. Many believed their voting was controlled by Democratic Party bosses or, even worse, by their religious leaders. Most of the Catholic community in Cincinnati supported the Democratic candidate, Stephen Douglas, for the presidency in 1860, even while Purcell himself publicly supported the Republican Party and Lincoln. Despite their political leanings, the immigrant population remained supporters of the Union and were optimistic that a peaceful compromise could be achieved.[44] "At least, let us beg if we cannot have Union, we may have peace, and that if these States cannot be sisters, they may be allies," Archbishop Purcell wrote on January 4, 1861.[45]

The *Catholic Telegraph* employed its editorial column to denounce both Northern abolitionists and Southern extremists,

---

42 On Father Edward Purcell's contributions to the slavery debate, see Joseph, "Father Edward Purcell and the Slavery Controversy," 25–54.

43 On the Rosecrans brothers, see William B. Kurtz, "'The Perfect Model of a Christian Hero': The Faith, Anti-Slaveryism, and Post-War Legacy of William S. Rosecrans," *U.S. Catholic Historian* 31, no. 1 (Winter 2013): 73–96; William B. Kurtz, "A Singular Zeal: William S. Rosecrans's Family in Faith, Triumph, and Failure," *U.S. Catholic Historian* 35, no. 2 (Spring 2017): 27–53.

44 Deye, "Archbishop John Baptist Purcell and the Civil War," 11; on Archbishop Purcell's support for Lincoln, see Creason, "United, Yet Divided," 65-67.

45 *Catholic Telegraph*, January 5, 1861.

beginning with an editorial on December 1, 1860.[46] Among the abuses that Purcell condemned while preaching at the cathedral were Harriet Beecher Stowe's distorted novel *Uncle Tom's Cabin*, Preston Brooks' brutal attack on Charles Sumner in the chambers of the Senate, and the violation of the Constitution by the secessionist states.[47] Purcell attacked radicalism wherever he believed it existed, both in the North and the South.

Since the *Catholic Telegraph* was one of the few Catholic newspapers published west of the Allegheny Mountains, the paper's readership extended westward through the North and South. By 1850 the weekly paper was published with the episcopal approval of the dioceses of Chicago, Cleveland, Detroit, Vincennes, and Louisville, representing most of the dioceses in the border region and points northward. The Diocese of Covington, Kentucky, later gave its approval but withdrew its support by November 1861, due to what it perceived as the paper's failure to maintain political neutrality.[48] Though published in Cincinnati, the *Catholic Telegraph* clearly depended on both Southern and Northern subscribers before the war and up to its onset, which may explain the paper's equal treatment of both Northern and Southern abuses before the rebellion.

As Purcell's opinion on the topic evolved and it became apparent that the forces of rebellion were seeking to destroy the Union, he became increasingly critical of the South. Little more than a week after promoting compromise with the rebellious states, Purcell addressed the officers of the Catholic Institute, a short-lived local educational institution, and condemned the "rattlesnake of secession." He was quoted in the *Cincinnati Commercial* as remarking, "When you look around this hall, and see the beautiful stars and stripes which adorn it, pray, oh pray! that the hideous rattlesnake may never sting them, but that the rattlesnake of seces-

---

46   *Catholic Telegraph*, December 1, 1860.
47   Deye, "Archbishop John Baptist Purcell: pre-Civil War years," 438.
48   Deye, "Archbishop John Baptist Purcell and the Civil War," 57; Hennesey, *American Catholics*, 153, asserts that Covington's Bishop George Carrell, S.J., withdrew his support of the *Catholic Telegraph* due to the paper's political activism.

sion may be crushed to death, even as the Ever Blessed Mother crushed the serpent that caused our fall."⁴⁹ At the same time, the *Catholic Telegraph* issued a more conservative response favoring peace. The paper cautioned, "It is hoped that in these times of excitement no Catholic will so far lose his reasoning powers as to suppose that our glorious institutions can be preserved and transmitted to posterity by fighting among ourselves."⁵⁰ Cincinnati Catholics remained hopeful that peace would prevail and that the dark clouds of secession would eventually dissipate.

The Sacred Duty to Defend the Union

After the attack on Fort Sumter, the hope for a peaceful compromise vanished. With the war beginning, the *Catholic Telegraph* came out in complete support of the Union and President Lincoln. The paper publicized a "Union Meeting" at Cincinnati's Catholic Institute to be held on April 20, 1861. An estimated 4,000 "Irish patriots" attended and pledged their "lives, fortunes, and sacred honor" to maintain the Constitution.⁵¹ Some of these Cincinnatians would be among the approximately 200,000 Catholic Americans who served in the war. Purcell also wrote in support of the Union cause. He was undoubtedly aware that perceived disloyalty on the part of Catholics, especially immigrants, could only increase nativist fervor. Rising to the challenge, Purcell proclaimed to his flock that the "President has spoken and it is our duty to obey him as head of the nation. . . . It is then our solemn duty as good and loyal citizens to walk shoulder to shoulder with all our fellow citizens in support of the national honor."⁵² To display public support for the cause, a star-spangled banner, ninety feet in length, was hung from the spire of St. Peter in Chains Cathedral on April 23.⁵³

Though the American hierarchy had among its ranks several Union men like Purcell, Rosecrans, and John Hughes of New

---

49 *Cincinnati Daily Commercial*, January 16, 1861.
50 *Catholic Telegraph*, January 19, 1861.
51 *Catholic Telegraph*, April 20, 1861; *Catholic Telegraph*, April 27, 1861.
52 *Catholic Telegraph*, April 20, 1861.
53 *Catholic Telegraph*, April 27, 1861.

York, their collective effort to boost Catholic enlistment achieved minimal results. As non-citizens, many immigrant Catholics were exempt from the draft; some opposed the war and eventually its aim of emancipating the slaves, while others had little concern for what they perceived as a contest for economic power by the affluent. Many Catholics who served in the war were lured by high enlistment bounties rather than support for the conflict.[54]

During the war, Purcell proved his loyalty to the Union in word and deed. Purcell and Rosecrans willingly visited Union army encampments, preached, administered the sacraments, and met with army chaplains.[55] Purcell's journeys to the field set him apart from other bishops who were often unwilling to act in a manner that might be construed as partisan. Throughout the conflict, the army was in dire need of priests to act as army chaplains, and Purcell helped fill the ranks of the Union chaplaincy by encouraging priests to volunteer. Some bishops refused to send chaplains; consequently, only forty priests were available to minister to the Union's Catholic soldiers.[56]

In late April 1861, the Third Provincial Council of Cincinnati, a meeting of the bishops from eight neighboring dioceses, was opened. Among the items discussed was the country's political situation. The pastoral letter drafted at the council spoke of the need for unity and peace. "While many of the sects have divided into hostile parties on an exciting political issue," the letter stated, "the Catholic Church has carefully preserved her unity of spirit in the bond of peace, knowing no North, no South, no East, and no West."[57] The letter specifically advised priests not to

---

54 Kurtz, *Excommunicated from the Union*, 46–47, 108–116.
55 David J. Endres, *A Bicentennial History of the Archdiocese of Cincinnati: The Catholic Church in Southwest Ohio, 1821–2021* (Milford, OH: Little Miami Publishing, 2021), 91.
56 Randall Miller, "Catholic Religion, Irish Ethnicity, and the Civil War," in *Religion and the American Civil War*, ed. Randall Miller, Harry Stout, and Charles Wilson (New York: Oxford University Press, 1998), 265–266; on the two Cincinnati priests (Father William T. O'Higgins and Father E.P. Corcoran) who served as chaplains, see Endres, *A Bicentennial History of the Archdiocese of Cincinnati*, 91–95.
57 *Catholic Telegraph*, May 11, 1861.

become involved in the political debate. "The spirit of the Catholic Church is eminently conservative," the bishops wrote, "and while her ministers rightfully feel a deep and abiding interest in all that concerns the welfare of the country, they do not think it their province to enter into the political arena."[58] The pastoral letter did not assign blame for the political crisis but highlighted wrongs by both the North and South. The primary author of the pastoral was Bishop Martin Spalding of Louisville, Kentucky, which explains its failure to support the president and the Union cause. If Purcell had authored the letter, it likely would have been more critical of secession.[59]

After the council's conclusion in June 1861, Purcell left Cincinnati for Rome and did not return until September of that year. During his visit, Purcell requested permission to retire, a request possibly born of the tension that accompanied his Union support. The pope, however, did not accept the sixty-one-year-old archbishop's request.[60] Upon his return, Purcell again spoke in favor of the Union cause, a position consistent with the general sentiments of the people of Cincinnati, though some had already sided with the Copperheads, the wing of the Democratic Party that supported peace.[61] The early months of the war brought with it a surge of patriotism, but the fervor began to die out as Cincinnati was plunged into an economic recession due to the cessation of trade along the Ohio River and the loss of Southern markets.[62] The recession put financial pressure on business owners and laborers who hoped for a quick end to the war. As the prospects for a swift Northern victory diminished, many former Union supporters began calling for peace, even if that meant Confederate independence. Anti-war sentiment, especially prevalent in the Ohio Valley, weighed on Purcell but did not cause him to waver in his Union support.

---

58   *Pastoral Letter of the Third Provincial Council of Cincinnati to the Clergy and Laity* (Cincinnati: John P. Walsh, 1861), 6.
59   Deye, "Archbishop John Baptist Purcell and the Civil War," 29–30.
60   Roger Fortin, *Faith and Action: A History of the Catholic Archdiocese of Cincinnati, 1821–1996* (Columbus: Ohio State University Press, 2002), 143.
61   Deye, "Archbishop John Baptist Purcell and the Civil War," 31.
62   Klement, "Sound and Fury," 101.

The Cincinnati *Catholic Telegraph*'s masthead, proclaiming, "In essentials, unity; in non-essentials, liberty; in all things charity." The newspaper became a more outspoken antislavery voice as the Civil War progressed (Archives of the Archdiocese of Cincinnati).

The *Catholic Telegraph* backed the war effort throughout the conflict, failing to ally with the Peace Democrats and the local anti-war movement that gained popularity and influence under the leadership of James Faran, the Irish American (but non-Catholic) editor of the *Cincinnati Enquirer*.[63] As a staunch Democrat, Faran opposed Lincoln from the start, but he gave qualified support to the Northern cause at the beginning of the war. Later he criticized how the war was being conducted and finally denounced the war entirely by 1863.[64] The other Catholic newspaper in Cincinnati, the German-language weekly *Der Wahrheits-Freund*, exhibited an editorial position distinct from both the official diocesan newspaper and the *Cincinnati Enquirer*. *Der Wahrheits-Freund* stressed neutrality, maintaining itself as a religious and not political newspaper.[65]

Though the *Catholic Telegraph* supported the war, it condemned the emancipation of slaves as a war aim. "The proposi-

---

63 Klement, "Catholics as Copperheads," 37.
64 Charles Wilson, *The Cincinnati Daily Enquirer and Civil War Politics: A Study in "Copperhead" Opinion* (Chicago: University of Chicago Libraries, 1934), 4, 8; Klement, "Sound and Fury," 106; Phillips, *Rivers Ran Backward*, 223, 273.
65 Deye, "Archbishop John Baptist Purcell and the Civil War," 88.

tion to emancipate the slaves as a war measure," the paper declared, "seems to us incendiary and stupid. . . . Do the American people believe that we could be a nation with 4,000,000 free negroes in our midst?"[66] Racism was widespread, and emancipation was an inconceivable war aim among the immigrant population. On July 10, 1862, violence erupted in Cincinnati after German and Irish river hands decided to strike for higher wages, and Black laborers were hired in their place.[67] Irish-Americans set homes on fire and assaulted inhabitants of "Bucktown," the Black section of the city located just east of downtown. African Americans retaliated in the neighborhood known as "Dublin," enacting similar violence.[68] Sympathizing with the rioters, the *Catholic Telegraph* wrote that Black labor was "fast undermining white labor along the Ohio. It is a question of bread and butter or starvation to thousands and nothing is more easily understood than jealousy in such a vital manner."[69] The newspaper clearly supported the interests of immigrant laborers, a position that it would later try to maintain even while supporting emancipation.

To the immigrant population, the suggestion of military conscription was almost as objectionable as emancipation. Though nearly every other Catholic newspaper denounced forced service, the *Catholic Telegraph* wrote in favor of the draft months before it was instituted.[70] "If you are drafted," the paper proclaimed, "*go you must*. When you talk of resisting the draft . . . you make yourself not only ridiculous but criminal."[71] Fortunately, riots did not erupt in Cincinnati as they had in New York City and elsewhere in response to the Conscription Act of March 3, 1863.[72] Though not responsible for a complete change in opinion, the leadership of Purcell and the attitudes voiced in the diocesan newspaper helped Cincinnati's immigrant population accept this government prerogative.

---

66 *Catholic Telegraph*, January 16, 1862.
67 Koehler, *Cincinnati's Black Peoples*, 57.
68 Klement, "Sound and Fury," 100.
69 *Catholic Telegraph*, July 23, 1862.
70 Klement, "Catholics as Copperheads," 48.
71 *Catholic Telegraph*, August 20, 1862.
72 Klement, "Catholics as Copperheads," 50–51; Kurtz, *Excommunicated from the Union*, 109–116.

In Answer to the Fatal Contrast

Upon returning from a second trip to Europe on September 1, 1862, three weeks before the Emancipation Proclamation was issued, Purcell delivered one of his most important speeches of the war. Reiterating the content of his 1838 speech delivered in Ireland, Purcell said that he believed "a people could not long survive the fatal contrast between the Declaration of Independence and the Constitution of the United States, the one asserting that all men are born free, sovereign and independent, that the other millions may be slaves." Going further, Purcell proclaimed that war could have been avoided if only the South would have compromised to abolish slavery "after a given period, say fifty, seventy, or a hundred years . . . and in the meantime, as the Northern States had done, fit her slaves, by education, to be men."[73] Since compromise was by then out of the question, Purcell went so far as to advocate emancipation of the slaves as a means of ending the war. While not demanding immediate emancipation, Purcell's address stood in forceful opposition to the thinking of his fellow Irish Catholics, some of whom had participated in anti-Black rioting just months earlier.[74]

These statements favoring gradual emancipation drew criticism from both Catholic and secular newspapers and helped to shape the opinions expressed in the *Catholic Telegraph*. At the time of Purcell's September 1, 1862 address, the diocesan newspaper was not seen as friendly to abolitionism, but it began to change its policy shortly thereafter by fiercely debating the journalists who were attacking the archbishop. Baltimore's *Catholic Mirror* reprimanded Purcell for his demands for emancipation, and the *Freeman's Journal* dubbed him a "political abolitionist."[75] The *Cincinnati Enquirer*, trumpeting the slogan, "The Constitution as it is, the Union as it was, and the Negroes where they are,"[76] also accused General Rosecrans of being an abolitionist. Ironically, the *Catholic Telegraph* became more outspoken against slavery as it

---

73 *Catholic Telegraph*, September 3, 1862.
74 Deye, "Archbishop John Baptist Purcell and the Civil War," 35.
75 [New York] *Freeman's Journal and Catholic Register*, February 6, 1864.
76 Deye, "Archbishop John Baptist Purcell and the Civil War," 34–35.

attempted to defend Purcell and Rosecrans by qualifying the position of each regarding emancipation.[77]

Not until April 1863 did the diocesan paper officially join Purcell in support of emancipation, though it had slowly been moving in that direction since September 1862. The editor, presumed to be Father Edward Purcell, wrote on April 8: "Slavery in every shape is condemned and reprobated by the Church." "What the Church would not or could not do," he continued, "the politicians have done. The door is now made open . . . and those who wish to despise the venerable Pontiffs and be the jailors of their fellow men, may endeavor to close and lock and bolt it. We take no part in any such proceeding."[78] With this proclamation, the *Catholic Telegraph* became the first diocesan newspaper to favor emancipation.[79] The newspaper, in effect, wished to wash its hands of the peculiar institution it had once approved. Having asserted its emancipationist views, the paper boasted, "If for telling these plain truths any subscriber wishes to withdraw his patronage, we hope he will do so at once."[80] In the face of sharp criticism from the *Freeman's Journal* and the *Metropolitan Record*, the *Catholic Telegraph* editor wrote, "We do not shape our cause to please any particular class of men, but we endeavor to follow the dictates of truth and justice as they present themselves to our minds."[81]

The *Quarterly Review*, published by convert and antislavery advocate Orestes Brownson, was the only other Catholic newspaper to support immediate emancipation.[82] Still, the reaction

---

77 Deye, "Archbishop John Baptist Purcell and the Civil War," 68.
78 *Catholic Telegraph*, April 8, 1863.
79 A short time later, Cincinnati's German Catholic newspaper, *Der Wahrheits-Freund*, also softened its view of emancipation, stating "the teachings of Christ in any case did not favor slavery" and Southern Know Nothings were a greater menace to Cincinnati Catholics than Northern abolitionists. See *Der Wahrheits-Freund*, August 5, 1863. I am grateful to William B. Kurtz for this reference.
80 *Catholic Telegraph*, April 8, 1863.
81 *Catholic Telegraph*, January 13, 1864.
82 On Brownson's *Quarterly Review* and his pro-emancipationist perspective, see Patrick W. Carey, *Orestes A. Brownson: American Religious Weathervane* (Grand Rapids, MI: William B. Eerdmans Publishing, 2004), 264–275.

toward the *Catholic Telegraph* was not wholly negative. Edward Purcell claimed that he had received letters from every part of the country expressing satisfaction that there was a Catholic newspaper unafraid to support "the most oppressed people on earth."[83] In writing to Archbishop Purcell on May 28, 1863, Father William O'Higgins, chaplain to the Tenth Ohio Volunteer Infantry, then stationed in Murfreesboro, Tennessee, voiced his agreement. O'Higgins wrote, "God bless Father Edward for the triumphant vindication of our dear old Mother Church from the advancing blotch of slavery. Yes, she always hated it. She hates it now, and would give the world's treasures to see such a rank smelling sin blotted from the face of the earth."[84]

The *Catholic Telegraph*, now emancipationist, attempted to maintain the precarious balance of supporting the interests of Cincinnati's immigrant population and the rights of enslaved people to be free. It argued that emancipation would be beneficial to slaves as well as laborers, reversing the position it had taken as late as 1862.[85] The paper favored limitations on African American migration to Northern states and assured its readers that countless immigrant families could make claims on Southern land after the fall of slavery and the plantation system.[86] It wrote in support of the white laborer and the free labor ideal. The restoration of peace, the paper concluded, should bring about "a peace profitable to the white man who earns his bread by the sweat of his brow. We wish to see him not so low, but that he may have one foot on the ladder by which he can ascend to fortune."[87]

---

83 *Catholic Telegraph*, June 10, 1863.
84 Father William O'Higgins to Archbishop John Purcell, May 28, 1863, box 13, RG 1.2, Archbishop John B. Purcell Papers, ser. 1.2-02, Historical Archives of the Chancery, Archdiocese of Cincinnati (hereafter ACA). On O'Higgins, see David J. Endres, "'With a Father's Affection': Chaplain William T. O'Higgins and the Tenth Ohio Volunteer Infantry," *U.S. Catholic Historian* 31, no. 1 (Winter 2013): 97–127; David J. Endres, "An Ohio 'Holy Joe': Chaplain William T. O'Higgins' Wartime Correspondence with Archbishop Purcell of Cincinnati, 1863," *Ohio Civil War Genealogy Journal* 13, no. 2 (2009): 73–78.
85 Deye, "Archbishop John Baptist Purcell and the Civil War," 73.
86 *Catholic Telegraph*, April 15, 1863; *Catholic Telegraph*, July 15, 1863.
87 *Catholic Telegraph*, January 20, 1864.

The paper also affirmed the dignity of African Americans. "Those colored men," it proclaimed, "have a right to life and liberty as much as the white men, and they who oppress them without reason, and only to gratify an insatiable and disgraceful prejudice, are the enemies of order and religion."[88] The newspaper proclaimed its unique new identity as "the largest Catholic journal in the United States; opposed to slavery and disunion; the advocate of justice and freedom."[89] Its abolitionist views, it maintained, were for the greater good of all peoples regardless of ethnicity or race.

In a pastoral letter written to the people of his diocese on January 27, 1864, Purcell stated his position in the clearest of terms: "We go with our whole heart and soul for the maintenance of the Union and the abolition of slavery—against neither of which does the Supreme Pontiff of Christendom utter a single word."[90] Bishop Spalding of Louisville, in particular, condemned the letter, saying that if Purcell could not produce a non-partisan pastoral letter, it would be best not to issue one. In fact, the opposition to Purcell was so significant that the bishops of the surrounding dioceses refused to attend the Provincial Council that Purcell had planned to take place in Cincinnati on the fourth Sunday after Easter 1864.[91]

Later that year, Purcell issued a Thanksgiving pastoral message in which he prayed for the abolition of slavery, voiced support for the draft, and condemned two Catholic newspapers, the *Freeman's Journal* and *Metropolitan Record*, for opposing the war and emancipation.[92] He blamed these papers for instigating their readers "to evil words and deeds" through deliberate duplicity and deception.[93] Among Purcell's correspondence can be found two letters of support for his Thanksgiving message. Two cler-

---

88 *Catholic Telegraph*, May 25, 1864.
89 *Catholic Telegraph*, January 11, 1865.
90 *Catholic Telegraph*, January 27, 1864.
91 Deye, "Archbishop John Baptist Purcell and the Civil War," 41.
92 *Catholic Telegraph*, November 16, 1864.
93 Archbishop John B. Purcell, Pastoral Letter: "Thanksgiving, Humiliation, and Prayer," November 13, 1864, in *Catholic Telegraph*, November 16, 1864.

ics—a Catholic priest and a Presbyterian minister—wrote letters on November 21, 1864, in response to Purcell's pastoral message that had appeared in the same newspapers that he had criticized. Father William Everett of New York City thanked the Cincinnati bishop "for the noble expression of patriotic sentiment" in denouncing "those impudent and wicked newspapers published in this city." Everett further argued, "Our people have been put in a false, disloyal, and essentially uncatholic position by the politicians whose lead they have followed like sheep—aided by such 'religious' papers as those you have named."[94] Reverend W. B. Sprague, a Presbyterian minister in Albany, New York, penned a similar note to Purcell. "I was previously aware of the honorable position you had taken on this subject," Sprague wrote, "and was the more deeply impressed by it from the fact that nearly all our Roman Catholic population in this part of the country have gone in the opposite direction. Your proclamation, my dear sir, will, of itself, I am sure, render your name imperishable in history."[95]

"Imperishable in History"

The prediction of Reverend Sprague begs the question of Archbishop Purcell's legacy to nation, church, and region: What was Purcell's impact on the Church and his flock during the years of the Civil War? Clearly, only a minority of his fellow bishops and the Catholic press accepted his opinions. Similarly, the vast majority of Cincinnati's Irish and German residents were unreceptive, remaining committed to the Democratic Party, opposed to abolitionism, and fearful of an African American exodus into Ohio.[96] The experience of Cincinnati Catholics throughout the Civil War years indicated that they were probably influenced more by local ethnic loyalties and economic real-

---

94 William Everett to Archbishop John Purcell, New York City, November 21, 1864, box 13, RG 1.2, Archbishop John B. Purcell Papers, ser. 1.2-02, ACA.

95 Reverend W. B. Sprague to Archbishop John Purcell, Albany, New York, November 21, 1864, box 14, RG 1.2, Archbishop John B. Purcell Papers, ser. 1.2-02, ACA.

96 Klement, "Catholics as Copperheads," 40.

ities than the moral and rational persuasion of their bishop and the *Catholic Telegraph*.

Though Purcell may have been unsuccessful in garnering widespread support for his ideals among Catholics, he brought attention to the moral and social ramifications of the slavery question. In emancipating the slaves, America's "fatal contrast" was resolved, and Cincinnati's conflict with race and religion diminished. Loyalty to the Union, especially among Catholics, was strengthened through Purcell's leadership, and the draft riots that had plagued other cities with large immigrant populations did not occur locally. Purcell also increased the visibility of the Catholic Church throughout the country, demonstrating that there were Catholics willing to stand in support of emancipation and the honor of the nation.[97]

The climate of extreme racism in Cincinnati was tempered under the archbishop's guidance. Near the end of the war, Purcell assisted in the formation of a Catholic church and school for African Americans known as St. Ann's. Under the leadership of a Jesuit priest, Francis Xavier Weninger, the parish was founded in 1866 as among the first Catholic parishes for Blacks in the United States. In September 1868, the *Catholic Telegraph* announced the formation of the Blessed Peter Claver Society, an organization founded to support St. Ann's School.[98] Purcell wrote that the students of St. Ann bear the fruits of their training and "prove this every year by public examinations and exhibitions to the aston-

---

97 See Ford, *Bonds of Union*, xi–xix, 14–63, 277–279. Though Ford does not expressly credit Purcell, she examines the forces that—despite tensions—helped forge bonds in the borderland region that included Cincinnati. As an example, she cites Catholic and Protestant participation in the Great Western Sanitary Fair held in Cincinnati, 1863–1864, which helped raise funds to care for Union soldiers.

98 Joseph Lackner, "St. Ann's Colored Church and School, Cincinnati, the Indian and Negro Collection for the United States, and Reverend Francis Xavier Weninger, S.J.," *U.S. Catholic Historian* 7, nos. 2–3 (Spring–Summer 1988), 145–147; on Weninger's efforts among African Americans, see David Komline, "'If There Were One People': Francis Weninger and the Segregation of American Catholicism," *Religion and American Culture* 27, no. 2 (Summer 2017): 218–246.

ishment and delight of the citizens of Cincinnati."[99] Though not viewed as equals, African Americans were beginning to be seen as capable of benefiting from education and participation in the life of the local Church.

The legacy of Purcell and his contribution to the slavery debate can be viewed in light of the words of Orestes Brownson: "Peace is a good thing, but justice is better. . . . Give us the noise and contention of life, rather than the peace and silence of the charnel-house."[100] Brownson preferred lively democratic debate to peaceful injustice, seeing it as the best hope for both nation and church. Purcell, too, preferred justice over peace and noise over silence if it could stir men and women to examine the most perplexing questions of the age. In the face of opposition, Purcell added his voice to the age's rhetorical dissonance, committing himself to following the dictates of truth and justice wherever they led. As a border state bishop who supported abolition, Purcell represents an important minority within the U.S. Church—one that should not be ignored when examining the Catholic contribution to the slavery debate.

---

99 Archbishop John B. Purcell, *Circular Letter to the Reverend Clergy and the Faithful People of the Diocese of Cincinnati*, September 9, 1877, ACA; printed in the *Catholic Telegraph*, September 13, 1877.

100 Orestes Brownson, "Education of the People," *Boston Quarterly Review* 2, no. 4 (October 1839), 423.

Catholic Responses to Lincoln's Emancipation Proclamation

ROBERT EMMETT CURRAN*

Prelude to Emancipation

In his 1899 memoir on the 9th Massachusetts Volunteers, Daniel George MacNamara recalled the Irish regiment's bivouacking in 1861 on the grounds of Robert E. Lee's Arlington plantation, just across the Potomac from the Capitol:

> ... many of us loitered around ... the slave quarters and held conversation with some of the slaves, learning for the first time many practical lessons from the living subjects themselves of the degradation of human slavery, which gave us food for thought on their aimless, animal-like life.... We ourselves felt then that the day of deliverance for the negro slaves of our land was near at hand....[1]

We could imagine that the encounter of Irish Catholic soldiers with Robert Lee's own slaves would have opened the eyes of the Irishmen to the "degradation of human slavery." This, however, seems a projection of MacNamara's thinking in the 1890s back onto his assumptions during the war's first months when few people, especially among the Irish, were reflecting on emancipation as an outcome of the war. When it did come in the form of Lincoln's proclamation a year and a half later, the Irish led the Catholic community in decrying the executive order that had changed the war.

---

* This essay was originally published as "'To tear down ... the Corinthian pillars of Constitutional liberty': Catholics and Lincoln's Emancipation Proclamation," *U.S. Catholic Historian* 37, no. 2 (Spring 2019): 109–136.

1 Daniel G. MacNamara, *The History of the Ninth Regiment: Massachusetts Volunteer Infantry, Second Brigade, First Division, Fifth Army Corps, Army of the Potomac, June 1861–June 1864* (Boston: E.B. Stillings, 1899), 45.

Charles Halpine's fictional poet, Miles O'Reilly, more accurately summed up the mind of the Irish at the war's beginning:

> To the tenets of Douglas we tenderly cling,
> Warm hearts to the cause of our country we bring,
> To the flag we are pledged—all its foes we abhor—
> And we ain't for the "nigger" but we are for the war.[2]

Even before Lincoln was sworn into office, the diocesan paper, the *Louisville Guardian*, in a December 1, 1860 editorial laid bare the inconvenient truth that was driving secession:

> We will not believe that the men of the North are ready to rush upon the evils of civil war on account of a mere idea ... of equal rights between the black and the white races on this continent. We will not believe that they are ready to sacrifice their own liberties through their efforts to give liberty to the slaves of the South.[3]

Lincoln, long before 1860, had made clear his conviction that slavery, as the root of the increasing division plaguing the country, was imperiling the existence of the country itself. As he observed during the 1858 debates with Stephen Douglas, "a house divided against itself cannot stand." In his inaugural address, President Lincoln announced that he had no intention of interfering with slavery in the states where it existed. But Lincoln knew the quarrel of the newly-formed Confederate States of America with his administration was not the status of slavery in the states but rather in the territories. Was slavery to be free to expand into those territories and be protected there as the seceded states insisted and the Supreme Court had ruled in its *Dred Scott v. Sanford* decision? Or was Congress to take the appropriate steps to preclude such expansion and protection, as the Republicans had pledged in their platform? Lincoln went on to point out that *Dred Scott v. Sanford*, the 1857 Supreme Court deci-

---

2 Robert B. Roosevelt, ed., *The Poetical Works of Charles G. Halpine* (New York: 1869), 289, cited in Frank L. Klement, "Catholics as Copperheads During the Civil War," *Catholic Historical Review* 80, no. 1 (January 1994), 37.

3 Judith C. Wimmer, "American Catholic Interpretations of the Civil War" (Ph.D. dissertation, Drew University, 1980), 108 n59.

sion that had sanctioned slavery in the territories, should not be the last word. "If the policy of the Government is to be irrevocably fixed by decisions of the Supreme Court...," he noted, "the people will have ceased to be their own rulers, having to that extent practically resigned their Government into the hands of that eminent tribunal." The president was suggesting that the Congress, the branch most beholden to the people, had the power to change that decision by their own action.[4]

When Congress met in July in special session, both houses passed resolutions that reaffirmed Lincoln's assurance that the government had no intention "of overthrowing or interfering with the rights or established institutions of [the seceded] States."[5] The day before the first of those resolutions, the stunning Confederate victory at Bull Run had been a distressing revelation that this would be no one-battle war won by 75,000 volunteers engaged for ninety days. That realization occasioned a rethinking by Congressional Republicans of how sacrosanct the institution of slavery should be in crafting a strategy for ultimate victory. Little by little, Congress began to take up Lincoln's threat to whittle away at slavery, both in the territories as well as in the seceded states themselves.

On August 6, less than three weeks after the Battle of Bull Run, Congress passed a Confiscation Act, which effectively treated as contraband any runaway slaves who had been employed by the Confederate armed forces. Eight months later it emancipated all 3,000 enslaved persons in the District of Columbia with limited compensation (a maximum of $300 per slave) to those who had held them as property and took the oath of allegiance.[6] For the first time in the country's history, the federal

---

4 Davis Newton Lott, ed., *The Presidents Speak: The Inaugural Addresses of the American Presidents from Washington to Clinton* (New York: Henry Holt and Company, 1994), 138–145; Richard Striner, "Lincoln's Threat to the Supreme Court," *New York Times*, Disunion Series, March 3, 2011, https://opinionator.blogs.nytimes.com/2011/03/03/lincoln-addresses-the-nation/.
5 *Congressional Quarterly*, 37th Congress, 1 Session, 222–223, 258–262, cited in James M. McPherson, *Battle Cry of Freedom: The Civil War Era* (New York: Oxford University Press, 1988), 312.
6 Mary Mitchell, *Divided Town* (Barre, MA: Barre Publishers, 1968), 60–61.

government had abolished slavery in a jurisdiction.[7] Then two months later, Congress took the bolder step of nullifying the *Dred Scott v. Sanford* decision by emancipating all bondspeople in the country's ten territories. In mid-July Congress passed a second Confiscation Act, authorizing the seizure of all the slaves of those engaged in rebellion, and a Militia Act, which approved the enlistment of African Americans.

For his part, Lincoln had been reluctant to embrace emancipation efforts that could have proven counterproductive. He had been quick to countermand emancipation orders by Union generals in South Carolina and Missouri in 1861–1862. Since early 1862 his own emancipation efforts had been concentrated on the border states where he had determined the key to defeating the South lay. If Lincoln could persuade Delaware, Kentucky, Maryland, and Missouri to accept compensated emancipation for their slaveholders, it would be a decisive signal to the Confederacy that these four states, whom it badly needed to prevail in the war, would not join their cause. For months, he tried to coax legislators from the border states to accept the compensated emancipation for their slaveholders which Congress had approved in April 1862. In the end, not one of the four was willing to participate.[8]

The Peninsula Campaign as Catalyst

The catalyst for abolition becoming a war goal was ironically the Peninsula Campaign, led by General George McClellan, who had written: "Help me to dodge the nigger, we want nothing to do with him." But events during the four-month campaign overtook McClellan's prejudice. The use of slave labor by the Confederates and the valuable intelligence runaways provided to the Federals during the campaign convinced many in Congress, including moderate and conservative Republicans, to advocate abolition as a war measure. The fierce Confederate resistance to

---

7 Paul Finkelman, "From Union to Freedom," *New York Times*, Disunion Series, October 5, 2012, https://opinionator.blogs.nytimes.com/2012/10/05/not-yet-freedom/.

8 William C. Harris, *Lincoln and the Border States: Preserving the Union* (Lawrence: University Press of Kansas, 2011), 159–189.

McClellan's grand army contributed to burying the prevailing notion within the Lincoln administration and beyond that secession had been the work of an extremist minority, and that a limited war which respected Southern property, including slaves, could persuade the seceded states to return to the Union.[9]

Had McClellan succeeded in taking Richmond and thereby virtually ending the war, it would have restored the Union "as it was antebellum." Instead, his failure on the Peninsula put pressure on Lincoln to pursue limited emancipation as a military necessity.[10] In early July he informed Senator Charles Sumner of Massachusetts, a leading abolitionist, that he hesitated to invoke such a policy for fear that half of his officers would "fling down their arms and three more States would rise" against the Union.[11] Further reflection apparently convinced Lincoln that the benefits that emancipation would bring to the Union's war effort outweighed any risk of defections among officers or border states. And accordingly, in late July he confided to his cabinet his plan to exercise his authority as commander-in-chief to free the three and a half million slaves in areas that were in rebellion against the United States. Such a proclamation, so Lincoln hoped, would undermine the Confederacy's use of slave labor to support Confederate armies.

Antietam and Promulgation

Lincoln was prepared to take action immediately but his secretary of state, William Seward, persuaded him to defer any public announcement of emancipation until the Union's military fortunes improved. That moment arrived in mid-September in Western Maryland. Along a five-mile stretch of Antietam Creek, Confederate and Union forces fought the bloodiest one-day battle in American history. At the end of the dawn-to-dark bloodlet-

---

9 Glenn David Brasher, *The Peninsula Campaign and the Necessity of Emancipation* (Chapel Hill: University of North Carolina Press, 2012), 69.
10 Brasher, *The Peninsula Campaign*, 203.
11 Charles Sumner, *The Works of Charles Sumner* (Boston: Lee & Shepard, 1872), VI: 215, cited in Stephen W. Sears, *Landscape Turned Red: The Battle of Antietam* (New York: Popular Library, 1985), 46.

ting, there were more than 23,000 casualties strewn about a "landscape turned red." In tactical terms, Antietam had been a standoff, even a remarkable Confederate success, given the overwhelming manpower advantage of the Union forces. In strategic ones, however, the apocalyptic battle was a victory for the Union. Robert E. Lee had been forced to abandon his invasion of Northern soil.

Union success, limited as it was, enabled Lincoln to make a preliminary proclamation of his intention to free all those slaves in areas still in rebellion against the United States government. If the Confederate States failed, by January 1, 1863, to call off their effort to gain independence, Lincoln would sign the order officially freeing, as a military necessity, all those held in bondage within Confederate lines. This changed the nature of the war. It may have physically freed not one enslaved person throughout the Confederacy, but psychologically it freed them all, both in the Confederacy as well as in the border states. It told the South and the world that abolition was now an explicit war goal of the United States government.

Catholics and Abolition

Nearly a year before Lincoln made his dramatic announcement regarding slavery, Archbishop John Hughes of New York had warned the secretary of war, Simon Cameron, that it would be a disaster if the administration widened the war's aims beyond restoring the Union "as it was." Adding abolition as a war goal, Hughes told Cameron, would immediately cost the administration Northern Catholic support.[12]

The Catholic position on slavery in the nineteenth century developed out of its traumatic experience with the forces of enlightened liberalism, epitomized by the French Revolution. "Catholics lumped immediate slave emancipation," John McGreevy has noted, "with a religious and political radicalism that threatened the foundations of society," including the hierar-

---

12 John Hassard, *Life of the Most Reverend John Hughes, D.D., First Archbishop of New York* (New York: D. Appleton and Company, 1866), 437.

chical order of which slavery was an evil necessity in a biracial society in which one race was superior to the other.[13] Publicly the American hierarchy in the antebellum period had regarded slavery as basically a political issue that the state alone could resolve. As Bishop John England of Charleston had confessed, he personally opposed slavery, but that was a "question for the legislature and not for me."[14] England's successor, Patrick Lynch, the most intellectually gifted among the American hierarchy of the Civil War era, dismissed abolition as a mere "speculative idea," with no bearing on the socio-political order. That all changed with Lincoln's election. The Republican Party's commitment to prevent the spread of slavery was its death warrant. The South, according to Lynch, had no choice but to strike out on its own.[15]

Northern Catholics may not necessarily have affirmed Bishop Lynch's explanation of the origin of the war, but by and large they shared his characterization of abolition as speculation that should have no place in government policy, especially in waging a war to reunite the country. As James McMaster, editor of the New York-based *Freeman's Journal*, editorialized in the fall of 1860: "It is not the business of the political power to settle moral questions."[16] Orestes Brownson, the leading intellectual among American Catholics, judged slavery "a great moral social and political wrong,"[17] but was highly skeptical of abolition, not only because of the anti-Catholic sentiments of most of its promoters, but also because Brownson considered Blacks, as moral and intellectual inferiors, to be problematic candidates for freedom. The war changed his thinking mightily. By the fall of 1861, he had concluded, as he wrote Senator Sumner, that it "is impos-

---

13   John T. McGreevy, *Catholicism and American Freedom: A History* (New York: W.W. Norton, 2003), 48–56.
14   William George Read, ed., *Letters of the Late Bishop England to the Hon. John Forsyth on the Subject of Domestic Slavery* (Baltimore: John Murphy, 1844), 23–24.
15   Patrick Lynch to John Hughes, Charleston, August 4, 1861, in *New York Daily Tribune*, September 5, 1861, 6.
16   *Freeman's Journal*, October 6, 1860.
17   Brownson, "Slavery and the War," in *The Works of Orestes A. Brownson*, ed. Henry F. Brownson (Detroit: Thorndike Nourse, 1885), 17: 163–164, cited in Cyprian Davis, *The History of Black Catholics in the United States* (New York: Crossroad Publishing, 1990), 59–60.

Orestes Brownson, a rare Catholic supporter of emancipation, is pictured here in a portrait by George Peter Alexander Healy, 1863 (Museum of Fine Arts, Boston).

sible to save both the integrity of the Nation and southern slavery. . . ." That same month his essay, "Slavery and the War," echoed this pronouncement in making a strong case for abolition as the only way to save the Union.[18] Like Lincoln, emancipation for Brownson became a military imperative.

The backlash was loud and immediate against Brownson's call for emancipation, including canceled subscriptions to his quarterly magazine, called-off engagements, and episcopal rejoinders. Archbishop John Hughes in the *Metropolitan Record*, under the cover of a *nom de plume*, deemed any call for the abolition of slavery an attack on the Constitution and humankind's experience. Slavery, Hughes pointed out, was an institution as old as man, which, in the African's case had been a civilizing experience for the race. He claimed to speak for all Catholics in

---

18   Brownson to Charles Sumner, October 23, 1861, I-4-H, University of Notre Dame Archives, Notre Dame, Indiana, cited in Wimmer, "American Catholic Interpretations of the Civil War," 176, n101.

denouncing the "idea of making this war subservient to the philanthropic nonsense of abolitionism."[19]

The Catholic press was virtually unanimous in its condemnation of the Congressional emancipation legislation. John Mullally of the New York *Metropolitan Record* denounced the Confiscation Acts as unconstitutional, part of the abolitionists' "grand project of social amalgamation and equality between blacks and whites. . . ."[20] *The Catholic Mirror*, the official paper of four Southern dioceses (Baltimore, Richmond, Wheeling, and Charleston), warned that the bill emancipating the slaves of the District of Columbia was but the first step toward a general emancipation which gave the lie to pre-war Republican claims that they would honor the Constitution by not interfering with slavery in the states.[21] The Boston *Pilot*, in its opposition to the first Confiscation Act, insisted, "The truth is no government suits the Negroes of the South, but the domestic government they have," that is, slavery.[22]

One Catholic weekly that came to be an outlier in supporting the abolition strategy of the Lincoln administration was the *Catholic Telegraph*, edited by Edward Purcell, clerical brother of Archbishop John B. Purcell of Cincinnati. As late as 1862 the *Telegraph* had denounced emancipation, even as a war measure, as both "incendiary and stupid." "Do the American people believe that we could be a nation with four millions of free negroes in our midst?" an editorial rhetorically asked.[23] That summer Archbishop Purcell was in Rome where he encountered Bishop Felix Dupanloup of Orleans, France, who had just issued an antislavery

---

19 Hughes later offered to administration officials the dubious explanation that he took such a negative stand on the issue to assure that Catholics would remain committed to the preservation of the Union (New York *Metropolitan Record*, October 12, 1861), cited in William B. Kurtz, *Excommunicated from the Union: How the Civil War Created a Separate Catholic America* (New York: Fordham University Press, 2016), 95–96.

20 Joseph George, Jr., "'A Catholic Family Newspaper' Views the Lincoln Administration: John Mullally's Copperhead Weekly," *Civil War History* 24 (June 1978), 118–119.

21 *Catholic Mirror*, April 19, 1862.

22 Boston *Pilot*, March 22, 1862.

23 Cincinnati *Catholic Telegraph*, July 23, 1862.

pastoral.²⁴ The meeting appears to have produced a sea change in Purcell's thinking. In a pastoral letter published in early September 1862, the archbishop flatly blamed the Southern states for starting the war. The South, he charged, had decades earlier decided upon secession as the best protector of slavery and systematically prepared for war beginning in the late 1850s. The North had no choice, according to Purcell, but to fight. And the only way to victory for the North lay through abolition.²⁵ Unlike his fellow prelates, Purcell now felt that slavery was a critical issue that the Church needed to address. Indeed, throwing caution to the wind, the archbishop added, "He who tries to perpetuate slavery disrespects the doctrine and example of Christ."²⁶

The Purcells spoke for a distinct minority among white American Catholics. A Fourth of July celebration of New York Democrats at a packed Tammany headquarters in 1862 represented mainline Catholic opinion. The program opened with a sung poem entitled: "The Union as it was, and the Constitution as it is." The anti-abolition message could not have been clearer. Judge Charles P. Daly told the crowd that the Democrats had a solemn duty to demand that the war be carried on "not as a political speculation, but as a great national work. . . ." Congress was wasting its time in devising measures for the confiscation of property and the emancipation of bondspeople of which the legislators had no possession. As it was, nothing less than the principles of republican government were on trial in "this great contest."²⁷

---

24 Kurtz, *Excommunicated from the Union*, 98–99.

25 For text of the pastoral, see *Pittsburgh Catholic*, September 20, 1862; Wimmer, "American Catholic Interpretations of the Civil War," 156–157.

26 William Henry Elder of Natchez, Mississippi, spoke for many of his fellow U.S. bishops when he accused Purcell of prolonging the war with his unconditional support for emancipation. The steep drop in subscriptions in the wake of Purcell's call for abolition was testament that many *Catholic Telegraph* subscribers agreed with Elder (Roger Fortin, *Faith and Action: A History of the Catholic Archdiocese of Cincinnati, 1821–1996* [Columbus: Ohio State University Press, 2002], 143).

27 *New York Daily Tribune*, July 5, 1862.

Catholic Reaction to the Preliminary Proclamation

Lincoln's preliminary announcement of the Emancipation Proclamation in late September 1862 galvanized opposition to the war. Stocks on Wall Street fell, as did enlistments. Democratic prospects in the fall elections considerably brightened. The public voices of the Catholic community were quick to vent their discontent with the president's executive action. Archbishop John Hughes vowed that "we Catholics, and a vast majority of our brave troops in the field, have not the slightest idea of carrying on a war that costs so much blood and treasure just to gratify a clique of Abolitionists."[28] In a paper that Hughes prepared on "The Emancipation Proclamation," the archbishop related a dream he had had in which a "big black beast" set fire to his former master's property before going on a violent spree. One needed little parsing of the prelate's text to discover the racist fears stoking his nightmare. Hughes added that Lincoln had made a grave mistake in judgment in issuing an order with such enormous consequences.[29]

Judge Daly dismissed the proclamation as a piece of paper which was meaningless against the animal-like loyalty that slaves had toward their masters. "Father [Bernard] O'Reilly," Judge Daly's wife, Maria, noted in her diary, "says we are under a worse despotism than they have in France or Russia. There is no law but the despotic will of poor Abe Lincoln because he is a *cover* for every knave and fanatic. . . . It is terrible. God help our unhappy country!"[30] Judge Daly was positive that the Irish would not fight

---

28 Susannah Ural Bruce, *The Harp and the Eagle: Irish-American Volunteers and the Union Army, 1861–1865* (New York: New York University Press, 2006), 137.

29 "The Emancipation Proclamation," Hughes Manuscript, Archives of the Archdiocese of New York, cited in Charles P. Connor, "The American Catholic Political Position at Mid-Century: Archbishop Hughes as a Test Case" (Ph.D. dissertation, Fordham University, 1979), 353. Archbishop Hughes agreed to join other conservative clergy in New York City to write public letters protesting Lincoln's new policy, but when the Protestant clergy withdrew from the effort, it was abandoned (Hassard, *Life of Hughes*, 440).

30 Maria Lydig Daly, *Diary of a Union Lady: 1861–1865*, ed. Harold Earl Hammond (Lincoln: University of Nebraska Press, 2000), entry for September 28, 1862, 179. Father Bernard O'Reilly, S.J., was a close friend of the Daly family and served as chaplain to the 69th New York, the Irish Brigade.

One of the earliest prints of Lincoln's executive order, March 1863 (Library of Congress).

for Blacks.[31] New York lawyer and politician Richard O'Gorman branded the preliminary proclamation "a barbarous, disgraceful, hideous violation of the morality of Christendom," predicted it would lead to "servile war," and insisted that abolitionists were doing more to destroy the country than anyone else.[32]

Of the sixteen major Catholic newspapers, only two of them, both housed in Cincinnati, supported the proclamation: the *Catholic Telegraph* and *Der Wahrheits-Freund*. The most critical of the Catholic weeklies was James McMaster's *Freeman's Journal*. About the proclamation it predicted:

---

31   Ernest A. McKay, *The Civil War and New York City* (Syracuse, NY: Syracuse University Press, 1990), 159–160; Daly, *Diary of a Union Lady*, entry for October 4, 1862, 181.

32   Albon P. Man, Jr., "The Irish in New York in the Early Eighteen-Sixties," *Irish Historical Studies* 26 (September 1950), 98–99.

Its effect at the North will be one of wide-spread demoralization of forces, and division of parties. As a document of State it is beneath either discussion or even simple contempt. Nevertheless, perhaps it is as well that it is out. It had to come. Abolitionism had to try its utmost before it could be made to feel its impotency in this agony of a great country.[33]

If some move toward universal emancipation was inevitable with the Lincoln administration, as McMaster strongly believed, then better that they expose their hand now, particularly with the fall elections looming, where the proclamation could become for the public a referendum on the Lincoln administration itself. The editor was very confident how any such vote would turn out, to the consternation of abolitionists and the Lincoln administration.[34]

Patrick Donahoe of the Boston *Pilot* displayed a whistling-past-the-graveyard bravado by predicting that the vast majority of the affected slaves would reject freedom.[35] For the leading Irish journal, the *Irish-American*, the Emancipation Proclamation was nothing more than a demonstration of the radical "Negrophilism" of the administration and "the irredeemable malignity of the Abolition hatred of our race." Putting Blacks on an equal level with whites meant for the Irish an increased competition for jobs and military service.[36]

Besides Archbishop Purcell, a few prelates spoke in support of the proclamation, notably bishops John Martin Henni of Milwaukee, Wisconsin, and Josue Young of Erie, Pennsylvania. Henni boldly defended Lincoln's order by linking its military necessity to the moral imperative of ending slavery. Union success in the war, Henni maintained, was vital "not only to prevent the extension, but to put an end to the existence of the great and crying shame upon all Christendom, the peculiar institution of

---

33 *Freeman's Journal*, October 4, 1862.
34 *Freeman's Journal*, October 4, 1862.
35 Boston *Pilot*, October 4, 1862, cited in Francis R. Walsh, "The Boston *Pilot* Reports the Civil War," *Historical Journal of Massachusetts* 9 (June 1981), 11.
36 *Irish American*, November 8, 1862; January 17, 1863, cited in Edward K. Spann, "Union Green: The Irish Community and the Civil War," in Ronald H. Bayor and Timothy J. Meagher, eds., *The New York Irish* (Baltimore: Johns Hopkins University Press, 1996), 203.

the South."³⁷ For Young, a New England convert and protégé of John Purcell, abolitionism was part of the cultural baggage he brought to his new faith. He drew criticism for his fiery sermons promoting the Union cause. Among the clergy, the outspoken advocates of abolition, like Sylvester Malone of Brooklyn, were the exception. Richard Burtsell, a New York priest, rued the "cowardice" that kept Catholic clergy and laity from supporting the abolition of slavery.³⁸ A rare Southern priest in support of the Emancipation Proclamation was Claude Paschal Maistre of occupied New Orleans. Maistre defied his archbishop, Jean-Marie Odin, by celebrating in April 1863 a Mass of Thanksgiving for the Emancipation Proclamation, during which he cited Lincoln's order as the first step on the road to equality between the races. The upshot of Maistre's witness for the proclamation was the mass exodus of his white congregants, his suspension from ministry, and interdiction of his church.³⁹

In his annual message to Congress at the beginning of December, Lincoln confused matters by renewing the prospects for compensated emancipation, even introducing a proposal for an amendment to the Constitution that would achieve that goal by the end of the century. However, his main focus was on the Emancipation Proclamation which would go into effect in a month unless the seceded states returned to the Union before the New Year. "In *giving* freedom to the slave, we *assure* freedom to the free," Lincoln said of his controversial executive order. The Emancipation Proclamation, borne of the "victory" at Antietam, was a stone in the structure that the American nation strove to be, a government of the people, by the people, for the people. As he told Congress: "In this war: We shall nobly save, or meanly

---

37 *Pittsburgh Catholic*, September 27, 1862, cited in Wimmer, "American Catholic Interpretations of the Civil War," 111 n65.

38 May 31, 1865, Diary of Richard Burtsell, Vol. I, Archives of the Archdiocese of New York; Robert Emmett Curran, "Prelude to 'Americanism': The New York *Accadèmia* and Clerical Radicalism in the Late Nineteenth Century," *Shaping American Catholicism: Maryland and New York, 1805–1915* (Washington, DC: Catholic University of America Press, 2012), 164–165.

39 Stephen J. Ochs, *A Black Patriot and a White Priest: André Cailloux and Claude Paschal Maistre in Civil War New Orleans* (Baton Rouge: Louisiana State University Press, 2000), 112–136.

lose, the last, best hope of earth." In freeing the slaves, he argued, we were honoring Jefferson's axiom that all men are created equal. The parameters of that freedom were still in flux as the nation struggled to comprehend the full dimensions of that equality. This, after all, was a republic constantly being redefined by citizens committed to the full realization of the American promise laid out in its founding documents.[40]

Lincoln's efforts to put Blacks on an equal level with whites through emancipation and enrolling them as soldiers were two straws too many for the *Pilot's* support of the war. The slaves, Donahoe insisted, did not want freedom: "They love their masters as dogs do." Nature intended the plantation to be their habitat.[41] The Boston weekly found common ground with the anti-war Copperheads, whom it regarded as the last "true representatives of Republican freedom today in this country."[42] For many Democrats, particularly Catholics, the series of reverses throughout the spring and summer of 1862 had fed the desire for peace, no matter what price the South demanded as a return to the Union. That growing peace movement was all the more infuriated by Lincoln's sudden announcement of the Emancipation Proclamation which, to them, ensured not only a much longer war but also one pursuing a policy of abolition that Democrats not only abhorred but read as the clearest evidence yet that Lincoln was shredding the Constitution. Lincoln was becoming the tyrant they had increasingly suspected he desired to be.

A Tipping Point

The blood bath the Army of the Potomac suffered on the hills behind Fredericksburg, Virginia, in mid-December 1862 left the nation sickened over the waste of so many lives in the suicidal charges up Marye's Hill. A Union chaplain, Joseph O'Hagan, wrote a fellow Jesuit five days after the disaster: "I never imag-

---

40   George Rable, *Fredericksburg! Fredericksburg!* (Chapel Hill: University of North Carolina Press, 2002), 129–130.
41   Boston *Pilot*, October 4, 1862.
42   Boston *Pilot*, April 4, 1863, in Thomas H. O'Connor, *Civil War Boston: Home Front and Battlefield* (Boston: Northeastern University Press, 1997), 38.

ined that so many dead could be left on our field. They were actually in heaps. . . . I am only surprised that the entire nation does not rise up against it unanimously."[43] The nation did not rise, but Fredericksburg proved the tipping point for many in the Catholic community, especially in the Irish neighborhoods of New York and other cities. The near annihilation of the Irish Brigade provided opponents of the Emancipation Proclamation with the opportunity to charge the Lincoln administration with sacrificing Irish lives in its desperate attempt to secure military success that would legitimize the unconstitutional executive order Lincoln was poised to put into effect in less than three weeks. Given the setbacks Republicans had experienced in the fall elections, together with Lincoln's own apparent second thoughts about the proclamation in his annual message to Congress, the Fredericksburg debacle gave hope in certain quarters that Lincoln might not promulgate it on January 1. The Boston *Pilot* could not suppress its racism in asking: "Can [Lincoln] ever make atonement for his unaccountable blunder?" in dismissing General McClellan from command of the Army of the Potomac to "satisfy the fanaticism of that herd . . . inflicted with the disease called 'Nigger on the brain.'" "For the sake of the union, let us have an armistice," the *Pilot* demanded.[44]

In his diary, New York lawyer George Templeton Strong, a few days after the Fredericksburg disaster, reflected on the widespread negative reaction to Lincoln's Proclamation:

> How strange that patriotic, loyal people should deny its expediency. This generation is certainly overshadowed by a superstition . . . that slaveholding rights possess peculiar sanctity and inviolability, that everybody who doubts their justice is an Abolitionist, and that an Abolitionist is a social pariah, a reprobate and caitiff, a leper whom all decent people are bound to avoid and denounce.[45]

---

43 O'Hagan to Bernard Wiget, near Falmouth, December 18, 1862, in *Woodstock Letters* 15 (1886): 112–113.
44 Bruce, *The Harp and the Eagle*, 140.
45 Allan Nevins and Milton Halsey Thomas, eds., *The Diary of George Templeton Strong*, Vol. 3, *The Civil War, 1860–1865* (New York: The Macmillan Company, 1952), entry for December 17, 1862, 284.

That reflection characterized the opinion of much of the Catholic community from the Northern states to the border areas to the Deep South. It came out in full when Lincoln made the proclamation official on January 1. With few exceptions, the Catholic response became increasingly alarmist about the horrific consequences emancipation would set loose.

Ever since Lincoln had made his initial gestures toward using African Americans in the military in the spring of 1862, Catholics had mounted strong protests against any such recruitment. *The Pilot* judged it as "a lasting disgrace to the nation." The last thing nature intended the African American to be was a soldier.[46] When seven months later the president included in his proclamation the enlistment of Blacks for military duties, Catholics, particularly in Baltimore, Philadelphia, Charleston, and other cities that had been sanctuaries for refugees from the slave uprising in Santo Domingo in the 1790s, found themselves revisiting the nightmarish tales that the emigres had spread abroad in their new communities. Lincoln's order threatened to revive on a vastly larger scale the slave terror and butchery that haunted the memories of the survivors and their progeny. Colonel Julius Garesché, chief aide to General William Rosecrans and descendent of Santo Domingo refugees, mindful of the horrors of their homeland that his family had passed down, vowed to resign should Lincoln go through with his threatened executive action on January 1. Garesché never had the opportunity. At the Battle of Stones River on the last day of 1862, a Confederate cannonball beheaded him.[47]

The Boston *Pilot* invoked the Emancipation Proclamation to stir fears of another Santo Domingo uprising. Add the specter of that horror to the catastrophic losses the American Irish had sustained in the unprecedentedly savage fighting in two theaters over the past six months, and it was incumbent, indeed patriotic, the editor concluded, for Catholics to oppose Lincoln and his administration in every way possible.[48] The *Pittsburgh*

---

46   May 10, 1862, cited in Bruce, *The Harp and the Eagle*, 137–138.
47   Louis Garesché, *Biography of Lieutenant Colonel Julius P. Garesché* (Philadelphia: J.B. Lippincott, 1887), 351–352.
48   Walsh, "The Boston *Pilot* Reports the Civil War," 11.

Catholic printed the full text of the president's proclamation without comment. On the same page, there was a brief note under the heading of "Loyalty." "Loyalty," the note explained, "here and now means devotion to the Union, the Constitution, and the legitimate Government of the United States. It does *not* mean the adoption of any peculiar theory as to the shortest way of putting down the rebellion." There could have been little doubt that the paper was taking the preemptive step of defending those Catholics who would oppose the introduction of abolition, under whatever pretext and howsoever limited, as a war goal.[49]

The editors of the *Catholic Mirror* simply ignored the president's action. In its first edition of January 1863, the principal editorial, "Radical Legislation," warned its readers of the Republicans' plans to pass "unjust and proscriptive confiscation laws," for which the Emancipation Proclamation was clearly paving the way. The editors returned to this topic several times in 1863, arguing in December 1863 that it would be in the economic interests of Southern planters to switch to free rather than slave labor since the former would not require the total lifetime support that planters provided their slaves. The free laborer, they pointed out, was "very far from getting the slave's share. . . ." The result was suffering and death at a rate the slave community never knew. Because of that paternal care, there was a mutual regard between "the Southerners and the colored race." It explained, the editors maintained, why gradual emancipation had proved a failure. "That which is effected rapidly," they concluded with an apparent reference to the Emancipation Proclamation, "cannot prove more so."[50] *The Irish American* reported in early January: "The Emancipation Proclamation is universally condemned as one of the worst acts of the president's administration . . . clearly illegal, it gives the South every incentive to fight with greater desperation than ever."[51] To the *Metropolitan Record*, Lincoln's proclamation

---

49   *Pittsburgh Catholic*, October 4, 1862.
50   *Catholic Mirror*, January 3, 1863; *Catholic Mirror*, January 24, 1863; *Catholic Mirror*, December 5, 1863.
51   *Irish American*, January 10, 1863.

was perverting a war to restore the Union into an "emancipation crusade."[52]

Eleven days after Lincoln made his proclamation official, Thomas Parkin Scott, a Baltimore lawyer, with ties to Santo Domingo refugees, gave a lecture to the city's Catholic Institute. His stated topic was "Authority and Free Will," but his actual remarks pertained much more to the president's recent executive action regarding slavery. The founders of the nation had deliberately restricted citizenship to white men, Scott began. Within that circle, all were indeed equal. More broadly speaking, society demands a hierarchical order to endure. So in any society, a certain subordination of some individuals to others is natural. "High and low, bond and free, are alike acceptable before the Deity; but a degree of subordination is necessary for the preservation of that order which is essential to the existence of society. "Slavery," Scott reflected, "has been with us as far back as we can reconstruct history, as both the Old and New Testaments attest." Given that lineage, "it is dangerous for one community to attempt to interfere with another, and in our case morally and legally wrong. Let it be left to the Christian charity of each community, to work out its own problem of social organization. The Negro family is certainly inferior to the White, and a persistent attempt at their immediate emancipation, without authority, and in violation of laws and solemn compacts, would be attended with fearful mischief, and end in their destruction. . . ." It would also justify a resistance to that government bent upon taking actions "without any warrant in the Constitution and the laws of the country to justify it."[53]

By late February, the Catholic General James Shields expressed to Judge Daly his fear that the proclamation was part of a Republican coup to consolidate power within the White

---

52   *Metropolitan Record*, January 3, 1863; January 10, 1863, cited in Albon P. Man, Jr., "The Church and the New York Draft Riots of 1863," *Records of the American Catholic Historical Society of Philadelphia* 62 (1951), 43.

53   T. Parkin Scott, *Authority and Free Will: A Lecture Delivered Before the Catholic Institute of Baltimore, February 11, 1863* (Baltimore: Kelly, Hedrin and Piet, 1863), 4–7.

House.⁵⁴ Another New York Catholic judge, John H. McCunn, at a meeting of Peace Democrats in April 1863, decried the wreckage of the economy that the war was causing. And for what? "The negro," he noted, "was a prince in the south compared to his situation at home."⁵⁵

To many, if not most Catholics, the association of abolitionists with anti-Catholic biases, together with the Church's teaching about slavery and memories of Santo Domingo, reinforced a racism that regarded Blacks as threats to their economic, social, and political status. That primordial prejudice had been on full display at a parade supporting Stephen Douglas in New York City in October 1860, when the marchers, mainly Irish, held aloft banners and images of Lincoln and other Republican leaders consorting with Black males and females in the crudest and most ribald fashion that rabid racism could conjure.⁵⁶ To the Northern Catholic working class, whether German or Irish, slavery was the best guarantee that Blacks would never become economic or social competitors.⁵⁷ Available evidence points to Lincoln's proclamation as a major reason for the rapid decline in commitment to the Union cause among Irish soldiers. Sergeant Charles Woolett noted the negative effect the proclamation had on his Irish-dominated 90th Illinois Regiment: "The emancipation policy and proposed arming of negroes is causing deep dissatis-

---

54   Daly, *Diary of a Union Lady*, entry for February 22, 1863, 221.
55   Tyler Anbinder, *Five Points: The 19th-Century New York City Neighborhood That Invented Tap Dance, Stole Elections, and Became the World's Most Notorious Slum* (New York: Free Press, 2001), 311.
56   Man, "Irish in New York," 100.
57   German Catholics in the North tended to be more rural, more Democratic in their political affiliation, and less likely to enlist for military service than other German immigrants. In the border states, limited evidence suggests that German Catholics were more to be found in Confederate armies than in their Union counterparts. These characteristics made them highly probable opponents of abolition in any form. See Walter D. Kamphoefner, "German-Americans and Civil War Politics: A Reconsideration of the Ethnocultural Thesis," *Civil War History* 37 (September 1991), 232–246, and Kristen Layne Anderson, *Abolitionizing Missouri: German Immigrants and Racial Ideology in Nineteenth-Century America* (Baton Rouge: Louisiana University Press, 2016).

faction, which, I fear will bear bitter fruits."[58] Peter Welsh, a recent enlistee of the 28th Massachusetts, a regiment of the Irish Brigade, wrote his wife in early February 1863 that there was "dissatisfaction and loud denunciation" of the president's proclamation. Welsh, a supporter of General McClellan, thought that if enslaved persons and slavery were disrupting the Union then the nation needed to "sweep both from the land forever rather than the freedom and prosperity of a great nation . . . should be destroyed." Welch was a conditional abolitionist, the condition being the deportation of all the emancipated, an event he fully expected to see accomplished, once the "incompetent . . . and fanatical nigar worshippers" of the Lincoln administration were turned out by the majority of citizens in the North.[59]

A rare unconditional Catholic supporter of the Emancipation Proclamation in the army was Colonel Patrick Guiney of the Massachusetts 9th. Guiney, a graduate of Holy Cross College and a lawyer, found his position on abolition at odds with the sentiment of his regiment. His worst fear was that the generals on both sides would agree to an armistice—"on God knows what terms"—in order to subvert Lincoln's proclamation. But Guiney's own ambition for military promotion apparently served to mute any resistance to the conspiratorial threats to the president's executive order.[60]

---

58   When Adjutant General Lorenzo Thomas informed the 90th Illinois in May 1863 that Lincoln's order to organize Black military units had now gone into effect, the regiment's response was a general hissing for which the lot of them was put under arrest (James B. Swan, *Chicago's Irish Legion: The 90th Illinois Volunteers in the Civil War* [Chicago: Southern Illinois University Press, 2009], 59–61).

59   Peter Welch to Margaret Welch, in camp near Falmouth, February 3, 1863; February 8, 1863, in Lawrence Frederick Kohl, with Margaret Cossé Richard, eds., *Irish Green & Union Blue: The Civil War Letters of Peter Welsh* (New York: Fordham University Press, 1986), 68–70.

60   It would be interesting to know the origins of Guiney's abolitionism. Was he at least one soldier of the 9th Massachusetts who was deeply affected by the regiment's stay at Mount Vernon? He went into the war a Democrat. By the time his three-year term of service expired in June of 1864, he was a Republican. During the 1864 presidential campaign, Guiney, on the stump for Lincoln, denounced slavery as an evil which "simmered, and burned into the very vitals of the nation, until . . . it raised up armies to fight

Colonel Patrick Guiney, Irish American commander of the 9th Massachusetts Regiment and ardent supporter of Lincoln's emancipation policy (College of the Holy Cross Archives, Worcester, Massachusetts).

Hostility to abolitionism became a test of tribal loyalty. As Orestes Brownson pointed out in the middle of the war: "The Catholic who does not throw his influence on the side of the pro-slavery party is read out of the pale of Catholic society, especially in the city of New York."[61] Brownson had had a taste of this ostracism the previous year when, in February 1862, Boston Jesuits had invited the famous convert to give a lecture only to rescind the invitation when Brownson announced that he would be speaking on the topic of abolition. As the superior, Charles Gresselin, S.J., informed Brownson, "For us to reject that theory

---

against our Republic. . . ." All those whose opposition to the government was undermining its war efforts, he concluded, were guilty of "a crime for which a life of penance cannot expiate" (Boston *Daily Advertiser*, October 7, 1864, cited in Christian G. Samito, ed., *Commanding Boston's Irish Ninth: The Civil War Letters of Colonel Patrick R. Guiney, Ninth Massachusetts Volunteer Infantry* [New York: Fordham University Press, 1998], xxxi).

61 *Brownson's Quarterly Review* 4 (1863), 369, in Edward K. Spann, *Gotham at War: New York City, 1860–1865* (Wilmington, DE: Scholarly Resources, 2002), 126.

[of abolition] is no moral or political sin."[62] When the Kentucky abolitionist, Cassius Clay, spoke at an Irish freedom rally in New York in October of 1862, he attempted to explain to the audience how their racism was self-defeating by showing how England depicted the Irish as inferior in order to oppress them. "I would not enslave neither the Irishman nor the negro. If you want to make labor respectable," he challenged, "make it free and God will prosper it." Clay received hisses, groans, and shouts for his removal as a return for his efforts.[63]

Spalding's Dissertation

To no prelate was the proclamation more repulsive than the bishop of Louisville, Martin John Spalding. Although a Southern sympathizer with several family members fighting for the Confederacy, he was of the firm belief that the hierarchy had no business involving itself in political matters. Spalding had accordingly adopted a public posture of strict neutrality during the early course of the war. The Emancipation Proclamation radically challenged Spalding's position. On the day the proclamation became official, Spalding wrote in his journal: "While our brethren are thus slaughtered in hecatombs, Abraham Lincoln coolly issues his Emancipation Proclamation, letting loose from three to four millions of half-civilized Africans to murder their masters & mistresses!! . . . —Verily this is a bloody New Year!"[64] Still, Spalding remained silent. Then in early April 1863, an editorial appeared in the Cincinnati *Catholic Telegraph* advocating the abolition policy presumably written by Edward Purcell, brother of the archbishop of Cincinnati. In subsequent weeks Purcell defended the administration's policy as a legitimate use of federal power to achieve victory in a civil war.[65]

---

62 Charles Gresselin, S.J., to Brownson, February 19, 1862, I-4-B, Archives of the Maryland Province of the Society of Jesus, cited in McGreevy, *Catholicism and American Freedom*, 67.
63 Man, "New York Irish," 98.
64 Journal of M. J. Spalding, Bishop of Louisville, et al., 1860-1864, p. 80, Associated Archives at St. Mary's Seminary and University, Baltimore, Maryland.
65 Satish Joseph, "'Long Live the Republic!' Father Edward Purcell and the Slavery Controversy: 1861–1865," *American Catholic Studies* 116, no. 4 (Winter 2005), 49–53.

The *Telegraph*'s editorials stirred Spalding to write, not to his own metropolitan, Purcell, but the metropolitan of the Baltimore Province, Archbishop Francis Kenrick. Spalding was seeking Kenrick's advice about writing to the Holy See's Propaganda Fide in order to persuade the Roman congregation to instruct prelates like Purcell not to engage in the discussion of political matters in the public square where, in Spalding's view, the archbishop was "run[ning] mad with this insane abolitionism."[66]

Kenrick, who had more than anyone in the antebellum era set the apolitical policy for the hierarchy, predictably encouraged Spalding to provide Rome with "a full and candid exposition of the facts."[67] Within the month Spalding had dispatched a twenty-three-page essay to Cardinal Alessandro Barnabò, prefect of Propaganda Fide. In his "dissertation," Spalding admitted that a principal cause of the war was slavery, a system that "all good and moderate men" recognize as a "great social evil." The problem was how to rid the country of it without bringing the country down in the process. If the United States were Catholic, Spalding went on, and guided by the Church's spirit and practice, real reform and gradual improvement in the lives and character of the enslaved would lead benevolent masters to emancipate them gradually. But, America being fundamentally a Protestant society, even were Catholic masters to emancipate their slaves, these freed persons would experience "moral and physical regression" in the North, where segregation and hostility to Blacks prevail. Immediate emancipation would immensely magnify the evil.

President Lincoln's Emancipation Proclamation, Spalding asserted, was nothing less than an instrument of terror to be employed against "obstinate rebels." It was an invitation to the more than three million slaves to rise up and massacre the whites in their midst, to replicate the horrors of Santo Domingo.

---

66 Francis Kenrick to Spalding, Baltimore, April 18, 1863, cited in David Spalding, "Martin John Spalding's 'Dissertation on the American Civil War,'" *Catholic Historical Review* 52, no. 1 (April 1966), 66; Spalding Journal, entry for April 21, 1863, pp. 85–87.

67 Kenrick to Spalding, April 18, 1863, 34-L63, Associated Archives at St. Mary's Seminary and University, Baltimore, Maryland.

Fortunately, the enslaved persons had repudiated the call to insurrection, in a striking affirmation of their loyalty to the peculiar institution of the South.

Spalding then took up the question of the Church's relation to the war. In a country that enjoyed the separation of church and state, religion and government had nothing to do with each other. During the war, he reported, Catholic prelates and priests, with few exceptions, had been faithful to their tradition of restricting themselves entirely to the spiritual sphere by praying "for the return of peace and prosperity." By inserting themselves into the "political agitation," Purcell and his allies were providing the enemies of the Church an excuse to renew the attacks in the postwar period that had plagued antebellum society by blaming Catholic leaders for the human and material losses that the war brought.[68]

Spalding had hoped that his arguments would lead Propaganda to censure Purcell and thus weaken the forces championing abolition as a war goal. The cardinal prefect did not do so, but he did share Spalding's piece with Pope Pius IX and had it published seriatim in the Roman newspaper *L'Osservatore Romano*. Spalding's "dissertation" proved to be a significant factor in changing the Holy See's opinion about the Civil War. Through the spring of 1863, Rome had harbored hopes of mediating the conflict. It took a Congressional resolution that declared that the government would be party to no foreign mediation toward a peace agreement to convince Rome that Washington would settle on nothing short of total victory. That, to the officials of the Holy See, meant a war whose length God alone could know and whose scale of destruction and casualties seemed to expand to ever more horrific dimensions, becoming ever less compatible with the standards that defined a just war. Spalding's lengthy report to Barnabò on the causes and consequences of the war had an immediate impact in confirming the Holy See's thinking about the conflict. Its prompt publication in *L'Osservatore Romano* was a clear indication of Church officials' desire to promulgate Spalding's interpretation of Lincoln's proclamation.

---

68 Spalding, "Dissertation," 69–84.

A Culmination to Catholic Opposition

As Rome shifted to a more negative opinion about the Lincoln administration, opposition to the war was rapidly rising within the American Catholic community. Randall Miller observes that by the middle of 1863:

> The redefinition of the war . . . created a sense of betrayal that fueled the Irish Catholics' doubts about the need to serve. War losses further cut into patriotism. When added to the straitened circumstances of many Irish families, amid inflation and job competition, the anger over Republican policies and the anxiety over family needs made for a highly combustible psychology among Irish Catholics, as indeed among many working-class Americans whatever their ethnic stripe. The Conscription Act of 1863 ignited the mix.[69]

The horrible carnage into which Irish Catholic soldiers had marched on fields like Antietam and Fredericksburg had drastically reduced enlistments in their communities. When conscription replaced recruiting, there was anger at the inequity in the system and a hunt for scapegoats. None came to the New York Irish mind sooner than the Blacks of the city; none—tragically—were more accessible and vulnerable.[70]

Catholic editors, notably James McMaster and John Mullally, had encouraged resistance to the draft as one way of expressing displeasure at the Emancipation Proclamation. When Federal officials began to draw names to be drafted in New York City in mid-July, violent resistance quickly turned into a reign of terror throughout much of uptown Manhattan for nearly a week. Scores died, most of them Blacks sought out by roving mobs, most of whom were Irish (Brownson thought

---

69 Miller, "Catholic Religion, Irish Ethnicity, and the Civil War," in Randall M. Miller, Harry S. Stout, and Charles Reagan Wilson, eds., *Religion and the American Civil War* (New York: Oxford University Press, 1998), 281.

70 Albon P. Man, Jr., "The Church and the New York Draft Riots of 1863," *Records of the American Catholic Historical Society of Philadelphia* 62 (1951), 33-46.

Destruction of the Negro Orphan Asylum, New York City. The Irish-dominated anti-draft riots of July 1863 represented the nadir of the opposition to Lincoln's making abolition a war goal (New York Public Library).

the Irish constituted 90% of the rioters).[71] The rioters lynched Blacks from lampposts. They burned down their orphanage. They dragged them out of their homes to beat them to death. This was racism in its most barbaric form. Some Catholic priests, including the Paulist founder, Isaac Hecker, performed heroic service in the streets of their parishes by pacifying rioters. Horace Greeley appealed to Archbishop Hughes to exercise his influence to restore order to the city. Hughes, in badly failing health, invited those rioting to come to the episcopal residence on Broadway and 36th Street to hear him. Five thousand turned out, but few, if any, among them were from the areas under siege. Only the arrival of 6,000 troops from Gettysburg put an end to the killing and anarchy.[72]

---

71 *Brownson's Quarterly Review* (October 1863), 386, in Shelley, *The History of the Archdiocese of New York* (Strasbourg: Editions du Signe, 1997), 208.

72 Shelley, *History of the Archdiocese of New York*, 208; Man, "The Church and the New York Draft Riots of 1863," 33–50.

McMaster, in defending the riot as a just opposition to an unconstitutional draft, pointed out the high crime rate among the Blacks of the city as a mitigating factor for the violence the Irish had displayed against them.[73] It fell to a virtually anonymous priest in the contiguous diocese of Brooklyn to get to the heart of what was at stake in the New York rioting. Joseph Fransioli in a sermon delivered at St. Peter's Church in Brooklyn on July 26 made no mention of the horrific events that had been transpiring on the streets of Brooklyn's sister city for nearly a week earlier that month. Fransioli instead focused on the social nature of being human, a societal orientation that Christianity in particular nurtures in its followers, he related. To be Christian is to have a deeply rooted responsibility to serve and protect one's country. Patriotism is embedded in the marrow of the Christian. Intrinsic to patriotism is an inherent commitment to the preservation of the whole of a nation, not identifying with one or another part. Being a patriot means being opposed to the dissolution of the whole nation, and affirmatively, the willingness to sacrifice, even the individual self, to preserve the nation, the source of our common good. "Patriotism," he told them, "is not an invitation or a choice but a duty." Fransioli would not have seen himself as engaging in the political sermonizing Martin Spalding detested. He was simply making deductions from general principles at the heart of the Catholic tradition. It was a simple plea for Catholics to dedicate themselves to the preservation of the Union from which they had so benefited. Disagreement with a particular war goal, even emancipation, was no justification for not doing one's share to enable the nation to prevail, much less for resisting that effort.[74]

Rome's Shifting Winds on Slavery

The Vatican had had no official comment on Lincoln's executive order. In a private audience that Bishop Patrick Lynch had with Pope Pius IX in July 1864, the pope, according to Lynch, con-

---

73 Kurtz, *Excommunicated from the Union*, 115.
74 Joseph Fransioli, *Patriotism, A Christian Virtue: A Sermon Preached at St. Peter's (Catholic) Church, Brooklyn, July 26th, 1863* (New York: Loyal Publication Society[?]: 1863).

fessed "it would be absurd to attempt, to cut the Gordian Knott [sic], by an Act of Emancipation. But still something might be done looking to an improvement in their position or state, and to a gradual preparation for their freedom at a future opportune time."[75] The pontiff's comments had only confirmed Bishop Lynch's conviction that, if the Confederacy ever hoped to secure European recognition, if not intervention in the South's behalf, it needed to reverse the negative image of slavery that prevailed across the Continent, thanks in large part to the Emancipation Proclamation.

So Lynch, a highly accomplished polemicist, set out to win hearts and minds by anonymously penning a pamphlet that presented slavery as something that any Christian nation should be proud to claim as an institution. Among the topics Lynch addressed was the response of the slaves within Confederate control to Lincoln's proclamation. The blunt reality, Lynch reported, was that "the Negroes have paid no attention whatever. . . ." If Lincoln's proclamation had been intended as an invitation to seek freedom, if not a call to arms, it had fallen on deaf ears. According to Lynch, Lincoln's appeal to the enslaved was but a more official form of strategy that Union military officers had pursued since virtually the war's start when General Benjamin Butler had declared runaway slaves on the Virginia Peninsula to be contraband of war. That strategy, Lynch insisted, had failed to entice slaves into deserting their masters, for the simple fact that the enslaved persons were content in their present condition: "So far as they could, [they] have kept out of the way of the Federal forces," he maintained. That is, the ones who were not already serving their masters on the front lines or working on fortifications behind them. Even those who had been "liberated" by Union troops, had, in many cases, so Lynch claimed, voluntarily rejoined their fleeing masters.[76] Should Lincoln's proclamation

---

75 Lynch to Judah Benjamin, July 5, 1864, copy in unclassified Lynch papers, Charleston Diocesan Archives, Charleston, South Carolina.

76 "A Few Words on the Domestic Slavery in the Confederate States of America by a Catholic Clergyman," 1864. The pamphlet was published in French, German, and Italian. An English translation is provided by David C.R. Heisser, ed., "A Few Words on the Domestic Slavery in the Confederate States of America by Patrick N. Lynch," *Avery Review* 2 (Spring 1999), 64–103; *Avery Review* 3 (Spring 2000), 93–123.

somehow become reality for the millions of Africans in bondage in the Confederacy, it would tragically assure a disastrous future for them. They had not the means to cope with the freedom suddenly thrust upon them, to provide for themselves, much less to compete with a superior, hostile white race. Race war, Lynch suggested, would inevitably result in a new enslavement or even extinction for the recently emancipated.

When the Rome-based Jesuit journal, *La Civiltà Cattolica*, pronounced Lynch's pamphlet the work of someone "impartial, superbly well-informed" and of "broad and just views," the bishop had to have been optimistic about its power to change opinion in the highest places in Catholic Europe, including the Vatican. Little did he know how the Roman curia, in its Byzantine manner, had already rendered his pamphlet a dead letter.

Apparently under the influence of Isaac Hecker, Louis B. Binsse, the Papal States' consul in New York, had been prodding Propaganda Fide to take up the slavery question in the wake of Lincoln's making abolition a war goal. Slavery, Binsse observed as though channeling Hecker, was a clear violation of natural rights.[77] The congregation finally did take up the question, it appears, nearly two years after Lincoln's proclamation by examining the 1861 pastoral of Natchitoches, Louisiana bishop, Auguste Martin, which had extolled slavery as a divine ordination. In the subsequent review, the Dominican Martin Gatti ruled that Bishop Martin's defense of slavery was untenable. Not even the blessing of Christianity could justify the "iniquity" which slavery entailed. His report explicitly condemned chattel slavery as well as slave trading. The pope thereupon condemned the pastoral but ordered the whole matter to be kept secret in order to give Martin the chance to retract his letter. Martin's subsequent retraction prevented any promulgation of Rome's ruling on slavery.[78] And so

---

77 Binsse to Alessandro Barnabò, New York, September 18, 1863, *Scritture*, 1864–1865, vol. 20, folios 213r–214rv, Archivo Di Propaganda Fide, Rome (hereafter APF); Binsse to Barnabò, New York, January 5, 1864, *Scritture*, 1864–1865, vol. 20, folios 503rv–506rv, APF.

78 Gatti, Minerva, November 25, 1864, *Scritture*, 1864–1865, vol. 20, fols. 1199r–1205v, APF.

the Church officially remained mute on the question of slavery, even as the United States prepared to abolish it in its Constitution. In January of 1865, as Bishop Lynch was still making arrangements to have his pamphlet published in France and Germany, the United States Congress passed the Thirteenth Amendment which brought the U.S. Constitution into accord with the reality that the course of the war and massive Black abandonment of the plantations and other venues of bondage had shaped. No longer did the fundamental law of the land sanction slavery. The United States had joined most of the rest of the developed world in legally renouncing forced labor as a means of production.

Catholics and the Legacy of the Proclamation

In the closing pages of his history of the 116th Pennsylvania, Medal of Honor winner General St. Clair Mulholland recounted the homeward march of the regiment from Appomattox. At Manchester, just south of Richmond, they came upon the remains of an auction block. Systematically the men of the 116th cut it up into small pieces, which they proceeded to burn, with all the purpose they could muster. "It seemed like a burnt offering on the altar of Liberty," Mulholland noted. "No man, no matter what his color, would ever again be bought or sold in all the land."[79] Mulholland, as William Kurtz has shown, was the major figure in shaping the memory of the Catholic contribution to the Northern war effort.[80] The tragedy is that this noble gesture of the 116th was not symbolic of the Irish contribution to the abolition of slavery. With notable exceptions, the Irish set their boats against the currents which brought down slavery. And no current did they oppose with as much primal determination as they did the one that the Emancipation Proclamation embodied.

The previous fall, Patrick Donahoe had commented that the fourth year of the war "presents the edifying picture of an agrarian sentimental policy which seeks to exalt a degraded, inferior

---

79 St. Clair A. Mulholland, *The Story of the 116th Regiment Pennsylvania Volunteers in the War of the Rebellion: The Record of a Gallant Command* (Philadelphia: P. McManus, Jr., 1903), 400.

80 Kurtz, *Excommunicated from the Union*, 146.

This photo, taken on January 1, 1863, was the first evidence of the emancipated slaves that Lincoln's proclamation had set in motion (Library of Congress).

race into equality with the white race, and to tear down personal security and property, the Corinthian pillars of Constitutional liberty."[81] Three and a half years into the war, nearly two years after Lincoln first announced the Emancipation Proclamation, and with an amendment before Congress to abolish slavery outright, the *Pilot* maintained that such steps toward abolition represented grave threats to our "Constitutional liberty," inasmuch as the respect for property rights, even where the property is human, was crucial toward maintaining the security and independence of the white race for whom the republic existed. And nothing guaranteed white supremacy like the chattel slavery which kept an inferior race in bondage *in perpetuum*.

Catholics, by and large, continued to regard abolition as did the editor of the *Pilot*. In the Catholic press, there was no celebration of the Congressional action, nor of the amendment's ongoing ratification as the states, seriatim, gave their approval. Beyond the

---

81 Boston *Pilot*, September 10, 1864, in Bruce, *The Harp and the* Eagle, 222.

press, there was no significant evidence that the Catholic public in general thought any differently. Not that their opinion set them apart from their fellow white citizens among most of whom rampant racism would prevail for decades to come. But this atavistic clinging to slavery as God-ordained and an ideal field for the display of Catholic paternalism was a mindset, if not peculiar to Catholics, at least one for which they had a special proclivity.

Martin Spalding's two-sphere model of society nurtured that proclivity in Catholic thought. It promoted an intellectual inertia which rendered it difficult to pursue any institutional reform, and unthinkable to contribute to any revolutionary change such as the Emancipation Proclamation initiated. Confining the Church strictly to the spiritual realm meant that government and the political sphere did not fall under the Church's moral judgment. All that the Church could teach about slavery involved the mutual fulfillment of obligations: for the enslaved persons, being faithful workers; for the owners, providing the proper material and spiritual care. What offended the Louisville prelate about the abolitionist clergy was their presuming to "intervene" in an area beyond their place in society, by preaching freedom for the slaves and working to persuade the Lincoln administration to change the laws to accomplish it. It was perfectly orthodox for prelates or clergy to express their desire for gradual emancipation, but they, in effect, could do nothing to bring it about, aside from influencing Catholic slaveholders to manumit voluntarily. The changing legal and economic conditions in the antebellum South had steadily diminished prospects of that happening on any significant scale. Once the war began, fast-moving events, climaxed by Lincoln's proclamation, rendered such benevolence irrelevant, indeed set the peculiar institution on the path to history's dustbin. Despite all of that, in the absence of any definitive judgment from Rome, Catholic opinion makers still tended to regard slavery as the ideal arrangement for a biracial society.[82]

---

82 While Pope Gregory XVI had written against the Atlantic slave trade in 1839, the Church's first public condemnation of the totality of slavery came in Pope Leo XIII's 1890 encyclical, *Catholicae Ecclesiae*, http://w2.vatican.va/content/leo-xiii/en/encyclicals/documents/hf_l-xiii_enc_20111890_ catholicae-ecclesiae.html.

Reconstruction's brave experiment to create a New South in which the races shared political power, social space, and economic opportunity had few overt Catholic supporters. Two notable exceptions were the New York priests, Sylvester Malone and Thomas Farrell, who made a tour of the South in 1869 in support of Reconstruction.[83] Far more Southern Catholics were contributors to Reconstruction's eventual demise in 1877. For most Catholics in North and South, home rule inevitably restored the natural hierarchical order, not by reviving slavery, but by instituting new forms of social, economic, and political control—Jim Crow, debt peonage, disenfranchisement—proper for a society composed of unequal races incapable of living together on a level playing field. The justice of the South's Lost Cause became the reigning narrative of the war. The Emancipation Proclamation went down the national memory hole, except among African Americans, for whom it remained a painful reminder of what might have been.

---

83 When Farrell made statements of solidarity with the freedpersons' struggle for freedom and equality, Philadelphia-born, John McGill, Bishop of Richmond, labeled him a "negrophile" (McGill to McCloskey, Richmond, June 14, 1869, Archives of the Archdiocese of New York, cited in Shelley, *History of the Archdiocese of New York*, 256).

The Church and Slavery: A Historical Chronology, 1452-2023

RONALD LAMARR SHARPS*

Fifteenth Century

1452 June 18   Pope Nicholas V promulgates *Dum Diversas*, authorizing Portugal and Spain to press into perpetual slavery the enemies of Christ, thus facilitating the slave trade in West Africa.

1455 January 8   Pope Nicholas V promulgates *Romanus Pontifex*, sanctioning Portuguese enslavement of native Saracens, pagans, and other enemies of Christ, while extending control of discovered lands in sub-Saharan Africa and the New World to Catholic nations.

1492 August 3–October 12   A Black Catholic who is not enslaved (identified interchangeably as Juan Prieto or Juan Moreno) accompanies Christopher Columbus on his first voyage to the New World. He also joins Columbus's 1493 expedition.

1493 May 4   Pope Alexander VI promulgates *Inter Caetera*, authorizing Portugal and Spain to colonize the discovered New World and enslave its inhabitants. According to the papal bull, by the "authority of Almighty God" and "the fullness of our apostolic power," lands not inhabited by Christians could be "discovered" and exploited by Christian rulers charged with evangelizing any Indigenous peoples. This "Doctrine of Discovery" becomes the basis of all European claims in the Americas and for the United States' western expansion. At the same time, Pope

---

* A portion of this chronology appeared as "Black Catholics in the United States: A Historical Chronology, 1452–2020," in David J. Endres, ed., *Black Catholic Studies Reader: History and Theology* (Washington, DC: Catholic University of America Press, 2021), 27–66.

Alexander VI issues *Eximiae Devotionis*, granting Spain control over much of the New World, including the right to appoint missionaries and bishops.

Sixteenth Century

1501 September 16   Catholic monarchs Ferdinand I and Isabella of Spain grant permission to Caribbean colonists to import enslaved Africans.

1526 October   The first slave rebellion in North America is initiated by African slaves at San Miguel de Gualdape (in present-day South Carolina), a settlement founded by Spanish explorer Lucas Vázquez de Ayllón in July of that year.

1537 June 2   Pope Paul III promulgates *Sublimis Deus*, forbidding enslavement of Indigenous peoples in the Americas and elsewhere, though colonists and conquistadors ignore the document. Paul III argues that man was created for eternal life and happiness through faith in Jesus Christ, but Satan deceived good men to believe that this should be done by any means, even reducing peoples to brute animals under the pretext that they lacked Catholic faith.

1565 August 28   As part of Pedro Menéndez de Avilés' colonizing expedition, the first Africans, free and enslaved, arrive in St. Augustine, Florida.

1573   Bartolomé Frías de Albornoz publishes *Arte de los Contractos* (*Art of Contracts*), including a section on slavery in which he says that he cannot find a reason for enslavement of West Africans, whether for war, crime, or destitution. The work is placed on the Index of Prohibited Books by the Holy See. Between 1573 and 1826 a number of books questioning tenets of slavery are listed in the Index.

1593–1609   Father Luis de Molina, S.J., of the University of Salamanca, Spain, compiles *De Justitia et Jure* (*On Justice and Law*) in six volumes, including the first theological treatise on the transatlantic slave trade.

Seventeenth Century

1627 Alonso de Sandoval, S.J., writes *De Instauranda Aethiopum Salute*, the first known book-length examination of enslavement and evangelization among Africans in the New World.

1634 March 25 Passengers of the British ships *Ark* and *Dove* arrive at St. Clement's Island to settle the colony of Maryland. Two Black indentured servants are aboard, including Mathias de Sousa, a Catholic indentured to members of the Society of Jesus (Jesuits). After securing his freedom, de Sousa is elected to the Maryland General Assembly in March 1641, the first Black to participate in a colonial British assembly. To support their mission to convert Indians, the Jesuits establish their first plantation on land gifted by Lord Baltimore in 1637. The last of their five Maryland plantations is gifted by James Carroll in 1729. Jesuits first operate their plantations with indentured servants but change to Black slave labor.

1673 Jesuit Jacques Marquette explores the Illinois Country. The Jesuits found a mission among the Kaskaskia Indians in 1675. The mission, established at different locations due to the movements of the Kaskaskia, eventually organizes a plantation that is first worked by Indigenous people, but by 1719 begins to utilize the labor of Africans and their descendants (often the result of intermarriage between Native Americans and Africans).

1678 Lord Baltimore (Charles Calvert) issues an edict requiring Catholic planters in Maryland to allow the enslaved to receive the sacraments. In 1664 and 1671, the colonial legislature passes laws affirming that slavery *durante vita* (for life) would be based on race regardless of baptismal status or marriage to a free spouse.

1681 French Capuchin Epiphanius of Moirans and Spanish Capuchin Francis Joseph of Jaca are imprisoned in Havana, Cuba, for attacking the instutution of slavery and calling for emancipation of slaves in the New World. The two missionaries observe that African slaves were baptized on ships without previous instruction in the faith to circummvent laws forbiding the sale of non-Christians in Spanish and Portuguese colonies. They argue their case in sermons and by refusing sacramental absolution to anyone refusing to free their slaves. The vicar of the bishop of Cuba eventually declares them excommunicated and imprisons them. With support of the Capuchin order, the two priests take their case to Rome in 1685 and are allowed to return to their order—their issue with slavery unresolved.

1684 March 6 Lourenço da Silva de Mendouça, Mbundu prince and Afro-Brazilian layman and procurator-general of the Confraternity of Our Lady Star of the Negroes (Madrid, Spain), petitions Pope Innocent XI to condemn perpetual slavery.

1685 March Louis XIV of France issues the *Code Noir*, first instituted in Saint-Domingue, outlining slavery in the colonies, limiting activities of free Blacks, and requiring conversion to Catholicism. Although largely unheeded, as the first formal codification of slave laws in the Americas, the *Code Noir* is applied to the West Indies in 1687 and Guyana in 1704.

1686 March 20 Under Pope Innocent XI, the Congregation of Holy Office of the Inquisition responds to an inquiry about the morality of enslaving innocent Blacks, condemning unjust enslavement, while recognizing just enslavement as a form of punishment. Rejecting the practice and trade in slaves, the pope urges slaveholders to emancipate and compensate Blacks "unjustly" enslaved.

1693 November 7 Charles II of Spain issues a royal decree offering freedom in Florida to enslaved runaways owned by British masters provided they convert to Catholicism. The first runaway slaves from the Carolinas arrive in St. Augustine, Florida, in October 1687. They convert to Catholicism, are assigned work, and paid for their labor, laying the foundation for Charles II's official policy.

Eighteenth Century

1722 French Capuchins Father Bruno de Langres and Brother Eusèbe de Chaumont, along with Father Christophe de Chaumont (to be assigned to Mobile) first arrive in New Orleans, Louisiana Colony. Capuchin Father Philibert de Vianden arrives in October 1722 for assignment to the Mississippi Valley. They justify slavery and their participation in owning enslaved persons as the result of the Africans' original sin, but they open their churches to all races (including Black slaves and freemen). Ecclesiastical jurisdiction over the European population and their slaves in Louisiana is granted to the Capuchins by the bishop of Quebec.

1723 April 17 Father Raphael de Luxembourg, French Capuchin major superior, arrives in New Orleans and begins work among Blacks on Catholic-owned plantations. He advocates for fair pay for Blacks and Native Americans.

1724 September 10 Governor Jean-Baptiste Le Moyne de Bienville, who founded New Orleans in 1718, publishes the first *Code Noir* initiated in the Louisiana Colony, requiring Catholic baptism and instruction of the enslaved. Slavery is abolished in the French colonies February 4, 1794, is reinstated July 16, 1802, and is abolished again on April 27, 1848.

1724 Francisco Menéndez, a runaway African slave from the Carolinas, arrives in St. Augustine, Florida. Converting to Catholicism, he joins the Spanish militia and defends the settlement from British attack.

1727 March Father Nicolas-Ignace de Beaubois arrives in New Orleans as Jesuit superior. His order's primary aim is to evangelize Native Americans, but like the Capuchins, they own Black slaves. He is appointed vicar general by the bishop of Quebec and establishes a model plantation to generate income for missionary work using slave labor. Although recalled the following year, Beaubois is reinstated in March 1732, only to be recalled again in 1734.

1727 August 7 Led by mother superior Sister Marie Saint Augustine (Marie Tranchepain), Sisters of the Order of St. Ursula found the Ursuline Monastery at New Orleans. Although owning slaves themselves, the nuns establish Ursuline Academy later that year, a school for Blacks and Indians (the oldest Catholic school established in colonial America).

1738 March 15 Governor of La Florida, Manuel de Montiano, establishes Fort Gracia Real de Santa Teresa de Mose as a community for freed enslaved persons who converted to Catholicism, the first legally sanctioned free Black community within the present U.S. boundaries.

1739 September 9 Kongolese (Congolese) Catholic slaves initiate the Stono Rebellion in South Carolina, the largest and deadliest uprising of the enslaved in the British colonies before the Revolutionary War.

1741 December 22 Pope Benedict XIV issues *Immensa Pastorum Principis* against enslavement of Indigenous peoples of the Americas and other countries, especially in lands under the control of Portugal.

1743 May 15 Benedict of Palermo, known also as Benedict the Moor, is beatified by Pope Benedict XIV. Born to enslaved Africans in Sicily, Benedict had joined a religious community of hermits, of which he became superior. He is canonized by Pope Pius VII in 1807.

1762 November Louisiana is ceded by France to Spain through the secret Treaty of Fontainebleau, transferring ecclesial jurisdiction to the bishop of Cuba and leading to the contentious but eventual replacement of French Capuchins by Spanish Capuchins. Slow to take control, the Spanish governor does not arrive until March 1766. The Spanish Capuchins, numbering six religious, first arrive in 1772. Unlike the French, Spanish Capuchins allow the marriage of white and free people of color.

1784 June 19 San Malo (Jean Saint Malo), an escaped slave (maroon) who led a community of approximately fifty runaways in Spanish Louisiana, is hanged because of his plantation raids and attacks on whites, typically to free Black slaves in transit. Clergy refuse to hear his final confession, but this becomes a day of remembrance for this defender of the oppressed in Louisiana.

1787 Pierre Toussaint, an enslaved man, arrives in New York from Haiti with his owner. He works as a hairdresser and becomes known for his charity, including the care of his master's widow and purchasing freedom for enslaved persons.

1789 May 31   Governor Esteban Rodriguez Miró of Louisiana promulgates "Instructions on Slaves for All of the Indies." It acknowledges that the enslaved have souls, requires Catholic baptism and instruction, and allows them to purchase their freedom.

1790 July 21   Led by Bernardina Matthews, Discalced Carmelite nuns establish a monastery in Port Tobacco, Maryland, where they maintain a plantation worked by slaves whom they instruct in the faith. This is the first community of women religious and the first monastery founded in the original thirteen British colonies.

1791   Toussaint Louverture/L'Ouverture (François Dominique Toussaint), a devout Catholic and former slave, joins and eventually leads a slave rebellion on the western side of French-controlled Saint-Domingue. He is taken prisoner in 1802. His lieutenant, Jean-Jacques Dessalines, completes the fight for independence, establishing the nation of Haiti on January 1, 1804.

1793 July 9   Black refugees from Haiti (Saint-Domingue) land in Baltimore, and Sulpicians associated with St. Mary's Seminary minister to them. Sulpician Father Louis William DuBourg starts a catechism class for Black children in 1794. Worship services are later held for Blacks in the Sulpician's basement-level "Chapelle Basse." While president of St. Mary's College (and in later roles), DuBourg purchases slaves and urges other priests and religious to acquire slaves, which he considers a necessity for the planting of Catholicism.

1794 February 4   Following the slave revolt in Haiti (Saint-Domingue), the French National Convention abolishes slavery in all of its colonies—the first European country to do so.

Nineteenth Century

1802 May 20   Appealing to settlers and needing workers to expand his empire, Napoleon Bonaparte reinstates slavery and the slave trade in the French colonies after taking control of France in a coup d'état in 1799. However, France's involvement in slavery and the slave trade is permanently abolished by the second republic on April 27, 1848.

1803 The first wave of refugees from the Saint-Domingue slave rebellion arrive in New Orleans.

1806 Father Edward Fenwick, O.P., establishes St. Rose Priory, Springfield, Kentucky, the first Dominican house in the United States. Fenwick, the future bishop of Cincinnati, had inherited from his family in Maryland enslaved persons, who he sold to purchase other slaves to build and operate the Kentucky priory.

1806 Archbishop John Carroll of Baltimore sells Alexis, his second of two slaves. He had willed the manumission of Charles, his first slave. Carroll, the first Catholic archbishop in the U.S., believed in gradual emancipation of slaves through manumission. His family had owned over 300 enslaved persons.

1812 April–June Father Charles Nerinckx, a Belgian priest, organizes the Sisters of Loretto in central Kentucky. They are the first American sisterhood without foreign affiliation. Dedicated to serving the frontier poor, they acquire enslaved persons through novices' dowries.

1814 September 20 Pope Pius VII writes *Inter Tot Ac Tantas*, a private letter to king of France Louis XVIII, condemning the transatlantic slave trade. The pope appeals to the king to follow the example of Great Britain and to support lessening the suffering and inhuman treatment of the Black African in the slave trade, an abominable situation according to Catholic faith. Again, urged by the British, Pius VII sends a similar letter, *Etsi Perspecta*, to Spain and Portugal on March 15, 1823, to end their trade in Africans.

1816 December 28 Teresa (Alice) Lalor, along with widows Maria McDermott and Maria Sharpe, take final vows for the Order of the Visitation in Georgetown, near Washington, D.C. Established in 1799, the order receives its American charter from Pius VII in 1816, and in 1817, Lalor becomes superior. The order follows the custom of members bringing their slaves, as well as buying, hiring out, and selling slaves to assist operating the monastery, working their farm, and building Georgetown Preparatory School for Girls. The sisters held more than one hundred enslaved persons between 1799 and 1862.

1821 Mother Eugénie Audé and Sister Mary Layton found the Society of the Sacred Heart convent in Grand Coteau, Louisiana, and begin a school. The first enslaved persons on the property were loaned to the founders by nearby Catholic families with daughters in the school. In 1823, Frank Hawkins is the convent's first recorded purchase of an enslaved person. When the Jesuits found a school in Grand Coteau in 1838, there is a steady exchange of slaves between their property and Sacred Heart.

1823 April 14 Jesuit Father Peter Verhaegen and several Jesuit novices leave Maryland to start a new novitiate and missionary headquarters in Florissant, Missouri. They bring with them six enslaved persons from their White Marsh plantation to help establish a seminary and farm. Additional Jesuit slaves are sent from Maryland to St. Louis in 1829, the year in which the order assumes charge of St. Louis College (now St. Louis University).

1829 July 2 Mary Elizabeth Lange, the daughter of a mulatto slave and a plantation owner's daughter, founds the Oblate Sisters of Providence, a religious community of free Black women dedicated to educating Black children in Baltimore, Maryland. It is the first community of Black sisters in the United States. In 1836, the community moves its chapel to a larger facility to better serve French-speaking Saint-Domingue and Haitian refugees, becoming the first permanent Black Catholic parish church in the U.S.

1830 Carmelite nuns sell about thirty slaves to pay their debts and remain on their Maryland plantation. Nonetheless, the plantation fails, requiring their move to Baltimore in 1831.

1836 November Sisters of the Presentation of the Blessed Virgin Mary, a community for free women of color, is founded in New Orleans by a free-born woman of color Henriette Diaz Delille and Haitian-born Juliette Gaudin. Formed to evangelize

Blacks, the community receives formal approval as the Sisters of the Holy Family on November 21, 1842. Delille had earlier attempted to enter religious life, but she sought to form her own community when her applications to the Ursulines and Carmelites were rejected because of her racial heritage.

1836 Father John Timon, the provincial of the newly-independent American province of the Congregation of the Mission (Vincentian Fathers) of St. Louis, Missouri, opposes slavery and attempts to reunite separated members of enslaved families. He begins selling the order's slaves to local Catholic families, phasing out their reliance on the enslaved. Although determined not to become a slaveholding order when the community was founded in 1818, the shortage of brothers led the order to accept its first gift of six female kitchen slaves from Bishop Louis William DuBourg in 1819. The shortage led to the acquisition of additional slaves to maintain the seminary, hire out to local people, and sell to priests and religious in the Mississippi Valley.

1837 July 20 Cincinnati priest Father John Martin Henni (later bishop of Milwaukee, Wisconsin) publishes the first issue of *Der Wahrheitsfreund*, a German Catholic weekly newspaper. Charging abolitionists with wanting to incite war, editor Henni opposes slavery in principle but rejects immediate emancipation. After vising Rome in 1862, Henni returns in support of immediate emancipation.

1837 October 29 Martin de Porres (Juan Martín de Porres Velázquez), a mulatto from Lima, Peru, is beatified by Pope Gregory XVI. Martin, who had become a Dominican lay brother in 1603, founded an orphanage and hospital, and ministered to enslaved persons brought to Peru.

1838 June 19 The Jesuits sell 272 slaves to cover the debt of Georgetown University.

1839 December 3 Pope Gregory XVI issues *In Supremo Apostolatus Fastigio*, condemning the Atlantic slave trade and future enslavement, but without explicit reference to those already enslaved.

1840 March 14 Bishop John England of Charleston, South Carolina, publishes an explanation of Pope Gregory XVI's apostolic letter in the periodical *United States Catholic Miscellany*, clarifying that it is not Christian to enslave individuals and treat them with underserved cruelty. However, he concludes that abolitionists are more unjust toward slaveowners than masters toward their slaves. In a series of eighteen letters, Bishop England challenges the assertion of U.S. Secretary of State John Forsyth that Pope Gregory supported abolition, distinguishing the slave trade from slavery and stressing slavery's compatibility with Christianity. Earlier, in December 1829, England had established the Sisters of Our Lady of Mercy (later Sisters of Charity of Our Lady of Mercy) and charged them with opening a school for free Blacks and offering religious instruction to enslaved persons.

1840 June 12–23 Irish Catholic Daniel O'Connell, champion of Catholic emancipation (political representation) in Ireland and agitator for Irish independence, strongly condemns American slavery when addressing the first World's Anti-Slavery Convention in London. He calls Irish Americans to support abolitionism, demanding immediate emancipation of Black slaves.

1842 October 9 St. Augustine Church in New Orleans is dedicated on land donated by the Ursuline Sisters (property formerly owned by Julie Moreau, a manumitted slave). Through pew rents, whites and Blacks compete for space in the church. Free people of color rent three times as many pews as whites and give access to the church to the enslaved, resulting in the nation's most integrated congregation.

1848 Catholic families settle Hidalgo Bluff, Texas, bringing ninety slaves with them. The enslaved persons are catechized and baptized, and in 1888, Father Martin Francis Huhn organizes a mission specifically for the African American community.

1850 July 16 Peter Claver is beatified by Pope Pius IX. The Spanish-born Jesuit worked in Cartagena (now in Columbia) ministering among enslaved Blacks for more than four decades.

1854 June 10 James Augustine Healy, son of an Irish immigrant father and an enslaved mixed-race mother, is ordained in

Paris for the Diocese of Boston. He is the first African American priest to serve in the U.S.

1858 December 15   Alexander Sherwood Healy, brother of James Augustine Healy, is ordained a priest in Paris for the Diocese of Boston. He serves as a theologian at the Second Plenary Council of Baltimore (1866) and at the First Vatican Council (1870).

1861 August 21   Bishop Auguste Marie Martin of Natchitoches, Louisiana, issues a pastoral letter "on the occasion of the War of Southern Independence." Martin defends slavery as "the manifest will of God" to bring salvation to "children of the race of Canaan" and argues that Catholics must repudiate abolitionism as an affront to God's plan.

1862 September 1   Cincinnati Archbishop John Baptist Purcell becomes the first U.S. Catholic bishop to publicly advocate for emancipation. On April 8, 1863, Cincinnati's *Catholic Telegraph* (edited by the archbishop's brother, Father Edward Purcell) becomes the first diocesan newspaper to support emancipation, arguing in a series of editorials that all men are created equal. Bishop Josue Young of Erie, Pennsylvania, a protégé of Purcell, also calls for emancipation.

1862   Upon her death, Mother Henriette Delille, foundress of the Sisters of the Holy Family, an order of free women of color, manumits her slave, Betsy.

1864 September 3   Patrick Francis Healy, S.J., another brother of James Augustine Healy, is ordained a priest in Belgium, becoming the first African American Jesuit. Graduating from Saint-Sulpice Seminary in Paris in 1865, he is the first Black American known to have earned a doctoral degree.

1864–1865   Bishop Patrick Lynch of Charleston, South Carolina, a slaveholder, serves during the Civil War as Confederate diplomatic emissary to the Holy See.

1866 September 2   Sisters of St. Joseph of LePuy, France, arrive in St. Augustine, Florida, to educate and catechize former slaves.

1866 October 7–21 The Second Plenary Council of Baltimore advocates for evangelization among Blacks and debates formation of separate Black churches (with the decision left to each bishop).

1869 April The Tenth Provincial Council of Baltimore adopts a proposal that each bishop build schools and churches for African Americans.

1874 July 31 Father Patrick F. Healy, S.J., is inaugurated president of Georgetown University in Washington, D.C.—the first African American to head a predominately white university.

1875 June 2 James Augustine Healy is ordained Bishop of Portland, Maine, becoming the nation's first African American bishop.

1877 November 21 Four Carmelite nuns arrive in Louisiana to found the Monastery of St. Joseph and St. Teresa of the Discalced Carmelites of New Orleans. The community of artists and artisans includes two Creole sisters, Louise J. Roman (Mother Teresa of Jesus) and Marie Eliza Tremoulet (Sister Marguerite).

1882 Eliza Healy (Sister Mary Magdalen), sister of James Augustine Healy, takes final vows with the Congregation of Notre Dame, Montreal, Canada. When named superior of a convent in St. Albans, Vermont, she becomes the first African American superior of a Catholic convent.

1886 April 24 Augustus Tolton, born into slavery, is ordained a priest in Rome. Tolton is the first recognizable Black priest in the U.S. and in 1893 founds Chicago's first Black parish, St. Monica.

1886 Daniel A. Rudd, born into slavery, begins the *American Catholic Tribune*, a publication for Black Catholics. It is published in Springfield, Ohio, and later in Cincinnati and Detroit.

1888 January 15 Peter Claver is canonized by Pope Leo XIII and proclaimed patron of missions among African Americans (and later, all Africans).

1888 May 5   Pope Leo XIII promulgates *In Plurimis*, lending support for the abolition of slavery in Brazil.

1889   The Sisters of the Third Order of St. Francis are established by Mother Mathilda Taylor Beasley in Savannah, Georgia. Born into slavery, Beasley organizes the first community of Black sisters in Georgia.

1890   November 20 Pope Leo XIII issues *Catholicae Ecclesiae*, calling for the abolition of slavery in Africa.

Twentieth Century

1912   As a gesture of healing, the Sisters of Charity of Nazareth in Nazareth, Kentucky, invite those they formerly enslaved and their descendants to celebrate the congregation's centennial.

1944   Saint Louis University in St. Louis, Missouri, becomes the first historically white university in a former slave state to admit Black students.

1952 August   The New Orleans Province of the Jesuits rejects the practice of racial segregation, subsequently integrating the order, as well as their schools, retreat houses, and parishes.

1953 March 15   Joseph Francis Rummel, archbishop of New Orleans, issues the pastoral letter "Blessed Are the Peacemakers," officially ending segregation in the archdiocese. Facing continued resistance, he repeats the call for racial justice in the pastoral letter "The Morality of Racial Segregation" (1956).

1953   The first monthly Hour of Reparation (later, Day of Reparation) is held at Xavier University in New Orleans to acknowledge the sin of racism and pray for conversion. The Hour of Reparation is conceived by Edmond Vales of the interracial lay organization, the Commission on Human Rights of the Catholic Committee of the South, which was founded in 1949 to remove obstacles to desegregation in the Catholic Church.

1962 May 6   Martin de Porres is canonized by Pope John XXIII and considered a patron saint of Blacks and people of mixed race. Earlier in 1945, Pope Pius XII named him a patron of social justice.

1964 October 30 Archbishop Alfred Schulte blesses and dedicates the Tomb of the Unknown Slave on the property of St. Augustine's Church, New Orleans. The shrine consists of outsized marine chains welded together with shackles and iron balls to form a huge, fallen cross.

1965 December 7 Pope Paul VI promulgates the Second Vatican Council's "Pastoral Constitution on the Church in the Modern World" (*Gaudium et Spes*), observing that "whatever is opposed to life" and insults human dignity—including forms of slavery—are a "supreme dishonor to the Creator."

1979 November 14 The United States Catholic bishops issue "Brothers and Sisters to Us: A Pastoral Letter on Racism in Our Day."

1985 August 14 During an address in Cameroon, Pope John Paul II apologizes to Black Africa for the involvement of white Christians in the slave trade.

1988 Henriette Delille, the foundress of the Sisters of the Holy Family, becomes the first native-born African American to be recognized as a Servant of God. On March 27, 2010, she is declared venerable by Pope Benedict XVI and in 2018 her cause for sainthood advances when documentation about a miracle attributed to her intercession is sent to Rome.

1989 December Cardinal John O'Connor of New York reintroduces Pierre Toussaint's cause for sainthood. The cause was first introduced by Cardinal Terence James Cooke in 1968, but no records could be found. In 1990, O'Connor exhumes and examines Toussaint's body as part of the canonization process before moving it to a crypt under the main altar at New York's St. Patrick's Cathedral, the first lay person so interred there. On December 17, 1996, Pope John Paul II proclaims Toussaint venerable, and in 2003, the Vatican accepts evidence of a miracle attributed to Toussaint's intercession.

1991 With approval of the Holy See, Cardinal William Keeler, archbishop of Baltimore, officially opens a formal canonization inquiry into the life of Mary Elizabeth Lange. In 2013, her remains are moved to the Our Lady of Mount Providence Convent Chapel in Baltimore. In 2020, Xaverian Brother Reginald Cruz completes the writing of the *positio*, detailing her life and showing evidence of her virtue, which is then submitted to Rome.

Twenty-first Century

2000 April 25 Sisters of Loretto in Nerinx, Kentucky, commission a monument to acknowledge mistakes of the past and honor Blacks whom the congregation held in slavery.

2000 December 8 The Sisters of Loretto, the Sisters of Charity of Nazareth, and the Dominicans of St. Catherine, all Kentucky-based religious communities, formally apologize for their use of enslaved persons prior to the Civil War.

2010 March 2 The canonization cause of Augustus Tolton is announced by the Archdiocese of Chicago, and Bishop Joseph Nathaniel Perry is named postulator. Tolton is proclaimed a Servant of God on February 13, 2012. On December 10, 2016, Tolton's body is exhumed at St. Peter's Cemetery, Quincy, Illinois. He is declared venerable by Pope Francis on June 11, 2019. In 2022, the Holy See sends representatives to the U.S. to investigate miracles attributed to Tolton.

2011 Archbishop Gregory Michael Aymond authorizes the Archdiocese of New Orleans to post on the internet thousands of African American Catholic (slave and free) sacramental records dating from 1718 to 1812.

2012 July Three Kentucky-based religious communities (Sisters of Loretto, Sisters of Charity of Nazareth, and Dominicans of St. Catherine) hold a joint reconciliation service to ask forgiveness for their congregations' role in slavery, pledging to continue to work to eliminate racism.

2012 Sisters of Charity of Nazareth, Kentucky, commission a monument to acknowledge mistakes of the past and honor Blacks whom the congregation enslaved.

2013 November Sisters of Loretto ask Pope Francis to "formally and publicly repudiate and rescind" the 1452 *Dum Diversas* bull and other bulls related to the "Doctrine of Discovery."

2014 February 8 The feast day of St. Josephine Bakhita becomes the International Day of Prayer and Awareness against Human Trafficking. Josephine had been kidnapped by slave traders in Sudan in 1877. She converted to Catholicism in 1890 and after finding that she could no longer be legally held as a slave, she took vows with the Canossian Daughters of Charity. She was canonized on October 1, 2000.

2014 December 2 Religious leaders from throughout the globe meet at the Vatican to sign a "Joint Declaration of Religious Leaders Against Modern Slavery." The aim of the document is to "inspire spiritual and practical action . . . to eradicate modern slavery across the world."

2015 September To further racial healing, Father Aidan McAleenan, pastor of the predominantly-Black St. Columba parish, Oakland, California, sends a letter to Pope Francis asking for an official apology for the Church's "acts of racial injustice . . . that have stained our history from the founding of our country, through the passing of the Civil Rights Movement of the 1960s to the present day."

2015 September John J. DeGioia, president of Georgetown University, establishes the Working Group on Slavery, Memory, and Reconciliation, led by Father David Collins, S.J., to better understand the university's connections to slavery and to make archival material regarding slavery more accessible to researchers. The Georgetown Slavery Archive is launched in February 2016.

2016 September 1 The Georgetown University Working Group on Slavery, Memory, and Reconciliation recommends renaming two campus buildings—Mulledy and McSherry Halls—that memorialized Jesuits connected to slavery. The rededicated buildings honor Isaac Hawkins, a slave sold by the Jesuits in 1838, and Anne Marie Becraft (Sister Mary Aloysius), a free woman of color who established a school for Catholic girls at Georgetown.

2016 October Father Robert L. Niehoff, S.J., president of John Carroll University in Cleveland, Ohio, convenes the working group "Slavery: Legacy and Reconciliation," to assess the slaveholding of Archbishop John Carroll, for whom the school was named. The working group issues its report and recommendations two years later.

2016 December 18 The cause for canonization of Julia Greeley is opened by the Archdiocese of Denver. Born into slavery in 1840 in Missouri, Greeley became Catholic in 1880 and joined the Third Order of St. Francis in 1901. She pursued a life of daily prayer and assistance to those in need. In 2017, her remains are moved to Denver's Cathedral Basilica of the Immaculate Conception.

2016 The GU272 Descendants Association is founded, composed of 10,000 known progeny of the slaves sold by the Jesuits in 1838. Cheryllyn Branche-Baker serves as president.

2016 The U.S. and Canadian Province of the Society of the Sacred Heart convenes a committee on Slavery, Accountability, and Reconciliation to investigate slavery in the order's early history in North America and to "commit to truth, healing and reconciliation for a better future." Primarily using sacramental records, they locate descendants of more than 150 former slaves who built and maintained Sacred Heart properties in Louisiana and Missouri.

2017 April 18 Father Timothy Kesicki, S.J., president of the Jesuit Conference of Canada and the U.S., publicly apologizes for the Jesuits' complicity in slavery and the mass sale of slaves in 1838.

2017 August 18 A statue of Roger Brooke Taney, first Catholic Chief Justice of the U.S. Supreme Court, is removed from the State House grounds in Annapolis, Maryland, because of his role in the proslavery *Dred Scott* decision (1857). The statue by William Henry Rinehart had been erected in 1872. On August 16, 2017, a recasting of the statue, which had been unveiled in Baltimore in 1887, is also removed.

2017 August   The United States Conference of Catholic Bishops establishes the Ad Hoc Committee Against Racism to address the evil of racism in our society and Church.

2017 September 21   Black Catholic Bishop Edward K. Braxton presents "The Catholic Church and the Racial Divide in the United States: Old Wounds Reopened" as part of a teach-in sponsored by the Catholic University of America's National Catholic School of Social Service. Braxton recalls that the Church in the U.S. once supported slavery and denied civil rights to African Americans, concluding that much remains to be done to heal the sin of racism.

2018 June 7   Pope Francis calls for people to "hear the cries" of modern slaves, the estimated forty million victims of human trafficking worldwide, in a public letter to Britain's Bishop John Sherrington.

2018 June 9   The GU272 Descendants Association, the offspring of enslaved persons who the Jesuits sold in 1838, hold a reunion in Iberville Parish, Louisiana.

2018 September 23   At the event, "We Speak Your Names," the Society of the Sacred Heart in Grand Coteau, Louisiana, and their former antebellum slaves' descendants remember and honor those who had been enslaved by the religious community.

2018 November 14   The U.S. bishops issue a pastoral letter against racism: "Open Wide Our Hearts: The Enduring Call to Love." It states, "Racist acts are sinful because they violate justice. They reveal a failure to acknowledge the human dignity of the persons offended, to recognize them as the neighbors Christ calls us to love."

2019 July 30   "The History of Enslaved People at Georgetown Visitation: Learning, Reflecting, and Teaching" is issued by Georgetown Preparatory School to begin a conversation about racial inequities and the Visitation sisters' involvement in slavery. The study's steering committee was formed in September 2016, with the school's archivist Susan Nalezyty as lead researcher.

2020 January 2 Catholic News Service distributes a plan of action for Catholic reparations for the Church's involvement in slavery as outlined by Black Catholic historian Shannen Dee Williams.

2020 June 1 The Conference of Major Superiors of Men, composed of leaders from over 200 U.S. Catholic religious institutes, issues a public statement against racism and calls for change.

2020 June Towson University, near Baltimore, Maryland, removes the names of slaveholders Charles Carroll and William Paca from two dormitories following a petition and student government resolutions. Carroll, a Catholic, had been a signer of the Declaration of Independence and congressional representative. The university convened a ten-member committee to recommend new names for the buildings.

2020 September 8 Loras College in Dubuque, Iowa, announces that because its founder, Bishop Mathias Loras, had enslaved a woman named Marie Louise, the college would establish a scholarship in her honor. The college also removed from campus Loras's statue until a community discussion could be held regarding its disposition.

2020 December 2 U.S. Congressman William Lacy Clay, a Black Catholic representing Missouri, cosponsors a resolution to remove a clause in the Thirteenth Amendment of the Constitution allowing for slavery and involuntary servitude as a criminal punishment. Sponsors of the legislation charge that this "punishment clause" has driven the over-incarceration of Blacks since the Civil War.

2020 December 30 The long running radio program "Morning Glory," hosted by Black Catholics Gloria Purvis and Deacon Harold Burke-Sivers, is cancelled by Catholic media conglomerate Eternal Word Television Network (EWTN) because of listener complaints. Purvis had defended calls for reparations and defunding of the police in the wake of the killing of George Floyd. Believing her positions consistent with Catholic teaching, Purvis emerged as a leading voice for social justice and human dignity.

2021 February "Forgive Us Our Trespasses" is initiated by the Archdiocese of St. Louis to research the archdiocese's involvement in slavery, including individuals enslaved by its bishops and priests.

2021 March 15 Father Timothy P. Kesicki, S.J., president of the Jesuit Conference of Canada and the U.S., and Joseph M. Stewart, acting president of the Descendants Truth and Reconciliation Foundation, announce a plan to distribute $100 million in reparations to descendants of enslaved persons previously owned by their order.

2021 July 13 The NETWORK Lobby for Catholic Social Justice joins representatives of the Presbyterian, Methodist, Lutheran, Evangelical, and Jewish communities in a press conference and ecumenical call to support the U.S. House of Representatives' "Commission to Study and Develop Reparation Proposals for African Americans." The National Council of Churches sponsors the event.

2021 December Loyola University Maryland (LUM) announces the formation of a presidential task force charged with guiding a university-wide examination of the school's connections to slavery. LUM joins the consortium Universities Studying Slavery (USS), which includes over ninety institutions.

2022 July 13 Kamm Howard, director of Reparations United, meets with Bishop Paul Tighe, secretary of the Vatican's Pontifical Council of Culture, to discuss the Catholic Church's involvement with the transatlantic slave trade and how it might make amends.

2022 October 26 Georgetown University offers a new plan for reparations. Through the support of alumni, the university's Reconciliation Fund will provide $400,000 each year to support community-based projects that aim to benefit the descendants of the GU272, the enslaved persons the university sold in 1838.

2023 January Members of Sacred Heart Catholic Church in Bowie, Maryland, partner with archaeologist Laura Masur of the

Catholic University of America to clear debris surrounding their church—property that was once part of the Jesuits' White Marsh plantation. They locate and flag more nearly 200 burials of enslaved and formerly-enslaved Black Catholics and their descendants.

2023 March 30 The Holy See officially repudiates the "Doctrine of Discovery," indicating that it is not part of the Catholic Church's teaching. In a statement, the Holy See acknowledges that the papal pronouncements that supported the doctrine "did not adequately reflect the equal dignity and rights of Indigenous peoples" and were used "to justify immoral acts against" them—including enslavement.

Uncomfortable Entries: Documenting Enslaved and Free Persons of Color in Sacramental Records

EMILIE GAGNET LEUMAS

Introduction

On March 20, 1829, an enslaved infant named Joseph William was baptized at St. Louis Cathedral in New Orleans, Louisiana. Attached to the baptism register was a document addressed to his master's attorney declaring that Joseph, the son of an enslaved mother, Becky, should be freed at the age of twenty-one because, as the owner stated, "it is too white to be a slave for life."[1]

While this kind of record may seem unusual, it illustrates how the Catholic Church's sacramental records document prejudices that researchers, scholars, and students—and the public at large— may find uncomfortable today. These sacramental entries not only record the slave-owning of bishops, priests, and religious orders but also reveal Catholic families that "passed for white." The records contain information regarding Catholic enslavers who fathered children with enslaved women and sometimes claimed paternity of their children. They also contain information about men—married or unmarried—who had long-term relationships with free women of color at a time when laws prohibited such liaisons.

Records of enslaved people receiving sacraments exist in many U.S. dioceses: Baltimore, Maryland; Louisville, Kentucky; St. Louis, Missouri; Mobile, Alabama; St. Augustine, Florida; Baton Rouge, Louisiana; and New Orleans, among others. Records may

---

  1 Correspondence document from S. M. Woolfolk to Mr. Field, affixed to Baptism of Joseph William, March 20, 1829, St. Louis Cathedral Baptism Register, volume 21, page 228, act 1682, Office of Archives and Records, Archdiocese of New Orleans, New Orleans, Louisiana (hereafter AANO).

be sparse or nonexistent in some places, but thousands of enslaved African and Native Americans were baptized throughout the United States. Many sacramental records, especially those from the hands of French and Spanish priests, record detailed information about the child, the parent(s), and the sponsors.[2]

Sacramental records are among the most important resources available to scholars researching the lives of enslaved and free persons of color. Recognized paternity, biological and fictive relationships, evidence of literacy, and manumissions are among the important pieces of evidence found in these archival records. In the Archdiocese of New Orleans, these records are extensive, well-maintained, and searchable.[3] They document baptisms, confirmations, marriages, and burials. Because these records detail the history of the local community over time, they are recognized as having unique and enduring value. Importantly, they illustrate the Catholic heritage of families across generations. To fully appreciate these records, one must be familiar with the laws, traditions, and practices that impacted their creation.

This essay will highlight the sacramental entries found in the registers at the Office of Archives and Records in the Archdiocese of New Orleans. It will detail how laws affected recordkeeping practices in Louisiana during the colonial and antebellum periods, and it will suggest how access to these records particularly benefits research of enslaved and free persons of color.

The Early New Orleans Church

New Orleans was founded in 1718 by Jean Baptiste Le Moyne de Bienville. Catholicism was bound up in its history from the

---

2 Father Cyprian Davis, O.S.B., explored the importance of sacramental records in understanding the identities of enslaved and free Catholic persons of color. He cited examples gleaned from the records of a variety of places, including St. Augustine, Florida; Natchitoches, Louisiana; Mobile, Alabama; Savannah, Georgia; and Baltimore, Maryland. See *The History of Black Catholics in the United States* (New York: Crossroad, 1990), 67–89.

3 Archdiocese of New Orleans, "Church Records: Digitized Sacramental Records in the Archives," https://nolacatholic.org/church-records.

beginning. Tradition has it that Bienville "traced the plan of the city on the ground with his sword and indicated the site for the building of a church and presbytery."[4] However, there is little existing evidence indicating this site was used from the founding of the city. Mass was celebrated during the first few years in a shed, a warehouse, and a beer tavern, among other buildings.[5] The earliest extant sacramental record from New Orleans is a marriage of French colonials recorded in 1720. The first St. Louis parish church at New Orleans was dedicated in 1727, but this early church was destroyed by fire in 1788, which resulted in the destruction of several early sacramental registers.

The Archdiocese of New Orleans, originally known as the Diocese of Louisiana and the Floridas (East and West Florida), was erected on April 25, 1793. Since Louisiana had passed from French control to the Spanish crown in 1763, the diocese was a joint creation of Charles IV, king of Spain, and Pope Pius VI. It was established less than four years after the founding of the Diocese of Baltimore, the first diocese in the United States. Having roots in the Catholic realms of Spain and France, the New Orleans archdiocese has a unique history, distinguishing it from dioceses that were established in the former English colonies amidst a Protestant majority. After the Louisiana Purchase of 1803, New Orleans became an "American" diocese, but older European traditions and practices would long survive. New Orleans Catholicism retained much of its earlier ethnic identity, with the cathedral, for instance, continuing to record sacraments in French until 1910.[6]

The early history of the Louisiana Catholic Church cannot be separated from the early Louisiana colonial period. As part of

---

4 Roger Baudier, *The Catholic Church in Louisiana* (New Orleans: Roger Baudier, 1939), 55.
5 Baudier, *The Catholic Church in Louisiana*, 56.
6 Emilie Gagnet Leumas, "Mais, I sin in French, I gotta go to confession in French: A Study of the Language Shift from French to English within the Louisiana Catholic Church" (Ph.D. diss., Louisiana State University, Baton Rouge, 2009), 18–19, 41; see Sylvie Dubois, Emilie Gagnet Leumas, and Malcolm Richardson, *Speaking French in Louisiana, 1720–1955: Linguistic Practices of the Catholic Church* (Baton Rouge: Louisiana State University Press, 2018).

the colonial empires of France and Spain, the settlers of Louisiana were required to be Catholic if they were to be faithful subjects. As Charles Nolan wrote, "The early residents of this area would have found our distinction between political and religious matters strange and unintelligible. War, a business or marriage contract, and a baptismal ceremony were both sacred and secular."[7]

New Orleans's history was steeped in the intermingling of sacred and secular, where births, marriages, and deaths were religious rites of passage. These rites of passage were marked for white and colored persons alike. And especially for generations of enslaved Africans and their descendants, these uncomfortable entries often provide the only individual record of their existence.

New Orleans and Race

The racial composition of New Orleans greatly impacted its governance, including the relationship of the Church to the local residents. In the eighteenth century's first half, more than 6,000 enslaved Africans were sent to colonial Louisiana. They soon outnumbered French residents. In 1732, enslaved people accounted for about 75% of French Louisiana's entire colonial population. By 1766, the number of enslaved persons decreased to 52% of the Louisiana population. In New Orleans, the trend was reversed, with an increase in the enslaved population from 12% in 1726 to 15% in 1766. The growth can be attributed to both natural increase and the development of urban slaveholding.[8] Under Spanish rule, New Orleans's enslaved population continued to increase. New African arrivals were joined by waves of Haitian refugees. By 1791, the enslaved population increased to 36%, while free persons of color accounted for 17% of the city's popu-

---

7   Charles E. Nolan, *A Southern Catholic Heritage: Volume 1, Colonial Period 1704–1813* (New Orleans: Archdiocese of New Orleans, 1976), xix.

8   Shannon Lee Dawdy, *Building the Devil's Empire: French Colonial New Orleans* (Chicago: University of Chicago Press, 2008), 175–176; Michael Pasquier, "Creole Catholicism before Black Catholicism: Religion and Slavery in French Colonial Louisiana," *Journal of Africana Religions* 2, no. 2 (2014): 272.

Illustration of a New Orleans slave auction (James Buckingham, *The Slave States of America* [London, 1842]).

lation. In 1805, under early American rule, the white population of New Orleans continued to decrease (43%) while the enslaved (38%) and free persons of color population (19%) increased.[9]

According to the 1823 New Orleans city directory, 29,000 residents lived in the city and an additional 14,000 lived outside of the city but in the parish (county). In total, 45% were white, 16% were free persons of color, and 34% were enslaved. The city residents were nearly evenly divided between white and African or of African descent. Of the 47% of the residents who were African or of African descent, 21% were free persons of color, and

---

9 Kimberly S. Hanger, *Bounded Lives, Bounded Places: Free Black Society in Colonial New Orleans, 1769–1803* (Durham, NC: Duke University Press, 1997), 22.

25% were enslaved. For those living beyond the city, only 6% were free persons of color, and 53% were enslaved.[10]

The *Code Noir* and Sacramental Practices Under French and Spanish Rule

The *Code Noir*, the legal regulation of relationships between colonists and enslaved persons, was first introduced in 1685 and was applied to French colonies in the West Indies in 1687, Guyana on the South American coast in 1704, and Réunion in the Indian Ocean in 1723. In 1724, King Louis XV promulgated the second version of the code and it was introduced to Louisiana. The Louisiana *Code Noir* outlined the laws and restrictions regarding religion and enslavement.[11] Several of its mandates are relevant to this study. The code required masters to provide religious instruction to the enslaved. It mandated that slaves be baptized in the Catholic faith, freed from work on Sunday, and treated humanely. It forbade its white subjects from marrying Blacks. Marriage of enslaved persons required proof of consent from their masters. Children inherited their enslaved condition from their mothers. Masters were required to have their Christian slaves buried in consecrated ground.[12] All of these mandates of the *Code Noir* are reflected in the colony's early sacramental records, adding to the richness of the information contained therein.

During the French colonial period (1718–1763) and up until 1777, the sacramental records of St. Louis Church, the predecessor of St. Louis Cathedral, were recorded in one book. The register contained entries for all people and separated entries only by the type of sacrament. Baptisms, marriages, and funerals were recorded chronologically—whether for White European colonists,

---

10   John Adams Paxton, *The New-Orleans Directory and Register* (New Orleans: Benjamin Levy, 1823).

11   Dawdy, *Building the Devil's Empire*, 145; Emily Clark, *Masterless Mistresses: The New Orleans Ursulines and the Development of a New World Society, 1727–1834* (Chapel Hill: University of North Carolina Press, 2007), 164–165.

12   Louis XV, *Le Code noir, ou Édit du Roi, servant de règlement pour le gouvernement et l'administration de la justice, police, discipline et le commerce des esclaves nègres dans la province et colonie de la Louisianne* (Paris: Imprimerie royale, 1727).

Canadians, Native Americans, or Africans. A typical page from the baptismal register of 1731, one of the earliest volumes of baptisms, illustrates the practice. Four entries are contained on the page dated January 1 through January 4. Catherine de Perier, born in Louisiana to a father who was a French military general and his wife, was recorded next to Henry Lacour, an infant born in Louisiana to French colonists. The next two entries are for persons of color: Anne, recorded as *negritte* (a young Black person), a slave owned by Jean Baptiste Leonard; and Marie, *negritte*, born to the legitimate marriage of Raphael, *negre libre* (free Black person), and his wife, Marie Gaspart.[13] This page illustrates the mixture of races within the population of New Orleans in the eighteenth century. The entries suggest how the mixing of races extended into religious, familial, and commercial life.

Sacramental records for enslaved persons contain significant personal information, while census records of the United States, France, and Spain, only counted the number of enslaved individuals. The United States federal census recorded the age and gender of enslaved persons under the enslaver's name in the slave censuses of 1850 and 1860. Information in the sacramental registers is much richer: it may include the date of birth, place of birth (sometimes even noting the African nation), name of mother and father, name of enslaver, and names of godparents and their relationship to the person receiving the sacrament. There may also be information about the status of the enslaved person or the skill/position they held.

In 1757, Philippe, a Black man enslaved by Capuchin missionaries, stood as a godfather at the baptism of Philippe, a one-month-old baby of Rose, who was enslaved by Sieur Dupart. Philippe, the godfather to the infant, signed his name below the baptism entry in the register.[14] In most situations, if an enslaved person signed the register (most probably at a marriage), it was with an "X," and the priest indicated it was the mark of a person

---

13   Entries for January 1–4, 1731, St. Louis Cathedral Baptisms, 1731–1733, page 1, AANO.
14   Baptism of Philippe, August 27, 1757, St. Louis Cathedral Baptismal Register, volume 3, page 80, AANO.

unable to write. What stands out is that Philippe not only signed his name but attempted to sign three times before correctly spelling "Philippe." This record is unusual because it indicates that he had the ability to write his name and had received some form of rudimentary education.

When the Spanish arrived and took possession of the colony, few changes were made to record keeping practices. In 1777, Spanish priests began keeping separate registers for white colonists and the enslaved and free persons of color, resulting in two sets of books. This practice is linked to the efforts of the Spanish crown to prevent "unequal" marriages.[15] In 1795, Bishop Luis Peñalver y Cardenas, the diocese's first bishop, decreed that sacramental books should be kept separately. On the first page of the separate baptismal register, it states: "Book where the baptisms of Black slaves and mulattos that have been celebrated in this parish church of St. Louis in the city of New Orleans beginning 1 January 1777 until the current year 1781."[16] This separation would last until the Civil War and, in some instances, several years beyond. By the early 1870s, all churches recorded sacraments in a single register, regardless of race.

The Spanish, like the French, continued the practice of documenting the baptism date, birthdate, place of birth, parents' names, and occupations. They sometimes entered additional details in the entries, noting grandparents. Both the French and Spanish were meticulous record keepers. One might assume that after the Louisiana Purchase in 1803, these practices changed, but they did not; Louisiana remained heavily influenced by Spanish priests and a new influx of French priests from Haiti and France. However, civil laws did change. Citizens were no longer required to be Catholic, but Catholicism remained the predominant religion in New Orleans.

---

15   Jennifer M. Spear, *Race, Sex, and Social Order in Early New Orleans* (Baltimore: Johns Hopkins University Press, 2009), 160.

16   Written in Spanish: "*Libro donde se asientan las partidas de baptismos de negros esclavos y mulatos que se han celebrado en esta Inglesia parroquial de Sr San Luis de la Ciudad de la Nueva Orleans des de el dia 1 de enero de 1777 que empezo hasta el ano de 1781 que es el corrente.*"

The Louisiana Civil Code of 1808

The Louisiana Civil Code affected what was recorded in the sacramental registers during the antebellum period. According to John T. Hood, the 1808 Louisiana Civil Code repealed "only those ancient laws of the Territory which were contrary to or irreconcilable with" the code. Later in 1817, the Louisiana Supreme Court held that all the Spanish laws that were formerly in effect and not contrary to the code were still in force. In 1822, the legislature appointed three attorneys to revise the 1808 Civil Code to reflect the prevailing laws. This revision was promulgated in 1824 and printed in 1825. This revised code contained an article nullifying the old Spanish laws. But the old laws were not so easily done away with. As disputes continued concerning the Spanish laws, the legislature attempted once again to repeal them through two acts adopted in 1828.[17]

Much of the *Code Noir* was retained in the Louisiana Civil Code, including laws regarding slavery. The code provided a definition for slaves, manumitted persons, and those persons noted as *statu liberi* (slaves for a time):

> Art. 35—A slave is one who is in the power of a master to whom he belongs. The master may sell him, dispose of his person, his industry, and his labor: he can do nothing, possess nothing, nor acquire any thing [sic] but what must belong to this master.
>
> Art. 36—Manumitted persons are those who, having once been slaves, are legally made free.
>
> Art. 37—Slaves for a time or *statu liberi*, are those who have acquired the right of being free at a time to come, or on a condition which is not fulfilled, or in a certain event which has not happened, but who, in the meantime, remain in a state of slavery.

This final state was that of Joseph William, the child of Becky, who was declared "too white." His master, Samuel Wool-

---

17 John T. Hood, "The History and Development of the Louisiana Civil Code," *Louisiana Law Review* 19, no. 1 (1958): 18–33.

St. Louis Cathedral, New Orleans, 1794 (from Henry C. Castellanos, *New Orleans As It Was: Episodes of Louisiana Life* [1895]).

fork, declared him freed at the age of twenty-one, but the condition of his freedom had not yet been fulfilled at the time of his baptism since he had not reached the age of manumission.

In 1827, the Louisiana code was again amended, and this amendment related to any person desiring to emancipate a slave. If emancipation were to occur, and the slave had not reached age thirty, then the master had to present to a parish (county) judge a petition explaining the motives for the emancipation. The Louisiana code tightened the laws concerning slaves and their emancipation throughout the antebellum period, finally deeming it illegal to emancipate in 1857.

Sacramental Registers of the Archdiocese of New Orleans

At the Office of Archives and Records in the Archdiocese of New Orleans, approximately 1,500 registers are preserved in a climate-controlled vault. In addition, more than 1,800 registers (dating after 1920) are maintained in the archdiocese's parish churches. Of the total registers in the vault, ninety-two books (6% of the registers) document the sacraments of enslaved persons and free persons of color. Of these, eighty-five separate sacramental registers refer to enslaved and free people of color, containing roughly 88,000 acts; the other seven books are from the French colonial era, in which the entries were recorded without separation. Fifty-seven of those volumes are from St. Louis Cathedral, compared to sixty-three volumes for entries of white persons for the same period. The number of registers for enslaved and free persons of color is 48% of the total number of registers for the cathedral. Baptisms and burials for persons of color seem to be roughly equal to the number of entries for white persons, while the acts of marriages for enslaved and free persons of color are far fewer than those identified as whites.

Baptisms

The state of Louisiana did not mandate the registration of births and deaths until 1918. Nonetheless, the city of New Orleans did establish the recording of births under the Spanish government in 1790, but the practice was not mandatory. Catholics relied on baptism as proof of birth and legal status. These sacramental records were often produced in court proceedings to establish paternity, marriage eligibility, heirship, and enslaved versus free status. In 1857, Father G. L. Duquesnay, the pastor of the St. Louis Cathedral, attested to the legal basis for the recording of baptisms. In a document witnessed by the vicar general of the diocese and the Consul of France at New Orleans, he wrote:

> I, the undersigned, Pastor of the Parish Church of St. Louis, of New Orleans, do certify that it is, and that it has always been, the constant practice at New Orleans, since the adoption of the code of 1808, [revised in 1823] that the acts of Baptism of Catholics are received and retained by the Priest Minister of the Sacrament, that these acts are never signed by any other than by the Priest alone, the signature of whom has ever been recognized as sufficient for proving the validity and the authenticity of the acts which are admitted as proof by all civil tribunals of the state.

It is also of constant practice that the priest only designates the name of the father, in the Baptismal record of a child born out of wedlock, when the father has personally appeared before him in order to acknowledge his child and has clearly displayed his intention in that respect.[18]

The Louisiana Code was specific regarding legitimacy and acknowledgment of paternity. It differentiated between children who were acknowledged by their fathers and those who were not. The term "natural child," indicating paternity, frequently appears in the sacramental registers. Understanding these nuances helps the researcher understand the entry. On the acknowledgment of illegitimate children, the code read:

> Art. 220—Illegitimate children who have been acknowledged by their father, are called natural children; and those whose father is unknown, are contra-distinguished by the appellation of bastards.
>
> Art. 221—The acknowledgment of an illegitimate child shall be made by a declaration executed before a notary public, in the presence of two witnesses, whenever it shall not have been made in the registering of the birth or baptism of such child.
>
> No other proof of acknowledgment shall be admitted in favor of children of color.

Other evidence of civil and ecclesiastical practices in the sacramental registers exists. Examples of children born to enslaved women who were freed at baptism by the enslaver are found throughout. As laws against manumission restricted the practice, fewer children were freed.

The baptism of Maria Alexandrina encompasses many aspects of civil law at the time of the record's creation. On January 16, 1828, Maria Alexandrina was presented at the cathedral for baptism. The register recorded:

---

18   Father G. L. Duquesnay, Correspondence, 1857-I/I-C-10/folder B, no. 9, AANO.

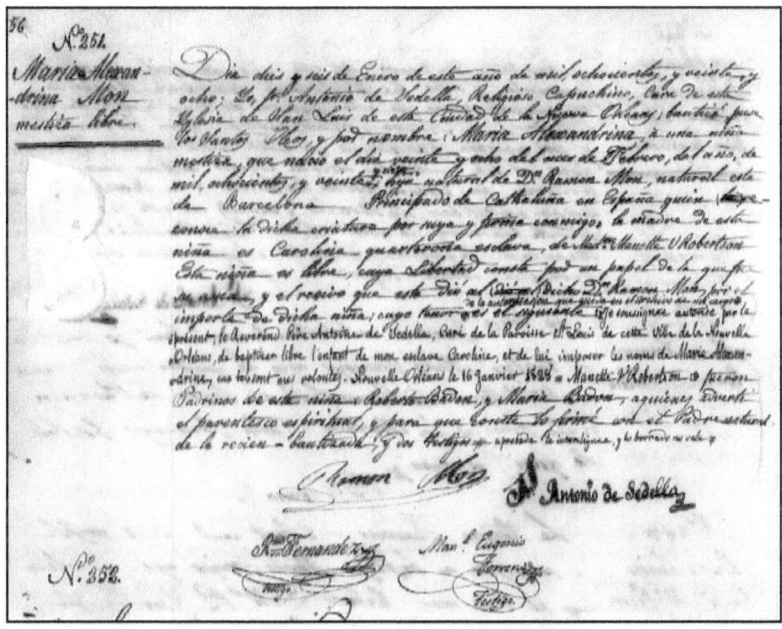

Baptism of Maria Alexandrina Mon, January 16, 1828, St. Louis Cathedral Baptismal Register, volume 21, page 56, act no. 251 (Archdiocese of New Orleans).

Maria Alexandrina, a girl, *mestiza*,[19] born on February 28, 1827, the natural daughter of Don Ramon Mon, a native of Barcelona, Spain, who signs with me. The mother of the child is Carolina, *quarteron*,[20] slave of Madame Manette V. Robertson, this child is free, whose freedom is granted in a document from her enslaver which is inscribed in the register, "I, the undersigned, authorize the Reverend Pere Antoine de Sedella, pastor of the parish of St. Louis of this city of New Orleans, to baptize free the infant of my slave Caroline, and to give her the name of Marie Alexandrine, with all my wishes. New Orleans the 16 January 1828 = Manette V. Robertson."[21]

---

19 *Mestiza* is a Spanish term denoting the person has Spanish and American Indian ancestry.

20 *Quarteron* is a Spanish term for a female quadroon, a person with twenty-five percent African ancestry.

21 Baptism of Maria Alexandrina, January 16, 1828, St. Louis Cathedral Baptismal Register, volume 21, page 56, act no. 251, AANO.

The entry was signed by Ramon Mon, Father Antonio De Sedella, and two witnesses. The entry is in Spanish, while the note appears in French.

This acknowledgment of paternity contains several layers of information, including the mother's enslaved status, the father's Spanish ethnicity, the child being of mixed race, and the mistress's granting of the child's freedom. This complexity is representative of many acts recorded in the registers. Acknowledgment of paternity is not an anomaly but follows a consistent practice based in both civil law and the Catholic Church's canon law.

Examples of baptisms that were amended to reflect an enslaved person's acquired freedom can also be found. For instance, one record indicates the July 4, 1824, baptism of three-month-old Joseph, son of Pierre Charles (Abelard inserted above name) and Saly, both enslaved by Mr. Sauvinet. Twelve years later, the baptism was amended to reflect that Joseph was freed on January 23, 1836, by an act passed before H. Paul Caire, notary of the city. Such entries, when they exist, are important evidence of manumission, though the reason for granting freedom is not always clear.

Marriages

Only fourteen sacramental registers record the marriages of enslaved and free persons of color in New Orleans between 1777 and 1880. Of these, nine are from St. Louis Cathedral, with 1,775 acts. The marriages of white persons held at the cathedral (more than 6,000 for the same time frame) outpace those of persons of color at a rate of three to four times, depending on the year.

Why the disparity in numbers? Both the *Code Noir* and the Louisiana Civil Code regulated marriages between enslaved persons, free persons of color, and white colonists. The *Code Noir* prohibited white subjects of both sexes from marrying Blacks under penalty of being fined and subjected to other forms of punishment. It forbade all curates, priests, missionaries, and even military chaplains to sanction such marriages. It also outlawed all white subjects, as well as manumitted or free-born Blacks, from living in a state of concubinage with Blacks. But many colonists disregarded this, as illustrated by the numerous baptisms of mixed-race children in the sacramental registers.

In a separate mandate, the *Code Noir* prohibited all curates from performing marriages between slaves without proof of consent from their enslavers; and it forbade all masters from forcing their slaves into marriages against their wills.

The Louisiana Civil Code maintained the same regulations:

> Art. 182—Slaves cannot marry without the consent of their masters, and their marriages do not produce any of the civil effects which result from such a contract.
>
> Art. 183—Children born of a mother then in a state of slavery, whether married or not, follow the condition of their mother; they are consequently slaves and belong to the master of their mother.

The earliest extant sacramental records from New Orleans are marriages of French colonials dating from the 1720s. Due to the original register's poor condition, a copy was made prior to the end of the French period. Fortunately, the copy survived the 1788 fire, while the original was destroyed. Contained in this volume are 390 marriage entries of colonists in New Orleans and the surrounding region. These entries provide a portrait of the inhabitants. Among the entries, there are eleven marriages for persons of color: five marriages where both parties were enslaved, three marriages where both parties were free, and three marriages where the groom was a free person and the bride was enslaved.

The earliest marriage for enslaved persons appears on November 1, 1721, when Louis and Catherine, enslaved by Mr. Croustilliad, were married by Father Joseph de St. Charles.[22] This entry is short compared to the next example: On August 4, 1725, Jean Baptiste Raphael and Marie Gaspart, both free Blacks, were

---

22 Marriage of Louis and Catherine, November 1, 1721, St. Louis Cathedral Marriages, volume 1, page 43, act 104, AANO.

married. Their daughter, Marie, was baptized in 1731 (noted earlier). Jean Baptiste Raphael was a native of Martinique, the son of Jean Raphael and Margueritte de St. Cristophe, both then living in Martinique. Marie Gaspart was the daughter of Jean Gaspart, drummer of the company of Mr. Le Blanc and Agnes Simon, both natives of Bruges in Flanders (present-day Belgium). After receiving the written permission of marriage from Mr. Pierre Dugué de Boisbriand, general commander of the colony, and knowing of no other impediments, Father Raphael de Luxembourg, a Capuchin priest and vicar general, imparted to the couple the nuptial blessing, with all the ordinary ceremonies of the church. The witnesses included Agnes Simon, mother of the bride; Nicolas Finaut, soldier of Le Blanc's company; Jean Joseph Lagrandeur D'Etain, drummer of the company of De Mandeville; and Jean Belair, a seaman of the Company of the Indies.[23]

This record keeper's meticulousness was matched by the priests who followed. In the last quarter of the 1700s, when New Orleans was under Spanish control, additional information was included about the parties. For example, in 1799, Carlos Simon, a free man of color and son of Ana Marta, married Francisca, a free woman of color and daughter of Maria Juana. The record declared that at the time of the wedding they had five children (Carlos, Luis, Simon, Eulalia, and Margarita) and were seeking to legitimize them. Attending the wedding were men active in the *Milicia de los mulatos* (militia of the free men of color), in which Carlos was a captain.[24] These militias played a vital role in defending New Orleans and promoted a sense of identity among the city's free people of color during the Spanish colonial and early American periods.[25] Carlos, forty years old, died soon thereafter; he was buried nineteen days after marrying Francisca.[26]

---

23 Marriage of Jean Baptiste Raphael and Marie Gaspart, August 4, 1725, St. Louis Cathedral Marriages, volume 1, page 89, act 200, AANO.

24 *Mulato* and *mulatresse* are terms used to denote persons of mixed race. See marriage of Carlos Simon and Francisca, March 7, 1799, St. Louis Cathedral Marriages, volume 3, page 17, act 49, AANO.

25 Hanger, *Bounded Lives, Bounded Places*, 109.

26 Funeral of Carlos Simon, March 26, 1799, St. Louis Cathedral Funerals, volume 5, page 28.

While the recording of marriages between enslaved persons was rare, one religious community encouraged marriage: the Ursuline sisters. The Ursulines arrived in Louisiana in 1727 with a mission to care for the patients of the Military Hospital and provide education for young girls and women. They educated not only the daughters of colonists but also enslaved and Indigenous girls. Historian Emily Clark, author of *Masterless Mistresses*, in exploring the history of the Ursulines' work in New Orleans from 1727 to 1834, documented and analyzed the enslaved people who were bought, sold, and worked on the Ursuline plantation. She explains the importance of marriage and family in the Ursuline community: "Family was clearly at the heart of this highly visible slave community. The most striking feature that emerges about the nuns' bondpeople is the predominance of the nuclear families anchored by a mother and father living together under the official blessing of sacramental marriage."[27]

When the Ursulines moved in 1824 from their convent in the French Quarter to a property located four miles downriver, known as the Dauphine Street Convent, they brought enslaved persons with them. In a volume titled, *Livres ou sont les noms et les années de la naissance des Nègres et Négresses qui sont venus au Couvent sur notre habitation le 2nd Octobre 1824*, the Ursulines recorded the names, ages, births, marriages, and deaths of the enslaved.[28] They continued to add vital information about these enslaved persons. Most of the additional notations date before 1864, but an additional entry was recorded in 1894: the death of Louis Gonzague, seventy-six years of age. Louis, once enslaved by the Ursulines, remained with them after emancipation, working for them until his death.

In the two small marriage registers that span the years 1837 to 1860, twelve marriages of enslaved persons, where one or both are enslaved by the Ursulines, are recorded. These marriage records are unusual because the enslaved person witnessing the marriage made "their mark" in the register. In 1858, when Theodore mar-

---

27 Clark, *Masterless Mistresses*, 170.
28 The sacramental registers from the Ursuline convent on Dauphine Street are housed in the Archives of the Archdiocese of New Orleans.

Marriage of Theodore and Augustine, June 12, 1858, Ursuline Convent Marriages, vol. 1854–1860, page 14 (Archdiocese of New Orleans).

ried Augustine, the marriage entry contained extensive family information:

> 12 June 1858, I the undersigned have given the nuptial benedictions to Theodore, widower of Rosalie, and Augustine, both belonging to the convent. Witness: Andria, brother of the groom, Louisson, his mother, Julien and other relatives and friends, who make their mark along with the groom and bride who don't know how to sign [their names]. N. J. Perche, priest.[29]

The Ursuline nuns may not have been the only religious order encouraging marriage among the enslaved. The sacramental registers of the Sisters of Charity Hospital record five marriages among enslaved people in 1840, though no other years contain entries for enslaved persons.[30]

---

29 Marriage of Theodore and Augustine, June 12, 1858, Ursuline Convent Marriages, vol. 1854–1860, page 14, AANO. Translated here from the French.

30 Marriages, 1840, Charity Hospital Sacramental Register Baptisms, 1836–1848, AANO.

Funerals and Burials

Though not sacraments, funerals and burials were often recorded in church registers. Funeral records were kept during the colonial period, but many were lost in the 1788 fire that destroyed the city. Funeral registers exist for St. Louis Cathedral from 1777 to 1843. After 1843, the parish church discontinued the practice of noting funerals in a sacramental register.[31] They did, however, keep bound volumes of funeral expenses from 1843 to 1871, noting information about burials and the purchase of tombs in the cemetery. Cemetery records, kept by the sextons, record vital information such as name, age, date of death, and cause. They sometimes provide information on the tomb's location, helping researchers find family tombs. Separate areas in the cemeteries were reserved for the burials of enslaved persons and free persons of color.

Eleven funeral registers, containing 20,227 entries for enslaved and free persons of color, span the years from 1777 to 1843, while fourteen registers exist for these years for white persons. Comparing the number of acts from 1832 to 1843 for each group indicates that twice as many burials were recorded for white persons (8,638 entries) compared to persons of color (4,102).

While the *Code Noir* regulated that baptized enslaved persons be buried in sacred ground, the Louisiana Civil Code was silent on the matter. In 1718, when the French established New Orleans, burials were made along the Mississippi riverbank. After the town was laid out by Royal Military Engineer Adrien DePauger in 1722, a cemetery was designated on the outskirts of the settlement along St. Peter Street, between today's Burgundy and Rampart Streets. During these early years, streets extended no farther than Dauphine Street, just five blocks from the river. A ditch, serving as a moat, was dug along this street, placing the cemetery outside the city. Burial in St. Peter Street Cemetery was entirely below ground, in contrast to the above-ground cemeteries that the locality is known for today. After accepting burials for nearly seventy

---

31 At the cathedral, the consistent practice of recording funerals in sacramental registers resumed in 1908.

years, St. Peter Street Cemetery became full and was closed in 1789 by royal decree of Charles IV, king of Spain.[32] The site was eventually used for the construction of houses, despite the protests of Louisiana's first bishop, Luis Peñalver y Cardenas.

One burial record tells the interesting story of a young girl enslaved by Monsieur de Lapommeray. Late in the spring of 1738, word came to Father Matthias of St. Louis Church that de Lapommeray, treasurer-general of New Orleans, had buried in his garden one of his slaves, a young girl about twelve or thirteen years old. This had taken place without the rites of Christian burial. Incensed at the violation of the laws of both Church and colony, Father Matthias filed a bill of complaint against de Lapommeray before the Superior Council. Father Matthias stated that the offender had interred the body outside of the cemetery, which was contrary to the ordinance of the French king and the *Code Noir*. The *Code Noir* of 1724 made it clear that Catholicism was the only religion of the colony, all slaves were to be instructed in the religion, and masters should have their baptized slaves buried in consecrated ground. Father Matthias demanded that the slave girl's body be disinterred and reburied with the rites of the Church. The court sided with Father Matthias, ordered the exhumation and transport of the body to the cemetery, and fined de Lapommeray thirty livres, the money to be applied to fencing the cemetery.[33]

In October 1733, thirteen burials were recorded in the sacramental registers of St. Louis parish church. This record offers a snapshot of the diversity of early New Orleans inhabitants, whether enslaved, free, white, African, or Native American:

> Jean Bouteillier dit St. Etienne, a soldier, from Toulouse, France, who died at the hospital.

---

32 Samuel Wilson, Jr., and Leonard V. Huber, *The St. Louis Cemeteries of New Orleans* (New Orleans: St. Louis Cathedral, 1963), 7–9.

33 Louisiana Digital Library, "1738-06-14 French Superior Council record, Louisiana State Museum, Records of the French Superior Council (1714–1769)," https://louisianadigitallibrary.org/islandora/object/lsm-p15140 coll60%3A1391.

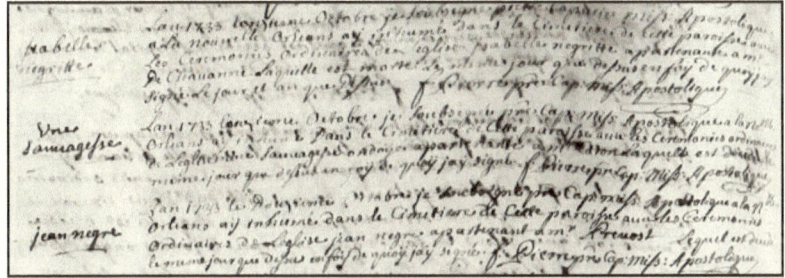

Excerpt of St. Louis Church Burials, October 1733, from St. Louis Cathedral Baptism, Marriage and Funeral Register, vol. 1, page 85 (Archdiocese of New Orleans).

Gilles Frechet, dit Liegois, son of Gilles Frechet and Catherine Ceron, a soldier, from Leige, France, who died at the hospital.
Charles Bourbeau, an 11-year-old boy, who died of smallpox.
Noel Fleuranjoye, son of Noel Fleuranjoye and Margueritte Poitier, a soldier, from Tours, France, who died at the hospital.
Jean Rian, son of Jean Rian and Marie Bougetre, a soldier from Nogent-le-Rotro, France, who died at the hospital after receiving the sacraments.
Isabel, a young slave girl, belonging to Mr. Chavanne.
Sauvagesse, a baptized Indian slave woman, belonging to Mr. Caron.
Jean, a slave, belonging to Mr. Provost.
Francois Servin, son of Francois Servin and Marie Francoise Lonery, a soldier, from Paris, France.
A baby, baptized simply with water, child of Mr. Raguet, councilor.
A slave belonging to Mr. Dubreuil.
Anne Marie LeQuintererck.
Etienne Giraud, son of Bertrand Giraud and Catherine Hemcy, a native of Ile d'Oleron, France.[34]

As the city grew in population, so did the need for additional cemeteries located outside the city. In 1789, the now-famous St. Louis Cemetery No. 1 was established, and in 1823, St. Louis No.

---

34   St. Louis Cathedral Baptism, Marriage and Funeral Register, vol. 1, page 85, AANO.

2 was opened. Many of the enslaved and free persons of color found in New Orleans's sacramental records are interred in these sacred spaces. The details offered by these records offer insight into the enslaved community, including their places of origin. For example:

> Victoire Macquimara of the Senegal tribe, age about 80 years old, died on February 21, 1832, and was buried the next day in the St. Louis Cemetery. She was enslaved by Jean Guilbert.[35]

Funeral entries supply information for persons who were formerly enslaved. For instance:

> Catarina, a creole, was buried in the St. Louis Cemetery on July 2, 1810, at the age of seventy years. She was a former slave of the "Capucin (sic) Mission of the province."[36]

> Miguel Rillieux was buried in the St. Louis Cemetery on June 5, 1812, at the age of sixty-four years. He was a former slave of Vizente Rillicux who, in his will, gave Miguel his freedom due to his "excellent service."[37]

Other entries indicate the mother was free, but the deceased was enslaved (and vice versa):

> Remi Veillon, age thirty-three years, was buried on January 30, 1824, in the St. Louis Cemetery. He was enslaved by J. B. Meilleur. His mother, Felicite, is a free woman of color.[38]

> Aimee Pognon Allain died at the age of fifty-five on November 19, 1834. She was buried two days later in the St. Louis Cemetery. Her mother, Babette, was still living, enslaved by Christoval de Armas.[39]

---

35 Funeral of Victoire Macquimara, February 22, 1832, St. Louis Cathedral Funerals, volume 16, page 222, act 1392, AANO.

36 Funeral of Catarina, July 2, 1810, St. Louis Cathedral Funerals, volume 9, page 17, act 118, AANO.

37 Funeral of Miguel Rillieux, June 5, 1812, St. Louis Cathedral Funerals, volume 9, page 111, act 1071, AANO.

38 Funeral of Remi Veillon, January 30, 1824, St. Louis Cathedral Funerals, volume 18, page 381, act 2580, AANO.

39 Funeral of Aimee Pognon Allain, November 21, 1834, St. Louis Cathedral Funerals, volume 18, page 381, act 2580, AANO.

Each of these examples illustrates the complexity and distinctions in funeral entries. While the basic format may be consistent, the specifics vary for each.

The Complementary Role of Civil Records

While using sacramental records to explain civil and ecclesiastical practices and procedures, one is left wondering what happened to those persons highlighted in this essay. The existence of civil, notarial, and other non-religious records allows the researcher to gain insight into the individual lives and communities of New Orleans. A sample of findings from other archival sources offers additional details about some persons mentioned in sacramental records.

"Joseph William, son of Becky," the youth mentioned at the beginning of this essay, is referenced in the will of Samuel Woolfork, slaveholder of Joseph and his mother. Woolfork, a native of North Carolina, was a slave trader who had relocated to New Orleans. His brother and sometimes business partner, Austin Woolfork, also traded in slaves and had been tasked with transporting to Louisiana the enslaved persons sold by the Jesuit community of Georgetown University, near Washington, D.C. Samuel Woolfork made his last will and testament in 1832 before William Boswell, notary of New Orleans, bequeathing to his "mulatress Beckey (sic) and her two children" freedom to be granted "as soon after his death as possible."[40] However, in 1836, he drafted a second will, voiding the first, containing no mention of Becky or her children. He did acknowledge his natural son, Richard Woolfork, "a free boy of color," who was born on October 25, 1824, and bequeathed $2,000 to be applied by his executor to Richard's support and education.[41] The fate of Becky and her children is unknown. Did Woolfork free them or sell them between 1832 and 1836, or did they perish in one of the typhoid or yellow fever epidemics? Extant records do not provide answers.

---

40 Will of S. M. Woolfork, October 27, 1832, William Boswell, notary, volume 19, 318–320, New Orleans Notarial Archives, New Orleans, Louisiana.

41 Will of S. M. Woolfork, December 7, 1836, David L. McCay notary, volume 2, 391–393, New Orleans Notarial Archives.

The fate of Maria Alexandrina Mon, the girl born to a Spanish father and enslaved mother, is similarly unclear. Two years after acknowledging the paternity of his daughter Marie Alexandrina, Ramon Mon married Marie Orosco, a native of Pensacola, Florida.[42] He died on November 2, 1832, and was buried in the St. Louis Cemetery.[43] On the day before his death, Ramon Mon made his last will and testament, declaring he was a merchant and had no living children. He listed six slaves, of which he declared George, *griffe*,[44] to be freed after an additional year of service to his widow. No mention is made of Maria Alexandrina; her mother, Caroline; or Caroline's owner, Manette V. Robertson.[45]

Joseph Abelard, who was freed at age twelve, is mentioned in numerous civil and sacramental records. Joseph's father, Pierre Charles Abelard, died on April 19, 1845, as a free man of color. His probate names three natural children: Joseph, Jules, and Zoe. He also had a mortgage with J. B. Sauvinet, his former master. There is no mention of Joseph's mother, Saly, in the record.[46] According to the 1850 federal census, Joseph and Saly, then age fifty-six, were living in the same household. Joseph married Melanie Balcet on January 5, 1871, at St. Augustine Catholic Church in New Orleans. Joseph and Melanie, both of whom the census describes as mulatto, were forty-eight years old at the time of their union. Joseph worked as a carpenter, while Melanie kept their home. They had no children. Joseph died on December 11, 1898.

---

42   Marriage of Ramon Mon and Marie Orosco, December 19, 1829, St. Louis Cathedral Marriages, volume 7, page 180, act 705, AANO.

43   Funeral of Ramon Mon, November 3, 1832, St. Louis Cathedral Funerals, volume 17, page 167, act 1007, AANO.

44   *Griffe* is a French term denoting a person who is of one-quarter European and three-quarters African descent, or possibly a person of both African and Native American ancestry.

45   "Louisiana, Orleans Parish Will Books, 1805–1920," Book 1824–1833, volume 4, City Archives & Special Collections, New Orleans Public Library, New Orleans, Louisiana, image 407 of 511 at https://familysearch.org/ark:/61903/3:1:3QSQ-G9MY-5S6?cc=2019728&wc=SJ76-W3D%3A341294301.

46   Probate of Pierre Charles Abelard, April 22, 1845, Orleans, Louisiana Parish Estate Files, Probate Court (Orleans Parish), New Orleans, Louisiana.

Additional information on Theodore and Augustine, the couple enslaved by the Ursuline nuns, is found in the records. Theodore, son of Andre and Louison, had been born on December 2, 1828, and was baptized at the Ursuline Convent on Dauphine Street. He married Rosalie, daughter of Honore and Adelaide, in 1849, and they had four children. Rosalie died in 1856, and two years later, Theodore married Augustine. The Ursulines documented that Theodore left the Ursulines on August 2, 1863, to "claim his freedom before the Federal authorities of New Orleans." Several days later, his children Honore and Adelaide (named for his first wife's parents) followed.[47]

While sacramental records reveal detailed information on individuals and families, they should not be viewed alone. Civil records, census records, and family papers are rich resources that provide additional information on enslaved and free persons of color.

Conclusion

Catholicism was mandated under colonial French and Spanish rule in Louisiana. It is apparent from the records that slaveholders took seriously the mandate to baptize enslaved persons. But once they were free from the colonial-era mandates and under American rule, why did they continue the practice? Were they concerned with the salvation of those they held in bondage? Did they connect the spiritual lives of their slaves with the salvation of their own souls? These questions may never be answered, but the sheer number of acts is a testimony to the importance of Catholicism in the lives of slave and free.

The sacramental registers of the Archdiocese of New Orleans contain more than 88,000 acts of baptisms, confirmations, marriages, and funerals. Each contains information for named individuals who were presented in the church to receive the sacra-

---

47 "Livres ou sont les noms et les années de la naissance des Nègres et Nègresses qui sont venus au Couvent sur notre habitation le 2^{ieme} Octobre 1824," Ursuline Archives, New Orleans; Ursuline Sacramental Registers, AANO.

ments. Civil laws and canonical norms impacted the ways the acts were recorded and used by individuals in civil matters. It seems evident by the number of acts that there was no discrimination at the baptismal font. Enslaved persons whose enslavers were Catholic were baptized and given a name, and their parents' identities and legal status were recorded. When positioned in the broader context of enslavement by Catholics—both individuals and institutions—these uncomfortable entries convey much about race, slavery, and the Church. They suggest significant possibilities for further research of free persons of color, enslaved persons, their enslavers, and the networks they created.

Contending with a Slaveholding Past: Slavery and U.S. Catholic Historiography

DAVID J. ENDRES*

AS AMERICANS HAVE COME TO REALIZE slavery's vast impact, historians of U.S. Catholicism have sought to appraise Catholicism's slaveholding past—a task made more pressing and challenging given the Church's role as a moral guide and its substantial entanglement in hereditary, race-based slavery. This study charts U.S. Catholic historians' assessment of slavery by analyzing historical literature from the early nineteenth century to the present. The first part examines the invisibility of slavery to historians, which lasted throughout the nineteenth century. Next, historians in the first half of the 1900s acknowledged Catholic slave owning and emphasized Catholic masters' purported kindness and the spiritual benefits offered to the enslaved. Lastly, from the 1960s to the present, Catholic historians have authored specialized studies of the Church and slavery, uncovering and clarifying the identities and relationships of Catholic-owned slaves. These studies have begun to shape surveys of U.S. Catholic history and have both prompted and amplified recent efforts by dioceses, religious communities, and Catholic universities to reconcile with their slaveholding pasts.[1]

---

* The author is grateful to Robert Emmett Curran and Maura Jane Farrelly for their helpful comments on a draft of this essay.

1 Few attempts have been made to chart a historiography of Catholic slaveholding. Thomas Murphy described the general contours, with Catholic historians first "championing it," then "measuring it" and "reconstructing its narrative," and finally "condemning it" and "using its example to shed light on pressing issues of today." See Thomas Murphy, S.J., *Jesuit Slaveholding in Maryland, 1717–1838* (New York: Routledge, 2001), xxiii. More recently, Kelly L. Schmidt has offered an excellent survey of the topic, discussing some historiographical issues: "The Pervasive Institution: Slavery and Its Legacies in U.S. Catholicism," *American Catholic Studies Newsletter* 49, no. 1 (Spring 2022):

An Unremarkable History, 1810-1910

For more than a century, historians of U.S. Catholicism viewed slaveholding as unremarkable. Early histories of the Church in the United States provide no sustained treatment of slavery. Texts composed from the nineteenth century through the early twentieth century rarely mention the topic, even when narrating the histories of states like Maryland, Kentucky, Missouri, and Louisiana, where Catholic slaveholding was prominent. When slavery is mentioned, it is discussed briefly and uncritically.

The Invisibility of Slavery

Jean Dilhet's *Beginnings of the Catholic Church in the United States* is the earliest attempt to chronicle the history of U.S. Catholicism. Composed about 1810, the book contains, unsurprisingly, scant reference to slavery. The text provides little information about the practice of Catholic slaveholding except for an acknowledgment of Maryland plantations where "Negroes do all the farm work" and a mention of a parish for Black Catholics in Baltimore (mainly composed of former slaves from Saint-Domingue) in which the members' spiritual "diligence" was "so edifying" that non-Blacks also attended.[2]

Various mid-nineteenth-century survey histories offer minimal mention of slavery, including the works of Thomas D'Arcy

---

11–22. Catholic historians' assessment of slavery shared some commonality with secular historians. Useful studies of the twentieth century "slavery debates" include James C. Morgan, *Slavery in the United States: Four Views* (Jefferson, NC: McFarland, 1985); Daniel C. Littlefield, "From Phillips to Genovese: The Historiography of American Slavery Before *Time on the Cross*," in *Slavery in the Americas*, ed. Wolfgang Binder (Wurzburg, Germany: Konigshausen and Neumann, 1993), 1–23; and Robert William Fogel, *The Slavery Debates, 1952–1990: A Retrospective* (Baton Rouge: Louisiana State University Press, 2003).

2 Jean Dilhet, *Beginnings of the Catholic Church in the United States*, trans. Patrick W. Browne (Washington, DC: Salve Regina Press, 1922), 25, 37–38. This text was originally published as *L'Etat de l'Eglise, ou du Diocèse des Etats Unis de l'Amérique Septentrionale*.

McGee, Xavier Donald MacLeod, and Charles I. White.[3] Even regional-specific texts exploring the history of Catholicism in Southern states sometimes overlook this aspect of their history.[4] Though written proximate to the Civil War and amid heightened disputes over slavery's continuation, these works focus on topics such as Catholic explorers, pioneer priests, early religious communities, and Native American missions. They lack the distance to adequately assess slavery's role, with the peculiar institution hidden in plain sight.

The magisterial work of John Gilmary Shea (1824–1892), an extensive four-volume *History of the Catholic Church in the United States* (1886–1892), evidences trace acknowledgment—and defense—of a slaveholding past. Written two decades after the Emancipation Proclamation, Shea's work testified to Jesuits' ownership of enslaved persons but insisted that the priests exercised a kind form of bondage: "The old Jesuit estates still held by the clergy were cultivated by slaves, the only form of labor to be obtained, but the rule of the clergy was so light that a 'priest's negro' was a proverbial expression for a slave who was pretty much his own master."[5] Elsewhere, he rebuffed the presumed false charge that the Jesuits "treated their negroes cruelly," claiming that the priests tended chiefly to pastoral duties. Quoting John Carroll, then prefect apostolic of the American missions, he related that the clergy "treat their negroes with great mildness and are attentive to guard them from the evils of hunger and nakedness; that they work less and are much better fed, lodged, and clothed than laboring men in almost any part of Europe. . . ."[6]

---

3 Thomas D'Arcy McGee, *Catholic History of North America* (Boston: Patrick Donahoe, 1855); Xavier Donald MacLeod, *History of Roman Catholicism in North America* (New York: Virtue and Yorston, 1866); C. I. White, "Sketch of the Origin and Progress of the Catholic Church in the United States of America," in J. E. Darras, *General History of the Catholic Church* (New York: P. O'Shea, 1865), 599–663.

4 For instance, William P. Treacy, *Old Catholic Maryland and Its Early Jesuit Missionaries* (Swedesboro, NJ: St. Joseph's Rectory, 1889).

5 John Gilmary Shea, *History of the Catholic Church in the United States*, Volume II, 1763–1815 (New York: J. G. Shea, 1888), 196.

6 John Gilmary Shea, *Life and Times of the Most Rev. John Carroll, Bishop and First Archbishop of Baltimore* (New York: J. G. Shea, 1886), 311–312, quote at 312.

John Gilmary Shea (Archives of the Catholic University of America).

It is striking that these sources provide little information on ministry to enslaved persons, but at least one nineteenth-century historian expounded upon the spiritual duty of the Catholic Church to those in bondage, noting the "sad state" of efforts to convert African Americans. While Blacks could be "good Catholics and excellent Christians," ministry to them was nearly non-existent—their souls languishing amidst a "vast and untilled field." The author asserted that ministering to the immigrant population detracted from efforts, including evangelizing Native American and enslaved persons, effectively rendering these populations less than visible to and within the Church.[7]

Criticizing Slavery

While criticism of slavery was generally rare, when Catholic historians showed concern, it was for its corruption by non-Catholic slaveholders, with the implication that slavery was not

---

7 Henry de Courcy, *The Catholic Church in the United States: Pages of Its History* (New York: Edward Dunigan and Brother, 1857), 115–116.

per se evil. Catholic slaveholding brought about the blessings of the true Christian faith; Protestant ownership led to infidelity and godlessness. Numerous historians asserted the institution's Protestant and English roots, with a resulting tendency toward bondspersons' unbelief and immorality. Father Jeremiah O'Connell, an Irish-born missionary who labored for decades in the South, blamed America's founders for slavery: "The blessings left behind by Protestant England were slavery, a corrupt Bible, savages on the war-path, and hatred of Catholicity."[8]

Father Thomas A. Hughes (1849–1939), an English-born but American-trained Jesuit, compiled a four-part history of Jesuits in North America in the early twentieth century. Though written forty years after the Thirteenth Amendment abolished slavery, his work was unapologetically supportive of Catholic ownership of the enslaved. Slavery's abuses were at the hands of non-Catholics, he contended. He wrote, "Worse than the cruelties inflicted on the negroes to the prejudice of life and limb was the guilt of systematically denying them Christian instruction and Baptism, in most of the English settlements." Catholic-owned slaves, however, were fundamentally different, graced by baptism and morally upright ownership.[9]

Most bondspeople, of course, were not Catholic-owned. And since an enslaved person's faith usually followed his master's, most of the enslaved were Protestant. This was slavery's chief ill, some historians believed. Henry de Courcy (1820–1861), in *The Catholic Church in the United States: Pages of Its History* (1857), lamented, "In general it is the fanaticism of Wesley that is preached with success to the colored people."[10] In a similar vein,

---

8   Jeremiah J. O'Connell, *Catholicity in the Carolinas and Georgia: Leaves of Its History* (New York: D. & J. Sadlier, 1879), 29.

9   Thomas Hughes, S.J., *History of the Society of Jesus in North America: Colonial and Federal* (New York: Longmans, Green, 1907): I: 281. On Hughes' approach as a historian, see Robert Emmett Curran, "From Saints to Secessionists: Thomas Hughes and *The History of the Society of Jesus in North America*," in *Studies in Catholic History in Honor of John Tracy Ellis*, ed. Nelson H. Minnich, Robert B. Eno, and Robert F. Trisco (Wilmington, DE: Michael Glazier, 1985), 239–259.

10   De Courcy, *The Catholic Church in the United States*, 116.

O'Connell argued that Protestants furthered the "abominable doctrine" that Blacks had no souls and should not be baptized, while Catholics recognized their God-given dignity. Slavery's only "redeeming feature," O'Connell contended, was Catholic acquisition of enslaved people, which assured a chapel, a priest, baptism, and Sunday catechism. Without it, the enslaved were inevitably reduced to unbelief.[11] Catholics were the only truly Christian owners of the enslaved: "It is only under Catholic governments, where the Church can regulate the relative duties between the servant and the master, that slavery can exist as a Christian institution, and the human being protected against the injustices and passions of the owner."[12]

The blessings of Catholicism to the enslaved notwithstanding, some historians claimed that slavery had a chilling effect on the Church's progress in the United States. It prevented Catholicism in the South from growing by discouraging immigration—the recognized lifeblood of the Northern Church. According to historian John O'Kane Murray, "The marvelous impulse which the tide of immigration gave to Catholicity in the North and West was wanting at the South. Slavery existed. Labor was cheap. The immigrants found but few inducements."[13] O'Connell, in characteristically hyperbolic language, echoed the sentiment: "Slavery, like another wall of China, isolated the Church in the Southern States from the world abroad, and during a century she sat in darkness and in the shadow of death."[14]

Slaves of Differing Complexions

Catholic historians at times used slavery as a metaphorical tool to criticize the status or treatment of Catholics in the United States, viewing Catholics—like the enslaved—as a persecuted minority. John O'Kane Murray wrote that Protestant bigotry had transformed colonial Maryland "into a penal colony—a land of

---

11 O'Connell, *Catholicity in the Carolinas and Georgia*, 629.
12 O'Connell, *Catholicity in the Carolinas and Georgia*, 72.
13 John O'Kane Murray, *A Popular History of the Catholic Church in the United States* (New York: D. & J. Sadlier, 1877), 252.
14 O'Connell, *Catholicity in the Carolinas and Georgia*, ix.

slaves!"[15] By that same token, Henry de Courcy insisted that Irish Catholic immigrants in America had been "reduced to the same condition of slavery as African negroes." In Virginia, he explained, anti-Catholic measures were so severe that they "sought means to degrade and insult [white Catholics], and devised a plan which rated them socially with their negro slaves."[16]

While offering sparse recognition of slavery's existence, these early texts downplay Catholic participation in race-based slavery and omit discussion of its morality, preferring to compare the experience of anti-Catholic prejudice to human bondage. Catholic scholars' omission of any serious discussion of slavery indicates that it was viewed as ordinary and unremarkable and, therefore, not worthy of historians' comment.

Acknowledging Catholic Slaveholding, 1910–1960

The failure to readily concede Catholic participation in slavery, including the many religious orders that enslaved people, was remedied in the twentieth century's first half. Histories of this period indicate a broadened understanding of slavery, including the details of Catholic-owned enslaved populations, their treatment—such as ministry efforts and sacramental reception—and American Catholic historians' earliest discussions of slavery's morality.

Catholic Owners, Catholic Slaves

In the early 1900s, and especially by the 1930s, U.S. Catholic historians more frequently mentioned the ownership and commerce of enslaved persons by Catholic religious orders, clergy, and laity. In writing about slave ownership, they unsurprisingly emphasized the role of masters rather than that of the enslaved and offered context for why Catholics, especially poverty-vowing men and women religious, would have engaged in the ownership of other humans.

---

15 Murray, *A Popular History of the Catholic Church in the United States*, 142.
16 De Courcy, *The Catholic Church in the United States*, 158–159.

In Louisiana, slavery was a remnant of its French and Spanish roots. Roger Baudier (1893–1960) offered an extensive treatment of slavery in Louisiana, exploring the role of Catholics, including Capuchins and Jesuits. He couched their property in its social, cultural, religious, and legal contexts, especially the parameters of the *Code Noir*, by which slavery was regulated. For Baudier, slavery was an established institution. The question was less in its existence and more in suppressing potential abuses, such as owners who did not catechize their bondspersons, forced work on the Sabbath, or prevented marriage.[17]

In frontier locations like Kentucky and Missouri, missionaries viewed participation in slavery as essential—as did the early-twentieth-century historians who wrote about them. These historians often explained that there were insufficient priests and sisters to serve lay Catholics' religious needs and perform the manual and domestic duties frontier life required. Father William J. Howlett, writing in 1915 of the Sisters of Loretto's foundation in central Kentucky, explained that slavery was a "necessity" for taming the frontier and advancing the work of the Church: "There was no support for the priest, sisters, or church without the land and the slaves to cultivate it."[18]

Historians did not always understand—or at least did not often convey—the extent of Catholic slaveholding, especially by clergy, but historians of this period began to quantify the Church's slaveholdings. Father Thomas Hughes' history of the Jesuits provides significant details of his order's dealings with slavery. Though insisting on masters' kind treatment, he offered some sense of how many enslaved persons worked on the Jesuits' Maryland plantations. The total, described as ever-increasing by the 1820s, was estimated at around 500, with the net worth of the Jesuits' human chattel at perhaps $100,000.[19] Baudier likewise

---

17 Roger Baudier, *The Catholic Church in Louisiana* (New Orleans: Roger Baudier, 1939), 206.
18 W. J. Howlett, *Life of Rev. Charles Nerinckx: Pioneer Missionary of Kentucky and Founder of the Sisters of Loretto at the Foot of the Cross* (Techny, IL: Mission Press, 1915), 153.
19 Thomas Hughes, S.J., *History of the Society of Jesus in North America: Colonial and Federal* (New York: Longmans, Green, 1910), I, Part II (Documents):

provided the number of enslaved persons on the Jesuits' Louisiana plantations at 140 in the mid-eighteenth century, though he explained that some were children, older men, or women unable to work.[20]

Historical works from the first half of the twentieth century acknowledged Catholic slaveholding but often underappreciated its pervasiveness. Madeleine Hooke Rice (1903–1999), in *American Catholic Opinion in the Slavery Controversy*, downplayed clergy ownership, writing, "In so far as the individual priests were concerned it was generally a case of ownership of one or two 'servants' for use about the rectory and church building." Holdings by religious orders, she admitted, were on a "somewhat larger scale" due to their agricultural activities.[21] Clergy ownership was deemphasized in other ways. For instance, the Dominican historian Father Victor Francis O'Daniel (1868–1960) did not often use the word "slave" to describe the persons held in bondage by his religious community. He preferred the term "colored servant," and when assessing the number of persons that his order enslaved in central Kentucky, he called the report that they held twenty-seven persons a "gross exaggeration," "the result of an oversight," or a Dominican superior's "fertile fancy."[22] The Jesuits also refrained from calling their bondspersons "slaves." Hughes explained that the terminology he utilized was not his choice but the language of the Jesuits themselves: "The missionaries seem to have avoided the term 'slaves.' The names used were 'servant men,' 'servant women,' 'the family,' 'creatures,' 'labourers,' 'negroes.'"[23]

---

749 n19. The number of persons the Jesuits enslaved may not have been that high. See Murphy, *Jesuit Slaveholding in Maryland*, xv.
    20   Baudier, *The Catholic Church in Louisiana*, 160, 164.
    21   Madeleine Hooke Rice, *American Catholic Opinion in the Slavery Controversy* (New York: Columbia University Press, 1944), 45–46.
    22   V. F. O'Daniel, *Light of the Church in Kentucky, Samuel Thomas Wilson* (Washington, DC: Dominicana, 1932), 220, 229, quote at 229. The actual number of enslaved held by the Dominicans was at least thirty-seven. See C. Walker Gollar, "Edward Fenwick: First Bishop of Cincinnati and Slaveholder," *U.S. Catholic Historian* 38, no. 1 (Winter 2020): 26 n1.
    23   Thomas Hughes, S.J., *History of the Society of Jesus in North America: Colonial and Federal* (New York: Longmans, Green, 1917), II: 560.

The number of bondspersons could also be downplayed with the assertion that fewer Catholics owned slaves than Protestants. Peter Guilday (1884–1947), cofounder of the American Catholic Historical Association and longtime editor of the *Catholic Historical Review*, wrote a magisterial work on proslavery Bishop John England. Guilday quoted England's letters profusely, iterating the bishop's assertion that "Catholics are generally too poor to possess [enslaved persons] or any other property."[24] When religious who had taken vows of poverty enslaved people, historians explained that their bondspeople were most often obtained through bequests or donations, not the slave trade.[25]

Overall, Catholic ownership was deemphasized. In some studies, historians were more likely to cite the religion of the enslaved rather than that of the owner, even if one followed the other. Guilday wrote, "A considerable number of slaves were Catholics but they were chiefly those who accompanied the French." Reframing the relationship as one of "accompaniment" and not ownership, the religion of the enslaved could appear to have unclear origins.[26] In the historical record, the agency of owners was paramount, but when Catholic slaves were mentioned, the details of the master-slave relationship could go unexplained.

Catholic Enslavers' Kindly Enslavement

When slavery was discussed, pains were taken to describe the qualitative difference in Catholic treatment of bondspersons. O'Daniel insisted that Protestants were careless toward their slaves' well-being, but Catholic-owned bondspersons were a "comparatively happier lot." Referring to those whom Catholic religious communities enslaved, he wrote, "In such places they received marked kindness, whilst their spiritual welfare was

---

24 "Report on the Charleston Diocese," January 30, 1833, in Peter Guilday, *Life and Times of John England, First Bishop of Charleston (1786–1842)* (New York: America, 1927), I: 526.

25 J. Herman Schauinger, *Stephen T. Badin: Priest in the Wilderness* (Milwaukee: Bruce Publishing, 1956), 40.

26 Guilday, *Life and Times of John England*, I: 506.

guarded with solicitude. In our own boyhood days it was a genuine pleasure to listen to the former colored servants . . . tell of the excellent treatment accorded them."[27] Guilday, in his extensive biography of Archbishop John Carroll, accepted uncritically Carroll's report that slaves were treated mildly, their morals carefully watched, and that during the "late war," the British provided the enslaved with the opportunity to desert, but they—except for two—chose to stay with the priests.[28]

Catholic owners were so kind, historians argued, that it could hardly be considered enslavement. According to Father Hughes, the Maryland Jesuits' bondspeople exhibited a "spirit of contentment." They were each gifted with a small plot of land on which they could raise chickens and vegetables. By selling what they produced, "The father of each family generally made from $80 to $100 per annum." Hughes emphasized, "This was clear gain to him, as he depended entirely on the manager for working clothes and provisions." A bondsperson could also benefit, he related, from the occasional theft of a pig, sheep, goose, or turkey or the selling of some tobacco, corn, or wheat.[29] Josephite Father John Gillard (1900–1942) reached the same conclusion: the Jesuit-owned bondspeople were not really slaves. "To refer to the Negroes as 'slaves' is hardly true; in some instances, they had practical freedom, jobbing on their own, the sick being cared for, and the aged provided for."[30]

More extensive treatment of the Church and slavery described the quality of ministry provided to enslaved persons, providing an opportunity to assert Catholic superiority over Protestantism. Francis J. Curran's *Major Trends in American Church History* summarized, "While the Protestant slave-holders in the United States were writing and rewriting arguments to prove

---

27 O'Daniel, *Light of the Church in Kentucky*, 222.
28 Father John Carroll to Archbishop John Troy, July 2, 1789, in Guilday, *Life and Times of John Carroll*, 319.
29 Hughes, *History of the Society of Jesus in North America*, II: 562–563, 565.
30 John T. Gillard, S.S.J., *Colored Catholics in the United States* (Baltimore: Josephite Press, 1941), 63.

that the Negroes were brutes and therefore should be enslaved as beasts of burden, the Catholics were accepting the Negroes as brethren and treating them as men."[31]

This recognition of shared human dignity required that Catholic-owned bondspeople receive the sacraments, be educated in the faith, and be free to foster marriage and family life. One historian lauded Catholic owners for their concern for the spiritual lives of the enslaved, calling their efforts a "domestic apostolate." He wrote, "Privately much was done by Catholic families . . . for the instruction and reception into the Church of their slaves or freed Negro servants. This domestic apostolate was a duty incumbent upon the head of the Catholic household."[32]

Baudier provided extensive documentation of ministry to the enslaved in Louisiana. Concentrating on bondspersons' instruction and reception of baptism, he asserted that parish registers are a "standing contradiction" that enslaved persons' religious life was neglected. Instead, he cited the example of thousands of slave baptisms, often occurring in groups of 75 or 100 on the vigil of Pentecost or Holy Saturday. While baptisms were numerous, he acknowledged that marriage seldom occurred, often because of masters' opposition to the accompanying obligation to prevent the separation of spouses.[33] Overall, he admitted that ministry to the enslaved, while significant, "was certainly far from what it should have been." It was "spasmodic and unorganized" and harmed by prejudice and racism.[34]

Father John LaFarge, S.J. (1880–1963), a pioneer of the interracial justice movement, offered a mostly positive view of Maryland Catholics' treatment of the enslaved. He contended that the Old Marylanders were urged to provide catechetical instruction for all in their households (including the enslaved), which was a

---

31 Francis J. Curran, *Major Trends in American Church History* (New York: America Press, 1946), 25.

32 C. E. McGuire, ed., *Catholic Builders of the Nation*, 5 vols. (Boston: Continental Press, 1923), V: 156.

33 Baudier, *The Catholic Church in Louisiana*, 185, 206.

34 Baudier, *The Catholic Church in Louisiana*, 433.

Father John LaFarge, S.J. (John J. Burns Library, Boston College)

frequent topic of sermons in the late eighteenth century. As he related, often the "entire personnel of the plantation, slaves and all" would gather together in the evenings for catechism.[35] Unlike Protestant faiths which saw no place for the enslaved among their members, bondspersons attended Mass in the same churches as their Catholic masters, though usually in separate seating to the side, back, or upper gallery of the church.[36]

Father Gillard explained that besides Quakers only Catholics promoted religion and education among the enslaved. In addition to emphasizing the necessity of baptism, Catholic masters sought to educate their bondspersons in the rudiments of the faith. According to Gillard, though in some localities it was illegal to teach enslaved persons, "Catholics frequently defied the laws

---

35 John LaFarge, S.J., "The Survival of the Catholic Faith in Southern Maryland," *Catholic Historical Review* 21, no. 1 (April 1935): 11.

36 LaFarge, "The Survival of the Catholic Faith in Southern Maryland," 14.

and instructed the slaves regardless of consequences." Gillard, however, admitted that enslaved persons' moral and spiritual development was slowed by "lack of priests and means with which to carry out an extensive missionary program."[37]

In central Kentucky, the clergy who ministered to the enslaved were also frequently enslavers. None apparently saw in this any conflict, nor did their biographers. Joseph Herman Schauinger (1912–1971), in authoring a work on the proto-priest of the United States Father Stephen T. Badin, acknowledged that he owned several persons who assisted him with domestic duties and farm work. His bondspersons credited Badin with their religious upbringing, noting that he had baptized them. As he had done, Badin expected others to do, admonishing Catholic owners who neglected the sacramental reception and religious education of the enslaved.[38] Father William J. Howlett, the biographer of frontier Kentucky missionary Father Charles Nerinckx, emphasized that the priest was active in his slaves' care. Nerinckx planned to establish an asylum for "old age, decrepit and useless slaves" and a religious community of freed African Americans.[39] Neither of these frontier Kentucky clergy, however, was an abolitionist. Badin opposed those who supported freedom for the enslaved, and Nerinckx, while being repelled by slavery, "appreciated the fact that the barrier of racial difference, being a natural one, should always be respected."[40]

As a credit to their excellent religious and moral upbringing, certain enslaved persons were lauded as especially pious. "Uncle Harry," owned by Father Badin, is mentioned in several sources as an exceptional Christian, devoted to prayer and charity—a model to all, whether slave or free.[41] Father LaFarge, too, explained the

---

37 John Gillard, S.S.J., *The Catholic Church and the American Negro* (Baltimore: St. Joseph's Society Press, 1929), 11–13, quotes at 12 and 13.
38 Howlett, *Life of Rev. Charles Nerinckx*, 114–115; Schauinger, *Stephen T. Badin*, 74.
39 Howlett, *Life of Rev. Charles Nerinckx*, 267, 389.
40 Schauinger, *Stephen T. Badin*, 36; Anna Catherine Minogue, *Loretto: Annals of the Century* (New York: America Press, 1912), 96.
41 Schauinger, *Stephen T. Badin*, 73. Most of the sources mentioning Uncle Harry seem to borrow from Martin John Spalding, *Sketches of the Early*

importance of "Negro nurses" in helping form their masters' children in the faith. Those of "more than ordinary piety and sanctity" were especially useful in teaching children to pray, reminding them of the importance of the sacraments, and modeling virtue. Such "chosen souls" were indispensable in passing on the Catholic faith and were "venerated by their white neighbors."[42]

Despite a proslavery apologetic highlighting Catholic ministry to the enslaved, a few historians recognized masters' inattentiveness to the moral and spiritual lives of bondspeople. This regret closely accompanied a general lament focused on slavery's inefficiencies and inherent difficulties.

Lamentations: Untangling Slavery from Catholic Life

Most, but not all, Catholic historians of the first half of the twentieth century failed to criticize slavery, concentrating on its potential spiritual benefits, but some writers insisted that these effects were largely theoretical—that slavery, as it was practiced in the United States (even by Catholics slaveholders), was so oppressive it canceled out any good that might have come from it. Father John Gillard, S.S.J., in attempting to balance the Church's theological tradition and U.S. Catholics' slaveholding, wrote, "As a proposition considered *in se*, when freed from all abuses, slavery is not intrinsically opposed to the natural or divine law. This is theoretical, however, since slavery rarely existed without abuses."[43] He acknowledged that "in many respects" Catholic slaveholders were no different from other enslavers and held "no loftier motives."[44] Peter Guilday, too, broached the topic of slaveholding as a moral failing, citing an 1813 letter that called priests' ownership of enslaved persons "no trifling occasion for scandal" and indicating that a "great portion

---

Missions of Kentucky; From their Commencement in 1787, to the Jubilee of 1826–7 (Louisville: B. J. Webb, 1844), 116–117. Spalding's text is unusual for highlighting—long before emancipation—an example of sanctity among the enslaved.

    42   LaFarge, "The Survival of the Catholic Faith in Southern Maryland," 15.

    43   Gillard, *The Catholic Church and the American Negro*, 76–77.

    44   Gillard, *Colored Catholics in the United States*, 43–44.

Father John T. Gillard, S.S.J. (Archives of the Oblate Sisters of Providence).

of the Catholics" lamented the ownership of enslaved people by bishops "in their corporate capacity" because it was "injurious to the character of their religion."[45]

Father Thomas Hughes explained that "for priests the marriage question and the preservation of the family introduced elements of anxiety and disturbance."[46] Similarly, Father John LaFarge wrote of the "tragically inconsistent position" of clergy enslaving people, which could include "painful and inhuman aspects" such as the separation of families and the sale of enslaved persons to masters who proved "faithless." Although LaFarge did not directly cite the Jesuits' tragic sale of 272 enslaved persons in 1838, he was undoubtedly aware of that blot on his order's history.[47]

---

45 Father John Ryan, O.P., to Archbishop John Carroll, April 12, 1813, in Peter Guilday, *The Life and Times of John Carroll, Archbishop of Baltimore (1735–1815)* (Westminster, MD: Newman Press, 1954), 684.
46 Hughes, *History of the Society of Jesus in North America*, II: 560.
47 LaFarge, "The Survival of the Catholic Faith in Southern Maryland," 18–19.

Madeleine Hooke Rice perhaps came closest to challenging the overall morality of the Catholic position on slavery when she asked, "In falling back upon the traditional policy of their church, were not Catholic leaders evading what was actually a moral issue, made so by the conflict between the inequities of the slave system and the rights of the slave as a human being?" She posed the question, though without attempting an answer.[48]

By the mid-twentieth century, an increasing number of U.S. Catholic historians lamented slavery, but more often for its practical difficulties than for its abuses. Most historians described slavery as an economic reality, invoking property rights and the cost of labor. The Jesuit historian Gilbert J. Garraghan (1871–1942) explained that by the 1830s and '40s members of his order were increasingly perplexed by their ownership of enslaved persons, citing the political agitation of the period and the fanaticism of abolitionists as reasons for transitioning to a free labor force to work their Missouri properties. But extricating themselves from slavery was not easy, absent emancipating their bondspeople (which apparently was not considered). Deciding when and where and to whom to sell became a vexing issue for Jesuit superiors, according to Garraghan. With the distance of a century from these discussions, Garraghan still refrained from considering its moral context.[49]

Those who questioned Catholic slaveholding emphasized that human bondage lacked economic benefit. Historians claimed that the cost of upkeep of enslaved persons, especially those of advanced years, rendered the institution unprofitable. As Garraghan maintained, slavery "as an economic institution failed to justify itself."[50] Historians frequently cited rebellious or lazy slaves, arguing that some took advantage of their kindly Catholic masters. Historians explained that Catholic slaveholders gradually abandoned slavery even before it became illegal. Especially in the Upper South and Mid-Atlantic regions, slavery was dying a

---

48   Rice, *American Catholic Opinion in the Slavery Controversy*, 158.
49   Gilbert J. Garraghan, S.J., *The Jesuits of the Middle United States* (Chicago: Loyola University Press, 1938), I: 617.
50   Garraghan, *The Jesuits of the Middle United States*, I: 617.

slow death, a casualty of economic realities more than moral conversion.[51]

The Reality of Slavery, 1960-2022

A heightened interest in slavery's history accompanied the civil rights and Black Power movements as historians became aware firsthand of the living legacy of hereditary, race-based slavery. As studies of slavery by secular historians proliferated, most of which focused on the slave experience, Catholic scholars followed by authoring specialized works on the role of religion in slavery and the spiritual lives of bondspersons. These studies, for the first time, move away from idealizing Catholic slaveholding and offer significant concern for its immorality and essential cruelty.

Humanity and Inhumanity

Father Cyprian Davis, O.S.B. (1930–2015), in his pathbreaking *History of Black Catholics in the United States*, lamented the Church's slaveholding and the lack of a coherent moral stance opposing it. Particularly troubling was the number of bishops, priests, and religious whose enslavement of others did not appear to trouble their consciences. As Father Davis wrote, ownership of enslaved persons by people of faith—and especially the forced break-up of enslaved families—evidenced not only slavery's inherent harshness but the "moral quicksand of expediency and inhumanity that sooner or later trapped everyone who participated in the ownership and buying and selling of human beings."[52]

The event that became symbolic of Catholic slavery's inhumanity was the Jesuits' sale of 272 enslaved persons "down river" to offset Georgetown University's debt. Robert Emmett Curran's work on the Maryland Jesuits' slaveholding, first published in 1983 and twice republished, contextualizes the decision and its

---

51 Contemporary historians have pushed back against this argument, however, offering evidence that slavery was never as profitable as on the eve of the Civil War.

52 Cyprian Davis, O.S.B., *The History of Black Catholics in the United States* (New York: Crossroad, 1990), 37.

Father Cyprian Davis, O.S.B. (St. Meinrad Archabbey Archives).

impact.[53] Curran explained that the decision evoked immediate outrage from certain Jesuits, mainly European-born and older American members. Though it was not unusual for an enslaved person to be sold, the Jesuits ordinarily did so to keep families from being separated or, more rarely, punish a bondsperson for disobedience. Curran described the reality of the mass sale: as the enslaved were informed of their fate, they resisted, having to be dragged to the boats that were to take them to Louisiana. Others

---

53   R. Emmett Curran, "'Splendid Poverty': Jesuit Slaveholding in Maryland, 1805–1838," in *Catholics in the Old South: Essays on Church and Culture*, ed. Randall M. Miller and Jon L. Wakelyn (Macon, GA: Mercer University Press, 1983), 125–146. The work was republished in Robert Emmett Curran, *Shaping American Catholicism: Maryland and New York, 1805–1915* (Washington, DC: Catholic University of America Press, 2012), 30–51, and Adam Rothman and Elsa Barraza Mendoza, eds., *Facing Georgetown's History: A Reader on Slavery, Memory, and Reconciliation* (Washington, DC: Georgetown University Press, 2021), 34–54. For a note on the essay's origination, see Curran, *Shaping American Catholicism*, 30.

escaped to the woods surrounding the plantations.[54] Though the Jesuits desired to exit from slaveholding, the sale *en masse* was not the only option. Curran pointed out that the Jesuits had allowed enslaved persons to work certain plots of land and keep the earnings, by which some eventually purchased their freedom. Others were granted "deferred emancipation" later in life, though such decisions were motivated more by practical considerations than moral ones.[55]

Building off of Curran's work, Father Thomas Murphy, S.J., authored an authoritative history of Maryland Jesuits' slaveholding. Murphy argued that the Jesuit relations to enslaved persons must be seen within the wider national and religious context. Viewing Jesuit slaveholding as a "contradiction," he wrote that Jesuits struggled with the tension between competing desires to defend slavery, on one hand, and to withdraw from ownership of enslaved persons, on the other. But even those Jesuits who questioned slaveholding and showed concern for bondspersons' well-being exhibited a mentality of white supremacy. This could lead to abuses, which though common, were viewed (even at the time) as morally problematic. As Murphy concluded, the Jesuits exhibited "a public emphasis on kind governance that masked a private harshness."[56]

Elsa Barraza Mendoza's essay "Catholic Slave Ownership and the Development of Georgetown University's Slave Hiring System" offers a stronger critique. In explaining higher education's reliance on enslaved laborers, she wrote, "Georgetown's entanglement with slaveholding can be examined as a microcosm of the rampant exploitation that spread across the nation." She related a contentious relationship between Maryland Jesuits and the enslaved, evidenced by at least twenty persons suing for their freedom on the grounds of illegal bondage.[57]

---

54   Curran, "'Splendid Poverty,'" 141–143.
55   Curran, "'Splendid Poverty,'" 131–134.
56   Murphy, *Jesuit Slaveholding in Maryland*, 93, 216–218.
57   Elsa Barraza Mendoza, "Catholic Slave Ownership and the Development of Georgetown University's Slave Hiring System, 1792–1862," in *Facing Georgetown's History: A Reader on Slavery, Memory, and Reconciliation*, ed. Adam Rothman and Elsa Barraza Mendoza (Washington, DC: Georgetown University Press, 2021), 55–77, quote at 57.

Rome and America: Transatlantic Contexts

Scholarship that emerged by the 1970s increasingly explored the transatlantic context of U.S. slavery and, in the case of Catholicism's relationship to slavery, the perspective of Rome (the Holy See). As slavery existed in many areas of the world, the impact of the Catholic Church's approach to the question was not limited to the United States. Consequently, Rome offered few statements about slavery in the antebellum era, aside from Pope Gregory XVI's 1839 apostolic letter *In Supremo Apostolatus*, which forbade Catholic participation in the slave trade. Rome weighed in on some regional disputes regarding slavery (as in the cases of proslavery Southern bishops Auguste Martin and Augustin Verot) but only with hesitation. The Italian historian Maria Genoino Caravaglios was among the first to study this dynamic. Using Roman archival sources, she traced the Church's response to slavery. At a time when American historians had little access to foreign sources, Caravaglios liberally excerpted or reproduced entire documents important to her study.[58]

Placing the American and Roman responses in comparative perspective, Robert Emmett Curran argued that American slavery was no higher a priority for Rome than it was for the American Church. When Rome did choose to intervene, it was only the occasional response to "*ad hoc* requests." Overall, "Rome respected the wisdom of the local Church that survival dictated silence and conformity."[59] More recently, Suzanne Krebsbach argued that Bishop John England of Charleston, South Carolina,

---

58 Maria Genoino Caravaglios, *The American Catholic Church and the Negro Problem in the XVIII–XIX Centuries*, ed. Ernest L. Unterkoefler (Charleston, SC: 1974). Caravaglios utilized Roman archival sources throughout her work and reproduced select copies in an appendix (221–351).

59 Robert Emmett Curran, "Rome, the American Church, and Slavery," in *Shaping American Catholicism: Maryland and New York, 1805–1915* (Washington, DC: Catholic University of America Press, 2012), 92–110, especially 103, 110. On Rome's response to Bishop Martin's pastoral letter, see Maria Caravaglios, "A Roman Critique of the Pro-Slavery Views of Bishop Martin of Natchitoches, Louisiana," *Records of the American Catholic Historical Society of Philadelphia* 83, no. 2 (June 1972): 67–81.

played an essential role in muting Rome's response to slavery, primarily through the prevention of a condemnation by Propaganda Fide, the Roman congregation that oversaw the Church in the United States. For its part, Propaganda Fide was more concerned with plans for evangelizing Blacks than offering a moral denunciation of slavery.[60]

In his influential work *The Civil War as a Theological Crisis*, Mark Noll dedicated a chapter to the Catholic response to slavery and the war. Maintaining that American Catholic opinion "was neither particularly distinctive nor rich," he turned to European influences, both liberal and conservative. Among liberal voices, he cited the French liberal tradition that both criticized slavery's incompatibility with Scripture and defended the Catholic record on slavery. Among the conservative voices was the German Catholic newspaper *Historisch-politische Blätter*, whose editor considered slavery "a pretext or smokescreen hiding the real issues" of America's lust for money and power—seen in the largely non-Catholic, Puritanical North.[61] These voices provide an additional perspective on the Church's approach to slavery, offering at times confirmation and at other times challenge to American Catholic viewpoints.

Identifying and Numbering

As historians expanded their geographic horizons, they also extended their methods. The turn to social history in the latter twentieth century opened new vistas for historians, who sought to emphasize the identities of enslaved persons—numbering, identifying, and exploring their perspectives, agency, and social networks. By mining census lists, sacramental records, and other primary sources, the extent of Catholic-owned slavery became much more evident. The recent availability of digitized documents and databases has enhanced the possibility of large-scale

---

60 Suzanne Krebsbach, "Rome's Response to Slavery in the United States," *Catholic Historical Review* 105, no. 2 (Spring 2019): 327–344.

61 Mark A. Noll, *The Civil War as a Theological Crisis* (Chapel Hill: University of North Carolina Press, 2006), 125–155, especially 132–155, quotes at 127 and 141.

studies, such as a recent effort to compare and analyze the sacramental record data of enslaved communities.[62]

Efforts to identify and accurately number Catholic-owned bondspersons became more successful as archives were better organized and accessibility increased. A few enslaved persons were named in earlier histories (Father Nerinckx's Tom, Father Badin's Uncle Harry, and the Missouri Jesuits' Tom, Polly, Moises, Nancy, Isaac, and Succy), but the vast majority were anonymous. Recent works have reproduced or cited archival documents with dozens of additional identities.[63]

In the 1980s, Father Cyprian Davis surveyed surviving sacramental records for enslaved persons and free persons of color, observing that a "careful examination of the registers for Black Catholics can often reveal names, family relationships, age, and origin."[64] In inspecting the records of St. Augustine, Florida; Natchitoches, Louisiana; Mobile, Alabama; Savannah, Georgia; and Baltimore, Maryland, he offered preliminary insights into the size of the Black population, racial intersectionality, and religious practice.[65]

Father Stafford Poole, C.M. (1930–2020) and Douglas Slawson carefully studied enslaved persons owned by the Congregation of the Mission (Vincentians). Their research enabled the reconstruction of families whose members served as "seminary slaves" at St. Mary's Seminary in Perry County, Missouri. The researchers tracked the intermarriage and child-bearing of enslaved persons, primarily using sacramental records. Though the number of persons owned or rented by the Vincentians is unknown—and appeared to fluctuate significantly—more than thirty bondspeople were identified.[66]

---

62 As an example, see Kelly L. Schmidt, "Enslaved Faith Communities in the Jesuits' Missouri Mission," *U.S. Catholic Historian* 37, no. 2 (Spring 2019): 49–81.

63 For example, Rothman and Mendoza, *Facing Georgetown's History*, 111–149.

64 Davis, *The History of Black Catholics in the United States*, 67.

65 Davis, *The History of Black Catholics in the United States*, 67–89.

66 Stafford Poole, C.M., and Douglas J. Slawson, *Church and Slave in Perry County, Missouri, 1818–1865* (Lewiston, NY: Edwin Mellen Press, 1986), 211–222.

Emily Clark, in her study of the New Orleans Ursulines, explored the relationships among those the nuns enslaved.[67] Utilizing hundreds of sacramental, civil, and community records, she found that the Ursulines strenuously promoted marriage and the nuclear family among their bondspeople—a rarity, even for Catholic religious. The result was a slave community composed of family groupings. In the case of two families, their members served as Ursuline bondspeople across five generations.[68] More so than other enslaved persons, the Ursuline bondspeople consequently enjoyed stability through bonds of blood and affection and contested the assertion that "families sacralized by the church were an unnecessary or unattainable ideal for the unfree."[69]

More recently, a thorough study of the enslaved persons owned by the Visitation Sisters in Georgetown/Washington, D.C., identified 107 persons—either by name or description.[70] An investigation of Sulpician-owned bondspersons in Maryland was less successful in determining identities but offered new information based on recently-uncovered records.[71] Georgetown University's extensive mining of archival sources has resulted in perhaps the most comprehensive picture of regional Catholic slaveholding, with more than 400 primary source documents digitized and available to scholars and the public.[72]

Enslaved Persons' Religious Experience

As history "from below" gained prominence, historians emphasized enslaved perspectives, including bondspeople's reli-

---

[67] Emily Clark, *Masterless Mistresses: The New Orleans Ursulines and the Development of a New World Society, 1727–1834* (Williamsburg, VA: Omohundro Institute of Early American History and Culture, 2007).
[68] Clark, *Masterless Mistresses*, 176, 178–179.
[69] Clark, *Masterless Mistresses*, 183–184, quote at 194.
[70] Susan Nalezyty, "The History of Enslaved People at Georgetown Visitation," *U.S. Catholic Historian* 37, no. 2 (Spring 2019): 23–48.
[71] Thomas R. Ulshafer, P.S.S., "Slavery and the Early Sulpician Community in Maryland," *U.S. Catholic Historian* 37, no. 2 (Spring 2019): 1–21.
[72] See Georgetown University, "The Georgetown Slavery Archive," https://slaveryarchive.georgetown.edu/. The archive continues to expand as documentation is found.

gious participation. While other historians had focused on Catholic ministry to the enslaved, studies from the 1980s and beyond highlight enslaved persons' religious experience and spiritual agency, often utilizing new sources and methods.[73]

Father Cyprian Davis's survey of sacramental records determined that while many enslaved persons were baptized, a much smaller number married in the Church. Since marriage required the master's permission and theoretically prevented the family unit from being broken apart by the sale of either spouse, fewer enslaved persons wed. Comparatively, a similarly small number were afforded burial from a church, and even fewer bondspersons received last rites.[74] Still, despite gaps in records, he noted signs of a lively faith for enslaved Catholics, including participation in religious societies that joined them together for prayer, education, and fraternity.[75]

Poole and Slawson's fine-grained analysis of slaveholding in Perry County, Missouri, focusing on Vincentian-held persons, found that the religious community utilized a dozen or more enslaved laborers or domestics at a time. The authors brought to light the religious experience and family life of enslaved Catholics, drawing from sacramental records and scant manuscript evidence. They determined that the most significant factor in the religiosity of the enslaved was their masters' faith practice (whether priests or lay Catholics), yet enslaved Catholics could also be found among non-Catholic and religiously-lapsed owners. And enslaved persons could be godparents for other enslaved persons, indicating the role of faith in a network of relationships among Catholic bondspeople. For their part, Catholic masters often attempted to dictate the religious lives of the enslaved, with compulsory Mass attendance and cessation of work on Sundays.[76]

---

73 See Schmidt, "The Pervasive Institution," 18–20.
74 Davis, *The History of Black Catholics in the United States*, 71, 80.
75 Davis, *The History of Black Catholics in the United States*, 86–88.
76 Poole and Slawson, *Church and Slave in Perry County, Missouri*, 59–93, 141–189.

Utilizing digital relationship-mapping tools, a study of the Missouri Jesuits' enslaved persons visually depicted familial and spiritual ties among dozens of individuals in two enslaved subcommunities. Kelly Schmidt, former research coordinator for the Jesuits' Slavery, History, Memory, and Reconciliation Project, utilized sacramental records to map how enslaved persons practiced their faith. She determined that certain enslaved persons were viewed as exemplary Christians and were chosen repeatedly as baptismal sponsors or marriage witnesses. As Schmidt concluded, "Few records survive to speak of the interior lives of the enslaved, but careful examination of surviving sacramental, sodality, and other records reveals that faith was part of a bondsperson's quest for an identity that distinguished him from mere chattel."[77]

In writing about enslaved Catholics in the nation's capital, Mary Beth Corrigan explained that Catholicism appealed to some enslaved persons, especially its sacramental system and devotion to the saints. Reception of the sacraments provided "spiritual recognition" of family ties between spouses and spouses and children, relationships that enslavement threatened.[78] Baptism, in particular, provided an opportunity to cement ties—to the Church and one another. By choosing baptismal sponsors, enslaved persons enacted personal and family bonds "in a setting acceptable to the white community." It is common to presume that the religious identities of slaves and masters were synonymous, but enslaved persons could show agency through religious choice. She argued that the religious influence of parents or grandparents became "far more important . . . than the outlook of slave owners or clergy. Many slaves embraced Catholicism even though their owners did not."[79]

Beatriz Betancourt Hardy, comparing Anglican and Catholic slaveholding in Maryland, contended that Catholic masters'

---

77 Schmidt, "Enslaved Faith Communities in the Jesuits' Missouri Mission," 49–81, quote at 81.
78 Mary Beth Corrigan, "Making the Most of an Opportunity: Slaves and the Catholic Church in Early Washington," *Washington History* 12, no. 1 (Spring-Summer 2000): 90–101, quote at 92.
79 Corrigan, "Making the Most of an Opportunity," quotes at 100 and 98.

enslaved persons were more likely to be instructed in the faith, receive baptism, and have their marriages recognized. While this was due partly to Catholic owners' sense of religious obligation to the enslaved, aspects of Catholicism (including the liturgical calendar, saints' relics, and prayers to saints) resembled West African traditions and rendered the Catholic faith more appealing.[80]

Recent archeological work has attempted to confirm the place of devotion in the lives of the enslaved. Anthropologist Laura Masur studied the rosaries, crosses, statues, and religious medals unearthed from the sites of Jesuit plantations in Maryland. Though it can be difficult to determine whether objects belonged to enslaved persons, artifacts begin to tell a story of how Black spirituality was shaped during the age of slavery. Masur concluded that "we cannot know with certainty what these objects meant to individuals," but they evidence a desire to "commune with the supernatural presences of gods, saints, and angels" in ways that were likely distinctive from their masters and other Euro-American Catholics.[81]

Memory and Reconciliation

Numerous dioceses, religious orders, and Catholic universities have sought to uncover the truth of their involvement with slavery.[82] This has resulted not only in historical explorations but also in reconciliation efforts through public apologies, prayer services, and even financial reparations. In 1912, the Sisters of Charity of Nazareth, based in central Kentucky, included formerly enslaved persons and their descendants in their centennial celebrations. It would be nearly a century before other religious followed. A nearby community, the Sisters of Loretto, dedicated a monument in 2000 to remember the enslaved persons who had

---

80   Beatriz Betancourt Hardy, "'The Papists . . . have shewn a laudable Care and Concern': Catholicism, Anglicanism, and Slave Religion in Colonial Maryland," *Maryland Historical Magazine* 98, no. 1 (Spring 2003): 4–33.

81   Laura E. Masur, "A Spiritual Inheritance: Black Catholics in Southern Maryland," in *Engaging Sources: The Tradition and Future of Collecting History in the Society of Jesus*, ed. Cristiano Casalini, Emanuele Colombo, and Seth Meehan (Boston: Institute of Jesuit Sources, 2021), 2, 23.

82   See Schmidt, "The Pervasive Institution," 20–21.

Formerly enslaved persons and their families return to the motherhouse of the Sisters of Charity of Nazareth, Kentucky, to mark the community's centennial in 1912 (Sisters of Charity of Nazareth Archival Center).

labored on the community's behalf.[83] In 2012, the Sisters of Charity of Nazareth, the Sisters of Loretto, and the Dominicans of St. Catherine (all headquartered in Kentucky) held a reconciliation service, asking for pardon for their roles in enslavement. Consequently, the narrative of these communities' histories has been enlarged to embrace the reality of slaveholding.[84]

Georgetown University, among the first Catholic educational institutions to apologize for its role in slavery, acknowledged in 2017 the sale of 272 enslaved persons to fund the college. In grappling with this reality, the university took steps to rename buildings and fund scholarships for the descendants of those the university enslaved.[85] The U.S. Jesuit Conference fol-

---

83 For the role of slavery in the community and its impact on the historical narrative, see Joan Campbell, S.L, *Loretto: An Early American Congregation in the Antebellum South* (St. Louis: Bluebird Book Press, 2015).

84 See Loretto Community, "We Repent," https://www.lorettocommunity.org/we-repent/.

85 Georgetown University, "Georgetown Reflects on Slavery, Memory, and Reconciliation," https://www.georgetown.edu/slavery/; Descendants

lowed with its Slavery, History, Memory, and Reconciliation Project, recognizing the vast entanglement of slavery with Jesuits and Jesuit ministries and the need for "truth-telling, reconciliation, and healing."[86]

As part of these efforts, several other Jesuit schools examined their slavery ties. Cleveland's John Carroll University explored its namesake's relationship to slavery, concluding in 2018 that Carroll had supervised and owned enslaved persons but had supported their gradual emancipation. The working group stopped short of recommending a name change for the school but supported a fuller exploration of Carroll and slaveholding.[87] At Xavier University in Cincinnati, a 2017 working group assessed the institution's slavery connections, including the use of slavery's profits to fund Southern students' tuition. Further dialogue resulted in the renaming of Fenwick Place, which had honored the first bishop of Cincinnati and the school's founder, who had been a slaveholder in Maryland and Kentucky.[88]

Dioceses have also begun to address their histories. The Archdiocese of St. Louis, Missouri, through the initiative "Forgive Us Our Trespasses," aims to acknowledge its slaveholding past and work for a future without racism.[89] In the Archdiocese of Baltimore, a working group contributed to the pastoral letter "The Journey to Racial Justice," which acknowledges significant

---

Truth and Reconciliation Foundation, https://www.descendants.org/; Rothman and Mendoza, *Facing Georgetown's History*.

86   Jesuit Conference of Canada and the U.S., "Slavery, History, Memory, and Reconciliation Project," https://www.jesuits.org/our-work/shmr/.

87   John Carroll University, "Final Report: Working Group: Slavery—Legacy and Reconciliation, Spring 2018," http://webmedia.jcu.edu/mission/files/2018/08/WGSLR-Final-Report-Spring-2018.pdf.

88   C. Walker Gollar, "What We Know About Xavier's Historical Connections to Slavery," August 20, 2020, https://libguides.xavier.edu/Fenwick; Xavier University, "Justice Hall," https://www.xavier.edu/mission-identity/xaviers-mission/buildings-statues-and-beauty/justice-hall. Also, Gollar, "Edward Fenwick: First Bishop of Cincinnati and Slaveholder."

89   Jennifer Brinker, "Archdiocese's research into history with slavery reveals three bishops, priests as slaveowners," *St. Louis Review*, June 17, 2021, https://www.archstl.org/archdioceses-research-into-history-with-slavery-reveals-three-bishops-priests-as-slaveowners-6587.

In 2012, the Sisters of Charity of Nazareth, Kentucky, erected a monument to the enslaved persons buried on the community's property (Sisters of Charity of Nazareth Archival Center).

historical ties to slavery.[90] As additional dioceses, religious communities, and institutions consider their pasts, such efforts will continue to impact remembrance, dialogue about race and racism, and historiography.

Conclusion: Historiography's Moral Development

The historiographical shifts outlined here have impacted contemporary historians who study the American Church.

---

90 Archdiocese of Baltimore, "Archbishop Releases Major Pastoral Document Encouraging Catholics to Bridge Racial Divides in Today's Society; Acknowledges Catholic Church's Historical Role in Slavery," January 22, 2019, https://www.archbalt.org/press-release-01-22-2019/; Archdiocese of Baltimore, "The Journey to Racial Justice," January 21, 2019, https://www.archbalt.org/racismpastoral19/.

Enslaved persons are increasingly visible in historical literature, including specialized works and the broader narrative of American Catholic history. And historians, more than ever, seek to engage with slavery's moral and theological dimensions—and what slavery's legacy might demand today.

Numerous contemporary studies engage Catholicism and slavery as a moral failing. Joseph Capizzi, in his 2004 article "For What Shall We Repent?," argues that U.S. Catholics, including members of the hierarchy, followed "what they believed to be church teaching" on slavery, citing the mixed reception of Pope Gregory XVI's 1839 condemnation of the slave trade. Even if Catholics operated out of the social, moral, and theological milieu of their age, he asserts that "we have grounds to question their actions" since their theological understanding "should have led them to greater criticism." He explains that attempts to mitigate slavery's abuses were rarely successful, as those who believed slavery could be practiced in a "moral" fashion usually did not follow their own standards. In the end, Catholic leaders "back[ed] themselves into an unnecessary complacency with a corrupt institution."[91]

John McGreevy's *Catholicism and American Freedom* shares Capizzi's concern for the morality of the practice. McGreevy offers a richly contextualized analysis of Catholicism and slavery, citing domestic and international influences while highlighting its moral dimensions. He balances an acknowledgment of Catholics' racist beliefs with the assertion that most conceived of slavery "as a legitimate, if tragic institution." As he explains, Catholics dismissed the idea that the enslaved were "biologically inferior"; they "frequently expressed doubts about the morality of slavery as it existed"; and they "almost never defended slavery as an unqualified good." But it was accepted nonetheless. By placing the question within the broader question of American freedom, McGreevy gives prominence to slavery's religious, moral,

---

91 Joseph E. Capizzi, "For What Shall We Repent? Reflections on the American Bishops, Their Teaching, and Slavery in the United States, 1839–1861," *Theological Studies* 65, no. 4 (December 2004): 767–791, especially 788–791.

social, and political aspects while ultimately casting it as a "theological problem."[92]

Christopher Shannon's *American Pilgrimage: A Historical Journey through Catholic Life in a New World* reminds his readers of Catholics' historical failure to object to slavery and the intersection of slavery with American Catholic life from the colonial period forward. Indeed, he writes, the "genteel, elite Catholic ideal flourished on an economic base that no Catholic today would find tolerable—namely, slavery."[93] Maura Jane Farrelly's essay "American Slavery, American Freedom, American Catholicism" argues for understanding the intellectual roots of the Church's failure to oppose slavery. She explains that U.S. Catholicism was born in a slaveholding context, which shaped and reinforced understandings of obligation, hierarchy, and mutual dependence and worked against opposing the chattel system.[94]

The moral problem of slavery, which historians so often failed to recognize, is now viewed as inextricable from its racist underpinnings. Contemporary historians acknowledge the cruelty of slavery and that owners' "kindly treatment" and plans for "deferred emancipation" were not morally tenable. The historiography of Catholic slaveholding has undergone a moral revolution, but its own past remains. To contend with the Church's slaveholding is to acknowledge that enslavement was viewed—sometimes long after its legal demise—as morally permissible and not evil or sinful. In operating from that flawed framework, historians were often guilty of the same racial prejudices that upheld antebellum Catholics' participation in the ownership of other human beings.

---

92 John T. McGreevy, *Catholicism and American Freedom: A History* (New York: W.W. Norton, 2003), 49–67, quotes at 52–56. See also John T. McGreevy, "Catholicism and Abolition: A Historical (and Theological) Problem," in *Figures in the Carpet: Finding the Human Person in the American Past*, ed. Wilfred M. McClay (Grand Rapids, MI: Eerdmans, 2007), 405–427, especially 424–427 on slavery as a "theological problem."

93 Christopher Shannon, *American Pilgrimage: A Historical Journey Through Catholic Life in a New World* (Greenwood Village, CO: Augustine Institute, 2022), 174, 251–252, 256, quote at 174.

94 Maura Jane Farrelly, "American Slavery, American Freedom, American Catholicism," *Early American Studies* 10, no. 1 (Winter 2012): 69–100.

Selected Bibliography

Agee, Gary B. *A Cry for Justice: Daniel Rudd and His Life in Black Catholicism, Journalism, and Activism, 1854–1933.* Fayetteville: University of Arkansas Press, 2017.

Allen, Cuthbert E. "The Slavery Question in Catholic Newspapers, 1850–1865." *Historical Records and Studies of the U.S. Catholic Historical Society* 26 (1936): 99–169.

Beckett, Edward F., S.J. "Listening to Our History: Inculturation and Jesuit Slaveholding." *Studies in the Spirituality of Jesuits* 28, no. 5 (November 1996).

Bell, Caryn Cossé. *Revolution, Romanticism, and the Afro-Creole Protest Tradition in Louisiana, 1718–1868.* Baton Rouge: Louisiana State University Press, 1997.

Blied, Benjamin J. *Catholics and the Civil War.* Milwaukee: St. Francis Seminary Press, 1945.

Brett, Stephen F. *Slavery and the Catholic Tradition: Rights in the Balance.* New York: Lang, 1994.

Brokhage, Joseph D. *Francis Patrick Kenrick's Opinion on Slavery.* Washington, DC: Catholic University of America Press, 1955.

Capizzi, Joseph E. "For What Shall We Repent? Reflections on the American Bishops, Their Teaching, and Slavery in the United States, 1839–1861." *Theological Studies* 65, no. 4 (December 2004): 767–791.

Caravaglios, Maria. *The American Catholic Church and the Negro Problem in the XVIII–XIX Centuries.* Charleston, SC: Caravaglios, 1974.

———. "A Roman Critique of the Pro-Slavery Views of Bishop Martin of Natchitoches, Louisiana." *Records of the American Catholic Historical Society of Philadelphia* 83 (1972): 67–81.

Carey, Patrick W. "Political Atheism: *Dred Scott*, Roger Brooke Taney, and Orestes A. Brownson." *Catholic Historical Review* 88, no. 2 (2002): 207–229.

Charles, Mark, and Soon-Chan Rah. *Unsettling Truths: The Ongoing, Dehumanizing Legacy of the Doctrine of Discovery.* Downers Grove, IL: InterVarsity Press, 2019.

Clark, Emily. *Masterless Mistresses: The New Orleans Ursulines and the Development of a New World Society, 1727–1834*. Williamsburg, VA: Omohundro Institute of Early American History and Culture, 2007.

Connor, Charles P. "The Northern Catholic Position on Slavery and the Civil War: Archbishop Hughes as a Test Case." *Records of the American Catholic Historical Society of Philadelphia* 96 (1986): 37–48.

Corrigan, Mary Beth. "Making the Most of an Opportunity: Slaves and the Catholic Church in Early Washington." *Washington History* 12, no. 1 (Spring-Summer 2000): 90–101.

Creason, Carl C. "United, Yet Divided: An Analysis of Bishops Martin John Spalding and John Baptist Purcell during the Civil War Era." *American Catholic Studies* 124, no. 2 (Spring 2013): 49–69.

Critchley-Menor, William, S.J. "Interview: How the Jesuits Are Working to Confront Their History of Slavery." *America*, February 26, 2021.

Curran, Robert Emmett. *American Catholics and the Quest for Equality in the Civil War Era*. Baton Rouge: Louisiana State University Press, 2023.

———, ed. *For Church and Confederacy: The Lynches of South Carolina*. Columbia: University of South Carolina Press, 2019.

———. "Rome, the American Church, and Slavery." In *Shaping American Catholicism: Maryland and New York, 1805–1915*, 92–110. Washington, DC: Catholic University of America Press, 2012.

Davis, Cyprian, O.S.B. *The History of Black Catholics in the United States*. New York: Crossroad, 1990.

Davis, Cyprian, O.S.B., and Jamie Phelps, O.P., eds. *"Stamped with the Image of God": African Americans as God's Image in Black*. American Catholic Identities: A Documentary History. Maryknoll, NY: Orbis, 2003.

Dewulf, Jeroen. *Afro-Atlantic Catholics: America's First Black Christians*. Notre Dame, IN: University of Notre Dame Press, 2022.

Din, Gilbert C. *Spaniards, Planters, and Slaves: The Spanish Regulation of Slavery in Louisiana, 1763–1803*. College Station: Texas A&M University Press, 1999.

Endres, David J., ed. *Black Catholic Studies Reader: History and Theology*. Washington, DC: Catholic University of America Press, 2021.

———. "'Three Cheers for the Union': Catholic Chaplains and Irish Loyalty during the American Civil War." *Catholic Historical Review* 108, no. 1 (Winter 2022): 92–117.

Farrelly, Maura Jane. "American Slavery, American Freedom, American Catholicism." *Early American Studies* 10, no. 1 (Winter 2012): 69–100.

Finn, Peter C. "The Slaves of the Jesuits in Maryland." Master's thesis, Georgetown University, 1974.

Gannon, Michael V. *Rebel Bishop: The Life and Era of Augustin Verot.* Milwaukee: Bruce, 1964.

Giles, Paul. "Catholic Ideology and American Slave Narratives." *U.S. Catholic Historian* 15, no. 2 (Spring 1997): 55–66.

Gollar, C. Walker. "The Controversial and Contradictory Anti-Slavery of Father John Thayer (1785–1815)." *Records of the American Catholic Historical Society of Philadelphia* 109, nos. 3–4 (Fall-Winter 1998): 113–146.

———. "Edward Fenwick: First Bishop of Cincinnati and Slaveholder." *U.S. Catholic Historian* 38, no. 1 (Winter 2020): 145–162.

———. "Father John Thayer: Catholic Antislavery Voice in the Kentucky Wilderness." *Register of the Kentucky Historical Society* 101, no. 3 (Summer 2003): 275–296.

———. "Jesuit Education and Slavery in Kentucky, 1832–1868." *Register of the Kentucky Historical Society* 108, no. 3 (Summer 2010): 213–249.

———. "The Role of Father Badin's Slaves in Frontier Kentucky." *American Catholic Studies* 115, no. 1 (Spring 2004): 1–24.

———. "The Role of Midwestern Christian Higher Education in the Abolition of Slavery." *The Cresset: A Review of Literature, the Arts, and Public Affairs* 70, no. 4 (April 2007): 22–33.

———. "Saint Louis University Slaves." *Missouri Historical Review* 105, no. 3 (April 2011): 125–140.

Grimes, Katie Walker. *Fugitive Saints: Catholicism and the Politics of Slavery.* Minneapolis: Fortress Press, 2017.

Hardy, Beatriz Betancourt. "'The Papists . . . have shewn a laudable Care and Concern': Catholicism, Anglicanism, and Slave Religion in Colonial Maryland." *Maryland Historical Magazine* 98, no. 1 (Spring 2003): 4–33.

Hayes, Diana. "Reflections on Slavery." In *Change in Official Catholic Moral Teachings,* No. 13, edited by Charles E. Curran, 65–75. New York: Paulist Press, 2003.

Heinlein, Michael R. *Black Catholics on the Road to Sainthood*. Huntington, IN: Our Sunday Visitor, 2021.

Heisser, David C. R. "Bishop Lynch's Civil War Pamphlet on Slavery." *Catholic Historical Review* 84 (1998): 681–696.

———. "Bishop Lynch's People: Slaveholding by a South Carolina Prelate." *South Carolina Historical Magazine* 102, no. 3 (July 2001): 238–262.

Heisser, David C. R., and Stephen J. White, Sr. *Patrick N. Lynch, 1817–1882: Third Catholic Bishop of Charleston*. Columbia: University of South Carolina Press, 2015.

Hemesath, Caroline, S.S.F. *From Slave to Priest: The Inspirational Story of Father Augustine Tolton (1854–1897)*. San Francisco: Ignatius Press, 2006.

Hooper, J. Leon, S.J. "Report of the Working Group on Slavery, Memory, and Reconciliation to the President of Georgetown University. Washington, D.C. Summer 2016." *Jesuit Higher Education: A Journal* 6, no. 1, article 17 (May 2017).

Joseph, Satish. "'Long Live the Republic!' Father Edward Purcell and the Slavery Controversy: 1861–1865." *American Catholic Studies* 116, no. 4 (Winter 2005): 25–54.

Kellerman, Christopher J., S.J. *All Oppression Shall Cease: A History of Slavery, Abolitionism, and the Catholic Church*. Maryknoll, NY: Orbis Books, 2022.

Kelly, Joseph. "Charleston's Bishop John England and American Slavery." *New Hibernia Review* 5, no. 4 (Winter 2001): 48–56.

Kraszewski, Gracjan. *Catholic Confederates: Faith and Duty in the Civil War South*. Kent, OH: Kent State University Press, 2020.

———. "Devout Catholics, Devoted Confederates: The Evolution of Southern Catholic Bishops from Reluctant Secessionists to Ardent Confederates." *Catholic Historical Review* 106, no. 1 (Winter 2020): 77–106.

Krebsbach, Suzanne. "Rome's Response to Slavery in the United States." *Catholic Historical Review* 105, no. 2 (Spring 2019): 327–344.

Kurtz, William B. *Excommunicated from the Union: How the Civil War Created a Separate Catholic America*. New York: Fordham University Press, 2016.

———. "'The Perfect Model of a Christian Hero': The Faith, Anti-Slaveryism, and Post-War Legacy of William S. Rosecrans." *U.S. Catholic Historian* 31, no. 1 (Winter 2013): 73–96.

Lalli, Anthony B., and Thomas O'Connor. "Roman Views on the American Civil War." *Catholic Historical Review* 57, no. 1 (April 1971): 21–41.

Masur, Laura E. "Plantation as Mission: American Indians, Enslaved Africans, and Jesuit Missionaries in Maryland." *Journal of Jesuit Studies* 8, no. 3 (April 2021): 385–407.

———. "A Spiritual Inheritance: Black Catholics in Southern Maryland." In *Engaging Sources: The Tradition and Future of Collecting History in the Society of Jesus (Proceedings of the Symposium Held at Boston College, June 11–13, 2019)*, edited by Cristiano Casalini, Emanuele Colombo, and Seth Meehan. Boston: Institute of Jesuit Sources, 2021.

Maxwell, John Francis. *Slavery and the Catholic Church: The History of Catholic Teaching Concerning the Moral Legitimacy of the Institution of Slavery.* Chichester, UK: Barry Rose, 1975.

McGreevy, John T. *American Jesuits and the World: How an Embattled Religious Order Made Modern Catholicism Global.* Princeton, NJ: Princeton University Press, 2016.

———. "Catholicism and Abolition: A Historical (and Theological) Problem." In *Figures in the Carpet: Finding the Human Person in the American Past*, edited by Wilfred M. McClay, 405–427. Grand Rapids, MI: Eerdmans, 2007.

———. *Catholicism and American Freedom: A History.* New York: W.W. Norton, 2003.

Mendoza, Elsa B. "Slaveholding and Jesuit Recordkeeping in the Maryland Province of the Society of Jesus, 1717–1867." In *Engaging Sources: The Tradition and Future of Collecting History in the Society of Jesus (Proceedings of the Symposium Held at Boston College, June 11–13, 2019)*, edited by Cristiano Casalini, Emanuele Colombo, and Seth Meehan. Boston: Institute of Jesuit Sources, 2021.

Miller, Randall M. "Black Catholics in the Slave South: Some Needs and Opportunities for Study." *Records of the American Catholic Historical Society of Philadelphia* 86, nos. 1–4 (March–December 1975): 93–106.

———. "Slaves and Southern Catholicism." In *Master and Slaves in the House of the Lord: Race and Religion in the American South, 1740–1870*, edited by John B. Boles, 127–152. Lexington, KY: University Press of Kentucky, 1988.

Miller, Randall M., and Jon L. Wakelyn, eds. *Catholics in the Old South: Essays on Church and Culture.* Macon, GA: Mercer University Press, 1983.

Miller, Randall M., Harry S. Stout, and Charles Reagan Wilson, eds. *Religion and the American Civil War*. New York: Oxford University Press, 1998.

Millett, Nathaniel. "The Memory of Slavery at Saint Louis University." *American Nineteenth Century History* 16, no. 3 (2015): 329–350.

Mills, Elizabeth Shown and Gary B. Mills. "Missionaries Compromised: Early Evangelization of Slaves and Free People of Color in North Louisiana." In *Cross, Crozier, and Crucible: A Volume Celebrating the Bicentennial of a Catholic Diocese in Louisiana*, edited by Glenn R. Conrad, 30–47. New Orleans: Archdiocese of New Orleans in Cooperation with the Center for Louisiana Studies, 1993.

Morrow, Diane Batts. *Persons of Color and Religious at the Same Time: The Oblate Sisters of Providence, 1828–1860*. Chapel Hill: University of North Carolina Press, 2002.

Murphy, Angela F. *American Slavery, Irish Freedom: Abolition, Immigrant Citizenship, and the Transatlantic Movement for Irish Repeal*. Baton Rouge: Louisiana State University Press, 2010.

———. "'Though Dead He Yet Speaketh': Abolitionist Memories of Daniel O'Connell in the United States." *American Journal of Irish Studies* 10 (2013): 11–38.

Murphy, Thomas, S.J. *Jesuit Slaveholding in Maryland, 1717–1838*. New York: Routledge, 2001.

Nalezyty, Susan. "The History of Enslaved People at Georgetown Visitation." *U.S. Catholic Historian* 37, no. 2 (Spring 2019): 23–48.

Noll, Mark A. *The Civil War as a Theological Crisis*. Chapel Hill: University of North Carolina Press, 2006.

O'Connell, Maureen. *Undoing the Knots: Five Generations of American Catholic Anti-Blackness*. Boston: Beacon Press, 2022.

O'Toole, James M. *Passing for White: Race, Religion and the Healy Family, 1820–1920*. Amherst: University of Massachusetts Press, 2002.

Panzer, Joel S. *The Popes and Slavery*. New York: Alba House, 1996.

Pasquier, Michael. "Creole Catholicism before Black Catholicism: Religion and Slavery in French Colonial Louisiana." *Journal of Africana Religions* 2 (2014): 271–279.

———. "'Though Their Skin Remains Brown, I Hope Their Souls Will Soon Be White': Slavery, French Missionaries, and the Roman Catholic Priesthood in the American South, 1789–1865." *Church History* 77, no. 2 (June 2008): 337–370.

Poole, Stafford, and Douglas J. Slawson. *Church and Slave in Perry County, Missouri, 1818–1865*. Lewiston, NY: Edwin Mellen, 1986.

Quinn, John F. "Expecting the Impossible? Abolitionist Appeals to the Irish in Antebellum America." *New England Quarterly* 82, no. 4 (December 2009): 667–710.

Raboteau, Albert J. *Slave Religion: The "Invisible Institution" in the Antebellum South*. New York: Oxford University Press, 1978.

Rice, Madeleine Hooke. *American Catholic Opinion in the Slavery Controversy*. New York: Columbia University Press, 1944.

Rothman, Adam, and Elsa Barraza Mendoza, eds. *Facing Georgetown's History: A Reader on Slavery, Memory, and Reconciliation*. Washington, DC: Georgetown University Press, 2021.

Rushforth, Brett. *Bonds of Alliance: Indigenous and Atlantic Slaveries in New France*. Chapel Hill: University of North Carolina Press, 2012.

Schmidt, Kelly L. "Enslaved Faith Communities in the Jesuits' Missouri Mission." *U.S. Catholic Historian* 37, no. 2 (Spring 2019): 49–81.

———. "The Pervasive Institution: Slavery and Its Legacies in U.S. Catholicism." *American Catholic Studies Newsletter* 49, no. 1 (Spring 2022): 11–22.

———. "'Regulations for Our Black People': Jesuit Recordkeeping on Slavery in Antebellum Missouri." In *Engaging Sources: The Tradition and Future of Collecting History in the Society of Jesus (Proceedings of the Symposium Held at Boston College, June 11–13, 2019)*, edited by Cristiano Casalini, Emanuele Colombo, and Seth Meehan. Boston: Institute of Jesuit Sources, 2021.

———. "Slavery and the Shaping of Catholic Missouri, 1810–1850." *Missouri Historical Review* 116, no. 3 (April 2022): 173–211.

———. "'Without Slaves and without Assassins': Antebellum Cincinnati, Transnational Jesuits, and the Challenges of Race and Slavery." *U.S. Catholic Historian* 39, no. 2 (Spring 2021): 1–26.

Sommar, Mary E. *The Slaves of the Churches: A History*. New York: Oxford University Press, 2020.

Spalding, David. "Martin John Spalding's 'Dissertation on the American Civil War.'" *Catholic Historical Review* 52, no. 1 (April 1966): 66–85.

Tate, Adam L. *Catholics' Lost Cause: South Carolina Catholics and the American South, 1820–1861*. Notre Dame, IN: University of Notre Dame Press, 2018.

———. "Confronting Abolitionism: Bishop John England, American Catholicism, and Slavery." *Journal of the Historical Society* 9, no. 3 (September 2009): 373–404.

Thomas, William G., III. *A Question of Freedom: The Families Who Challenged Slavery from the Nation's Founding to the Civil War*. New Haven, CT: Yale University Press, 2020.

Ulshafer, Thomas, P.S.S. "Slavery and the Early Sulpician Community in Maryland." *U.S. Catholic Historian* 37, no. 2 (Spring 2019): 1–21.

Wilder, Craig Steven. "War and Priests: Catholic Colleges and Slavery in the Age of Revolution." In *Slavery's Capitalism: A New History of American Economic Development*, edited by Sven Beckert and Seth Rockman, 227–242. Philadelphia: University of Pennsylvania Press, 2016.

Williams, Shannen Dee. "The Church Must Make Reparation for Its Role in Slavery, Segregation." *National Catholic Reporter*, June 15, 2020.

———. "Religious Orders Owning Slaves Isn't New—Black Catholics Have Emphasized This History for Years." *America*, August 6, 2019.

Wimmer, Judith C. "American Catholic Interpretations of the Civil War." PhD diss., Drew University, 1980.

Woods, James M. *A History of the Catholic Church in the American South: 1513–1900*. Gainesville: University Press of Florida, 2011.

Zanca, Kenneth J., ed. *American Catholics and Slavery, 1789–1866: An Anthology of Primary Documents*. Lanham, MD: University Press of America, 1994.

Index

A

Abelard, Joseph
 224, 234
Abelard, Pierre Charles
 224, 234
Abelard, Saly
 224, 234
abolitionism
 Catholic participation in, 51, 98, 103, 147–48, 150, 153, 162–64, 168, 175, 199, 202; link to anti-Catholicism, 37, 57, 112–13, 114, 123, 133–34, 174; as a movement, 37, 95–96, 98–99, 105–15, 122, 126, 134–35, 253; opposition to, 25–26, 38, 52, 75–77, 102, 104, 122–24, 125, 137, 151, 161–64, 176–78, 186–87, 198, 199, 200
 See also antislavery; emancipation
Adams, John Quincy
 101
Adams, Peter
 80
Africa
 abolition of slavery in, 202; native traditions similar to Catholicism, 263; and racial theory, 54, 193; slave trade, 8, 37, 90–94, 102, 189, 190, 191–92, 195–96, 203, 214
African Americans
 and Irish, 146, 167, 174, 180–82; ministry to, 50, 55, 201, 240, 258; as soldiers in Civil War, 158, 171
 See also freed Blacks
Alabama
 slavery in, 4, 29, 211, 259
Albornoz, Bartolomé Frías de
 190
Alexander VI (pope)
 189–90
Allain, Aimee Pognon
 232
Amistad
 96
Anderson, Francis S.
 69

Anglicans
 slaveholding by, 262–63
Angola
 slave trade in, 8
anti-Catholicism
 75, 103; abolitionists as anti-Catholic, 29, 37, 57, 112–14, 123, 161, 174, 243; threats and violence against Catholics, 25, 133, 243
 See also Know-Nothings; nativism
Antietam, battle of (1862)
 159–60, 168, 180
antislavery
 opposition from Catholics to, 76, 99, 113, 115–16, 120–21, 123, 128, 133–37, 199; support from Catholics for, 94, 95, 97, 99, 106–14, 116–17, 122, 125–28, 130–32, 147–53, 163–64; ties to anti-Catholicism, 29, 37
 See also abolitionism
Anwander, Thaddeus, C.Ss.R.
 50
Armas, Christoval de
 232
Aubin, Thomas
 91, 95
Audé, Mother Eugénie
 197
Ayllón, Lucas Vázquez de
 190
Aymond, Gregory Michael
 204

B

Badin, Stephen Theodore
 69, 71–72, 78, 250, 259
Bakhita, St. Josephine
 205
Balcet, Melanie
 234
Baltimore, Maryland
 Catholic (arch)diocese of, 43–44, 213, 265–66; education of Black children in, 197; parish for Black Catholics in, 238; plenary and provincial councils of Catholic bishops in, 37, 98, 127, 138, 200,

201; refugees from slave rebellion in, 171, 195; sacramental records of, 211, 259; women religious in, 41, 43, 50, 197
baptism
enslaved persons as sponsors for, 70–71; freeing of enslaved at, 222, 224; received by the enslaved, 48–49, 53, 70–71, 78–79, 83, 86, 191–93, 195, 199, 211–12, 214, 216–18, 220–26, 235–36, 241–42, 248–50, 261–63
Barada, Louis
18
Bardstown, Kentucky
Black parish in, 87; Catholic school for Blacks and whites, 72; opposition to slavery in, 74, 76; slavery at Saint Joseph College, 18–21; slavery in, 67, 73–74, 81, 82
Barnabò, Alessandro
178, 179
Baton Rouge, Louisiana
211
Baudier, Roger
244–45, 248
Bayou Boeuf, Louisiana
23–25
Beall, Richard
84
Beasley, Mother Mathilda Taylor
202
Beaubois, Nicolas-Ignace de, S.J.
193
Beckx, Pieter Jan, S.J.
28
Becraft, Anne Marie (Sister Mary Aloysius)
59, 205
Bedini, Gaetano
133
Beecher, Lyman
133
Belair, Jean
226
Benedict of Palermo (Benedict the Moor)
194
Benedict XIV (pope)
37, 93, 194
Benedict XVI (pope)
203

Bible
and slavery, 36, 92, 105, 173, 258
Bienville, Jean-Baptiste Le Moyne de
193, 212–13
Binsse, Louis B.
184
Black Codes
See Code Noir
Boone, Charley
69
Boston, Massachusetts
abolitionist meeting in, 108–9; African American priest of, 200; Irish Repeal Association in, 114; proslavery in, 163, 167, 170, 171, 176–77
Boswell, William
233
Branche-Baker, Cheryllyn
206
Braxton, Edward K.
207
Brazil
90, 202
Brent, William
103
Brooks, Preston
141
Brown, Mary (Polly/Molly)
1, 2–3, 6, 9–11, 13, 14
Brown, Thomas
1, 2–3, 6, 9–11, 13, 14
Brownson, Orestes
38, 39, 52, 120–22, 148, 153, 161–62, 176–77, 180–81
Buchanan, James
118, 121
burials
of enslaved persons, 60, 86, 210; in sacramental records, 71, 79, 86–87, 212, 216–17, 221, 229–33, 235, 261; separate for enslaved and free persons of color, 229
Burke-Sivers, Harold
208
Burtsell, Richard
168
Butler, Benjamin
183

Index | **279**

C

Calvert, Charles
191
Cameron, Simon
160
Campbell, Alexander
132
Capizzi, Joseph
267
Capuchins
194, 226; antislavery, 191–92, 193; as slaveholders, 41, 49, 192–93, 217, 232, 244
Caravaglios, Maria Genoino
257
Carberry, Joseph, S.J.
47
Carmelite nuns
198, 201; as slaveholders, 41, 43, 195, 197
Carroll, Charles
208
Carroll, James
191
Carroll, John
39, 48, 196, 206, 239, 247, 265
Catholic Church
and Civil War (U.S.), 179; condemnation of slavery, 93–94, 97; development of doctrine, 58; "Doctrine of Discovery," 189, 205, 210; and Emancipation Proclamation, 182–83; failure to condemn U.S. slavery, 36, 75–76, 184–85, 187, 268; ministry to enslaved, 48–51, 199, 248–50; morality of slavery, 267–68; theological justification for slavery, 77–78, 92, 105–6, 193, 251; U.S. bishops and slavery, 37–38, 97–100, 122–23, 136–38, 161
Catholic Committee of the South
202
Catholic University of America (Washington, D.C.)
207, 209–10
Charleston, South Carolina
111; Catholic diocese of, 98, 100; education of Black children in, 49, 72; refugees from slave rebellion in, 171; women religious in, 41, 49

Chaumont, Christophe de
192–93
Chaumont, Eusèbe de
192–93
Cincinnati, Ohio
African Americans in, 134–36, 152–53, 201; anti-Catholicism in, 133–34; Black Catholics in, 152–53; Black students in, 27; Catholic (arch)diocese of, 130–32, 139–40; connections to South, 27, 136, 144; demographics of, 132; free from slavery, 27, 131; immigrants in, 132–36, 140, 142, 146, 149, 151; Irish Repeal Association in, 111–14, 119, 123; provincial councils of Catholic bishops in, 138, 143–44, 150; religious landscape of, 132–33; support for emancipation in, 98, 125–28, 147–50, 166, 177, 200; support for slavery in, 134, 136, 147, 151; support for Union in, 140–46
Civil War (U.S.)
28, 34–35, 37–38, 52–53, 76, 128, 142–47, 150–52, 155–88, 200, 258
Clark, Emily
227, 260
Claver, St. Peter
97, 199, 201
Clay, Cassius
177
Clay, William Lacy
208
clergy
antislavery, 168, 187, 191–92; Black, 109, 112, 200, 201; as Civil War chaplains, 143; ministry to the enslaved, 49, 55–56, 70; pacifying draft rioters, 181; political impartiality of, 143–44, 179; proslavery, 113, 194; as slaveholders, 1, 4, 6, 11–12, 18, 45, 47–48, 195, 198, 209, 211, 239, 242–45, 247, 250–52, 254, 261
See also Capuchins; Jesuits; Sulpicians; Vincentians
Code Noir (Black Codes)
7, 192, 193, 216–18, 219, 224–25, 229, 230, 244
Collins, David, S.J.
205

colonies
  British, 74, 130, 191, 194, 213, 242; French, 7, 49, 74, 192–93, 195–96, 212–14, 216–17, 221, 225, 230, 235; slavery in, 189, 190; Spanish, 190, 192, 213–14, 218, 221, 226, 235
Columbus, Christopher
  189
Confederate States of America (Confederacy)
  28, 38, 144, 156–60, 177, 183–84, 200
confession, sacrament of
  5, 25, 194
confirmation, sacrament of
  30; received by the enslaved, 70–71, 86, 235; sacramental records of, 70–71, 212, 235
Connelly, Cornelia
  23, 26
Connelly, Pierce
  23, 26, 27
conscription, military
  143, 146, 150, 180; riots against, 146, 152, 180–82
Constitution (U.S.)
  and property rights, 186; and secession, 141; and slavery, 53, 123, 147, 162–64, 168–70; support for, 142, 164, 172–73; Thirteenth Amendment to, 185–86, 208
Cooke, Terence James
  203
Copperheads
  144, 169
  See also Peace Democrats
Corrigan, Mary Beth
  262
Covington, Kentucky
  141
Cruz, Reginald, C.F.X.
  204
Curran, Francis J.
  247–48
Curran, Robert Emmett
  122, 254–56, 257

D

Daly, Charles P.
  164, 165–66, 173

Daughters of Charity
  49–50, 51, 205
  See also Sisters of Charity
Daughters of the Cross (Cocoville, Louisiana)
  as slaveholders, 42, 49
Davis, Cyprian, O.S.B.
  254–55, 259, 261
DeAndreis, Felix, C.M.
  40, 55
De Courcy, Henry
  241, 243
DeGioia, John J.
  205
DeLeeuw, Theodore, S.J.
  25
Delille, Mother Henriette Diaz
  50, 197–98, 200, 203
Deluol, Louis-Regis, S.S.
  51
Democratic Party
  101–3, 105, 108, 118, 133–34, 140, 144, 145, 151, 164, 165, 169, 174
DePauger, Adrien
  229
Dessalines, Jean-Jacques
  195
De Theux, Theodore, S.J.
  18–19
Dilhet, Jean
  238
Dominican Friars
  68–70, 196, 245
Dominican Sisters of St. Catherine (Kentucky)
  reconciliation efforts by, 60, 204, 264; as slaveholders, 41, 47
Donahoe, Patrick
  167, 169, 185–86
Douglas, Stephen
  118, 140, 156, 174
Douglass, Frederick
  116
Doyle, E. J. "Patrick"
  74–76
Drady, Ann Jarboe
  68
draft
  See conscription
Dred Scott v. Sanford
  121, 156–57, 158, 206
DuBourg, Louis William
  3, 9, 40, 195, 198

Duchesne, Philippine
42
Duerinck, John Baptist, S.J.
18
Dugué de Boisbriand, Pierre
226
Dupanloup, Felix
163–64
Duquesnay, G. L.
221
Dzierozynski, Francis, S.J.
45

E

Eccleston, Samuel
98, 99
emancipation
deferred, 44, 256, 268; of enslaved by owners, 80, 129, 256; gradual, 38, 53, 56, 147, 172, 178, 187, 196, 265; laws regarding, 220; opposition to, 77, 96, 125, 134, 136, 147, 150, 155–88; support for, 38, 126, 128, 140, 147–49, 152, 182, 191–92, 198, 199, 200; as war measure, 143, 145–47, 157–58, 160, 182, 184 *See also* manumission
Emancipation Proclamation
147, 155–88
Emmitsburg, Maryland
41, 128
England
condemnation of slave trade, 89–93, 95, 102–4, 196; depiction of Irish by, 177; enslaver of Ireland, 109; and Holy See, 93, 95, 102, 103; origin of slavery, 130, 241
England, John
approach to slavery, 72–73, 98–100, 103–6, 113, 115–18, 120, 123, 137, 161, 199, 246, 257–58; ministry to Blacks, 49, 72, 137, 199
enslavers
abuse of enslaved, 5, 38, 83–84, 244; and enslaved religious participation, 16, 29–30, 63–64, 73–74, 77, 87, 216, 230, 241, 249, 261–63; treatment of enslaved, 5, 53, 56, 77–78, 83–86, 106, 187, 216, 237, 241–42, 246–51
Epiphanius of Moirans
191

Eternal Word Television Network (EWTN)
208
Everett, William
151

F

Faran, James
145
Farrell, Thomas
188
Farrelly, Maura Jane
268
Fenwick, Benedict
98
Fenwick, Edward D.
70, 196, 265
Fillmore, Millard
118
Finaut, Nicolas
226
Florida
ministry to freed Blacks in, 200; runaways in, 192–93; slavery in, 190, 194, 211, 234, 259
Florissant, Missouri
Jesuit novitiate at, 3, 9–11, 13, 14, 20, 197
Floyd, George
61, 208
Fordham University (New York)
16
Forsyth, John
72–73, 90, 102–6, 115–17, 120, 199
France
antislavery in, 163–64, 258; colonists from, 213, 225; control of Louisiana, 194, 213–14, 229, 235; outlawing of slavery, 90, 195–96; slavery in colonies, 7, 41–42, 192–93, 195–96, 216–17, 230, 235, 244, 246
Francis Joseph of Jaca
191
Francis (pope)
204, 205, 207
Fransioli, Joseph
182
Fredericksburg, battle of (1862)
169, 170, 180
freed Blacks
13, 80, 82, 96, 123, 128, 191, 217;

Catholic practice of and ministry to, 30, 40, 48, 49, 193, 194, 195, 248; discrimination against, 136, 192; education of, 72, 98–99, 197; purchased freedom, 14–15, 29, 68, 194, 195, 256; in religious life, 40, 197, 250; in sacramental records, 68, 70, 79, 222–24, 225–26, 232, 234
See also emancipation; manumission
Frémont, John C.
117–21
fugitive slaves
82–83, 129, 135, 157, 158, 183, 192, 193, 194

G

Garesché, Julius
171
Garraghan, Gilbert J., S.J.
253
Garrison, William Lloyd
108–12, 113–14, 123
Gaspart, Jean
226
Gaspart, Marie
217, 225–26
Gatti, Martin, O.P.
184
Gaudin, Juliette
197
Georgetown Preparatory School (Washington, D.C.)
197, 207
See also Visitation Sisters
Georgetown University (Washington, D.C.)
22, 51, 201; enslaved persons held by, 256; GU272 Descendants Association, 206, 207, 209; reconciliation efforts by, 59, 205, 209, 264; sale of enslaved persons, 58–59, 198, 205, 206, 207, 233, 252, 254–56, 264; slavery archive, 205, 260
See also Jesuits
Georgia
Catholic Church in, 202, 259; support for slavery in, 90, 102, 105

German Americans
approach to slavery, 132–35, 145, 151, 198; conflict with Blacks, 134–35, 146, 174; immigrants to U.S., 89
Gettysburg, Pennsylvania
181
Gillard, John T., S.S.J.
247, 249–52
Gough, Ignatius
22–26
Gough, Stephen H.
22
Graham, Richard
19
Grand Coteau, Louisiana
22–26, 42, 47, 197, 207
Grayson Gough, Sally
22–23, 26–27
Greeley, Horace
181
Greeley, Julia
206
Gregory XVI (pope)
117; condemnation of slave trade, 37, 72–73, 89–100, 104–5, 108, 110, 113–15, 117, 118, 122, 131, 136–37, 198, 199, 257, 267
Gresselin, Charles, S.J.
176–77
Grimmer, Nicholas Charles
22
Guerin, Mother Theodore
54–55
Guilbert, Jean
232
Guilday, Peter
137, 246, 247, 251–52
Guiney, Patrick
175–76
Guyana
Code Noir in, 192, 216

H

Haiti
194, 197, 218; refugees from, 50, 195, 197, 214; slave rebellion in, 195
See also Saint-Domingue
Halpine, Charles
156
Hamilton, Leonard
83

Hardy, Beatriz Betancourt
  262–63
Harrison, William Henry
  101–2, 105
Haughton, James
  95, 107–8
Hawkins, Frank
  197
Hawkins, Isaac
  59, 205
Healy, Alexander
  200
Healy, Eliza (Sister Mary Magdalene)
  201
Healy, James A.
  199–200, 201
Healy, Patrick Francis, S.J.
  200, 201
Hecker, Isaac Thomas
  52–53, 181, 184
Henni, John Martin
  167–68, 198
Hill, Thomas
  63, 80
historiography and Catholic slaveholding
  8, 237–268
Holy See
  and Civil War (U.S.), 178–79, 200; and Emancipation Proclamation, 182–83; and slavery, 90–91, 93, 136–37, 190, 257–58
  See also papacy
Hood, John T.
  219
Howard, Kamm
  209
Howlett, William J.
  244, 250
Hughes, John
  110, 123, 142–43, 160, 162–63, 165, 181
Hughes, Thomas A., S.J.
  241, 244, 245, 247, 252
Huhn, Martin Francis
  199
Hunter, George, S.J.
  53

I

immigrants
  economic competition with Blacks, 123–24, 135–36, 146, 242; prejudice against, 133–34, 142, 243; and slavery, 96, 108–10, 114, 133–35, 143, 146, 149
  See also German Americans; Irish Americans
Indigenous peoples
  enslaved interaction with, 6, 9, 12–13, 191; enslavement of, 8, 93, 104, 190, 193, 194, 231; evangelization of, 5, 7, 31, 189–90, 191, 193, 227, 239, 240; ministry to, 212, 227; sacramental records of, 212, 216–17, 230
Innocent XI (pope)
  192
In Supremo Apostolatus (1839)
  97, 198, 257; composition of, 89–94; interpretation of, 99–100, 104–5, 113–16, 118, 122–24, 136–37, 199
  See also Gregory XVI
Irish
  as abolitionists, 37, 95–96, 106–8, 199; bishops and slavery, 97
Irish Americans
  antislavery, 74–75, 98, 114, 118–19, 130; and Civil War, 142, 155, 170–71, 174–76, 180; compared to enslaved, 177, 243; conflict with Blacks, 108, 134–35, 146–47, 174, 180–82; opposed to abolition, 96, 98–99, 110–12, 114–15, 123–24, 155–56, 165–67, 170, 172, 180–81, 185; opposed to conscription, 180; political identification, 133, 145, 151, 174; as slaveholders, 67
Irish Brigade
  170, 175
Irish Repeal Movement
  89, 108–16, 119, 123, 130

J

Jacobs, Harriet
  88
Jamison, Francis
  129

Jefferson, Thomas
  17, 169
Jesuits (Society of Jesus)
  African American, 200; as Civil War chaplains, 169–70; end racial segregation, 202; enslaved persons held by, 1–32, 35, 39–40, 41, 43–48, 49, 51, 54, 191, 193, 197, 209–10, 239, 244–45, 247, 253, 256, 259, 262, 263; ministry to enslaved and freed Blacks, 49, 53, 152; opposition to abolitionism, 51, 176–77; reconciliation efforts by, 4–5, 29–32, 59, 205–6, 209, 264–65; sale of enslaved persons by, 11, 20–22, 43–45, 58–59, 198, 207, 233, 252–56, 264
  See also Georgetown University
John Carroll University (Cleveland, Ohio)
  206, 265
John Paul II (pope)
  203
Johnson, Henry
  45
Johnson, William
  78
Joubert, James, S.S.
  50

K

Kaskaskia, Illinois
  7, 191
Keeler, William
  204
Kelly, C. C.
  84
Kenney, Peter, S.J.
  46, 47, 54
Kenrick, Francis P.
  38, 77, 115, 120, 123, 178
Kenrick, Peter R.
  131–32
Kentucky
  Catholics in, 39, 63–88, 141, 144, 196; laws against educating Blacks in, 27–28; religious communities' ownership of enslaved persons in, 4, 15, 18–19, 21, 39–41, 43, 47, 60, 196, 202, 204, 244, 245, 263–66; slavery in, 40, 41, 43, 47, 51, 60, 63–88, 158, 196, 202, 204, 211, 238, 244, 245, 250, 263–66
Kesicki, Timothy, S.J.
  206, 209
Know-Nothings
  25, 37, 118, 133–34
  See also anti-Catholicism; nativism
Krebsbach, Suzanne
  257–58

L

Lacour, Henry
  217
LaFarge, John, S.J.
  248–49, 250–51, 252
Lagrandeur D'Etain, Jean Joseph
  226
Lalor, Teresa (Alice)
  196
Lambruschini, Luigi
  91–93
Lancaster, Charles
  68
Lancaster, Nancy
  68
Lange, Mary Elizabeth
  197, 204
Langres, Bruno de
  192–93
Lapommeray, Monsieur de
  230
Layton, Mary
  197
Lebanon, Kentucky
  15–17
LeConnait, Mother Hyacinth
  42, 49
Lee, Robert E.
  155, 160
Leo XIII (pope)
  201, 202
Leonard, Jean Baptiste
  217
Lincoln, Abraham
  34, 77, 126–27, 140, 142, 145; and Emancipation Proclamation, 155–88
Loras, Mathias
  208
Loras College (Dubuque, Iowa)
  208

Lord Baltimore
  39, 191
Louisiana
  abrogation of Spanish law in, 219; Catholic Church in, 3, 213–14, 220–33; Civil Code (1808), 219–20, 222, 224, 225, 229; *Code Noir* in, 216–19, 224, 225, 229, 230, 244; demographics of, 214; reconciliation efforts in, 206, 207; record keeping practices in, 212, 214, 216–36; slavery in, 4, 7, 16, 22–26, 40–42, 45, 49–51, 55, 74, 192–95, 197, 233, 244–45, 248, 255
Louisville, Kentucky
  20, 21, 63; Catholic (arch)diocese of, 141, 144, 150, 156, 177, 187; sacramental records of, 211
Lovell, Rebecca
  85
Loyola University Maryland
  209
Luxembourg, Raphael de
  193, 226
Lynch, Patrick N.
  53, 161, 182–85, 200

M

MacLeod, Xavier Donald
  239
MacNamara, Daniel George
  155
Macquimara, Victoire
  232
Madden, R. R.
  96–97, 108, 110
Maistre, Claude Paschal
  168
Malone, Sylvester
  168, 188
manumission
  clergy/religious and, 51, 129, 187, 196, 199, 200; laws regarding, 219–20, 222; in sacramental records, 212, 224
Maréchal, Ambrose
  43
Marquette, Jacques, S.J.
  191
marriage
  of enslaved, 48–49, 68, 70–72, 79, 85–86, 221, 224–28, 248, 252, 259–63; enslaver's consent required for, 55, 216, 225, 226, 244, 261; and family composition of enslaved, 78–79; intermarriage of differing races, 191, 194, 259; laws for Blacks regarding, 27–28, 86, 216, 218, 221, 224–25; in sacramental records, 212, 216–17, 221, 224–28, 261; and separating enslaved families, 19–22, 38, 45, 78, 81–82, 87, 137, 198, 252, 254–55, 261–62
Marshall, Adam, S.J.
  46
Martin, Auguste Marie
  184, 200, 257
Martin, de Porres, St.
  198, 202–3
Martinique
  slavery in, 7, 226
Maryland
  Catholic Church in, 39, 242–43; Civil War in, 159–60; founding of, 191; Jesuit ownership of enslaved in, 1–4, 6, 7, 10–11, 14, 22, 39–40, 43–47, 49, 54, 191, 197, 244, 247, 254–56, 263; reconciliation efforts in, 206, 208, 209; slavery in, 39–41, 43, 49, 74, 128–30, 158, 191, 195, 196, 197, 209–10, 211, 238, 248–49, 259, 260, 262–63, 265
Mass
  69, 168, 213; enslaved participation in, 9, 47–49, 249, 261; freed Black participation in, 30
  See also prayer; preaching; sacraments
Massachusetts
  regiments in Civil War, 155, 175–76
masters
  See enslavers
Masur, Laura
  209–10, 263
Mathew, Theobald
  108, 110
Matthews, Bernardina
  195
Mattingly, William
  81
McAleenan, Aidan
  205

McClellan, George
 158–59, 170, 175
McCunn, John H.
 174
McDermott, Maria
 196
McGee, Thomas D'Arcy
 238–39
McGreevy, John
 160–61, 267–68
McHatton, Charles G.
 14
McLean, Edward
 84
McMaster, James
 122, 161, 166–67, 180, 182
Meilleur, J. B.
 232
Mendouça, Lourenço da Silva de
 192
Mendoza, Elsa Barraza
 256
Menéndez de Avilés, Pedro
 190
Menéndez, Francisco
 193
Metcalf, Elisha
 83
Metcalfe, Thomas
 84
Millard, Henry Jackson
 26
Mill Hill Fathers
 74
Miró, Esteban Rodriguez
 195
Missouri
 emancipation order in, 158; laws against educating Blacks in, 27–28; slavery in, 3–6, 9–16, 18, 20–21, 40, 42, 197, 198, 206, 244, 253, 259, 261–62
Mobberly, Joseph, S.J.
 54
Mobile, Alabama
 sacramental records of, 211, 259; slavery in, 29, 192–93
Molina, Luis de, S.J.
 190
Mon, Maria Alexandrina
 222–23, 234
Mon, Ramon
 223–24, 234

Montiano, Manuel de
 194
Moreau, Julie
 199
Moreno, Juan
 189
Mosley, Joseph, S.J.
 54
Mount St. Mary's College (Emmitsburg, Maryland)
 128–30
Mozambique
 slavery in, 8
Mulholland, St. Clair
 185
Mullally, John
 163, 180
Mulledy, Thomas F., S.J.
 44–46, 205
Murphy, Thomas, S.J.
 256
Murphy, William Stack, S.J.
 27–28
Murray, John O'Kane
 242–43

N

Nalezyty, Susan
 207
Nash, Michael, S.J.
 16
Natchitoches, Louisiana
 Catholic diocese of, 184, 200; sacramental records of, 259
Native Americans
 See Indigenous peoples
nativism
 25, 37, 118, 133–34, 142
 See also anti-Catholicism; Know-Nothings
Nerinckx, Charles
 71–72, 196, 250, 259
Nerinx, Kentucky
 204
Nesbit, Charles
 12
NETWORK Lobby for Catholic Social Justice
 209
Neumann, John
 50

New Orleans, Louisiana
168; Catholic Church in, 199, 201, 202, 204, 211–14, 216–18, 220–33, 235–36; educational and charitable outreach to enslaved in, 50–51, 197–98; racial composition of, 214–16, 230–31; reconciliation efforts in, 203; sacramental records of, 211–33, 235–36; slavery in, 7, 29, 40, 41, 50, 55, 83, 192–93, 196, 260

New York City
antislavery in, 118, 151, 168; Blacks in, 180–82, 194; draft riots in, 146, 180–82; proslavery in, 110, 122, 160, 161, 163, 164, 166, 170, 174, 176, 177

Nicholas V (pope)
189

Niehoff, Robert L., S.J.
206

Noll, Mark
258

Northup, Solomon
23, 25

nuns
See women religious

O

Oblate Sisters of Providence
41, 50, 197

O'Brien, D. W.
114

Ochs, Stephen J.
74

O'Connell, Daniel
37, 95–96, 102, 107–14, 116–17, 119, 122, 123, 130, 199

O'Connell, Jeremiah
241–42

O'Connor, John
203

O'Daniel, Victor Francis, O.P.
245, 246–47

Odin, Jean-Marie
168

O'Gorman, Richard
166

O'Hagan, Joseph, S.J.
169–70

O'Higgins, William T.
149

Ohio
connections to South, 136, 144; fear of African American exodus to, 151; free from slavery, 27, 131

Ohio River
1, 9, 20, 63, 135, 136, 144, 146

Olivier, Charles Napoleon
22

O'Reilly, Bernard, S.J.
165

O'Reilly, Miles
156

Orosco, Marie
234

P

Paca, William
208

Paddington, George
109

papacy
apology for slavery, 203, 205; approval of slavery, 189; Catholics' allegiance to, 75, 133; and Civil War, 179, 182–83; condemnation of slave trade, 72–73, 89–124, 131, 136–37, 192, 196, 198–99, 257, 267; condemnation of slavery, 37, 190, 194, 202, 203, 207; and "Doctrine of Discovery," 189, 205; and question of abolition, 182–85, 192
See also Gregory XVI (pope); Holy See

Paul III (pope)
93, 190

Paulists (Missionary Society of Saint Paul the Apostle)
52, 181

Peace Democrats
145, 174
See also Copperheads; Democratic Party

Peñalver y Cardenas, Luis
218, 230

Pennsylvania
antislavery efforts in, 111–12, 167, 185, 200; enslaved labor in, 4, 6, 39–40

Perier, Catherine de
217

Perry, Joseph Nathaniel
204

Philadelphia, Pennsylvania
  Catholic (arch)diocese of, 38, 77, 115; refugees from slave rebellion in, 171
Phillips, Wendell
  89, 109–10, 111, 114
Pius II (pope)
  37, 93
Pius VI (pope)
  213
Pius VII (pope)
  90–91, 93, 194, 196
Pius IX (pope)
  117, 179, 182–83, 199
Pius XII (pope)
  203
Poole, Stafford, C.M.
  259, 261
Portugal
  antislavery efforts and, 95; colonization by, 189; participation in slavery, 8, 89, 90, 99, 189, 191–92, 194, 196
prayer
  enslaved participation in, 2, 69, 73–74, 77, 250–51, 261, 263
  See also Mass; sacraments
preaching
  antislavery, 132, 187, 191–92; concern for religious practices of enslaved, 248–49; condemning abolitionists in, 52, 141; during Civil War, 143, 168, 182
Price, Joseph
  81
priests
  See clergy
Prieto, Juan
  189
Protestantism
  and the American founding, 52, 241; and antislavery, 52, 74–76, 151; divisions over slavery, 75, 127; and slavery, 53, 75–76, 127, 241–42, 246–49, 262–63
Purcell, Edward
  98, 138–40, 148–49, 163, 177, 200
Purcell, John B.
  168; approach to slavery, 98, 125–32, 138–53, 163–64, 167, 178–79, 200
Purvis, Gloria
  208

Q

Queen, Augustine
  21
Queen, "Big" Peter
  17, 18–21
Queen, Jack
  10, 18
Queen, Marian
  19
Queen, Mary Hoppins
  20–21
Queen, Moses
  1, 2–3, 6, 9–11
Queen, Nancy
  1, 2–3, 6, 9–10
Queen, Sally
  10, 18
Queen-Hawkins, Anny
  10, 18, 32
Queen-Hawkins, Isaac
  1, 2–3, 6, 9–11
Queen-Hawkins, Margaret
  14, 15
Queen-Hawkins, Peter
  14, 15
Queen-Hawkins, Proteus
  10, 18, 32
Queen-Hawkins, Susanna
  1, 2–3, 6, 9–10

R

racism
  Catholic Church's opposition to, 61, 203, 204, 207, 208, 265; and Catholics, 5, 29, 39, 58, 60–61, 152, 165, 174, 248, 267–68; and Irish, 96, 174, 177, 181
Raphael, Jean
  226
Raphael, Jean Baptiste
  225–26
Read, William George
  115–16, 117
Reconstruction era
  188
Religious of the Sacred Heart (Society of the Sacred Heart)
  11–12, 22, 42, 47, 59, 197, 206, 207
Remond, Charles Lenox
  108, 110

Republican Party
    117–19, 133–34, 140, 156–58, 161, 163, 170, 172, 173–74, 180
Reynolds, Ignatius
    117
Rice, Madeleine Hooke
    245, 253
Richmond, Virginia
    51, 159, 163, 185
Rillieux, Miguel
    232
Rillieux, Vizente
    232
Rinehart, William Henry
    206
Robertson, Manette V.
    223, 234
Roman, Louise J. (Mother Teresa of Jesus)
    201
Rosati, Joseph
    12, 54, 55–56
Rosecrans, Sylvester
    139–40, 142–43
Rosecrans, William Starke
    140, 147–48, 171
Rudd, Daniel A.
    74, 201
Rummel, Joseph Francis
    202
Ryder, John, S.J.
    51

S

sacraments
    admonishing enslavers who neglect, 250; received by enslaved persons, 55, 56, 68, 70–72, 74, 78–79, 86–87, 191, 221, 248, 251, 260; records of, 204, 206, 211–36, 258–59, 261–62
    See also baptism; confession; confirmation; marriage
Saint Charles, Missouri
    11, 18
Saint Charles College (Grand Coteau, Louisiana)
    22–23, 26
Saint-Domingue
    Code Noir in, 192; refugees from, 171, 173, 195, 196, 197, 238; slave rebellion, 171, 178–79, 195; slavery in, 7, 195
    See also Haiti
Saint Joseph College (Bardstown, Kentucky)
    18–21, 26, 27, 74
Saint Louis University (St. Louis, Missouri)
    4, 11, 13, 14, 18, 26, 27, 29, 197, 202
Saint Mary's College (Lebanon, Kentucky)
    15–17
Sandoval, Alonso de, S.J.
    191
San Malo (Jean Saint Malo)
    194
Sansbury, Louis
    68
Sauvinet, J. B.
    224, 234
Savannah, Georgia
    202, 259
Schauinger, Joseph Herman
    250
Schmidt, Kelly
    262
Schulte, Alfred
    203
Scott, Thomas Parkin
    173
secession
    Northern Catholic opposition to, 139–42, 144; and slavery, 156, 157, 159, 164
    See also Civil War (U.S.)
Second Vatican Council (Vatican II)
    33, 36, 203
Sedgwick, Jane
    53
Seton, St. Elizabeth
    49
Seward, William
    159
sexuality
    84–86, 134; child-bearing of enslaved, 191, 259; concubinage with Blacks outlawed, 211, 224–25; exploitation of enslaved, 38, 84–85; illegitimacy and acknowledgment of paternity, 211, 222, 224; mixed-race/mulatto (creole), 9, 26–28, 40, 55, 84, 197, 199, 201, 203, 218, 224, 225, 233–34
    See also marriage

Shannon, Christopher
  268
Sharpe, Maria
  196
Shea, John Gilmary
  239, 240
Sherrington, John
  207
Shields, James
  173–74
Simon, Agnes
  226
Simon, Carlos
  226
Sisters of Charity (Emmitsburg, Maryland)
  as slaveholders, 41, 49–50
Sisters of Charity (Nazareth, Kentucky)
  reconciliation efforts by, 202, 204, 263–64, 266; as slaveholders, 41, 43
Sisters of Charity (New Orleans)
  228
Sisters of Loretto (Kentucky)
  reconciliation efforts by, 60, 204, 205, 263–64; as slaveholders, 12, 41, 42, 196, 244
Sisters of Our Lady of Mercy (Charleston, South Carolina)
  41, 199
Sisters of Providence of Saint Mary-of-the-Woods (Indiana)
  54–55
Sisters of Saint Joseph (Cahokia, Illinois)
  12
Sisters of St. Joseph (LePuy, France)
  200
Sisters of the Holy Family (New Orleans)
  50–51, 197–98, 200, 203
Sisters of the Presentation of the Blessed Virgin Mary (New Orleans)
  197–98
  See also Sisters of the Holy Family
Sisters of the Third Order of St. Francis (Savannah, Georgia)
  202
slavery
  economics of, 253–54; insurrections, 23–26, 83, 171, 178–79, 190, 194, 195, 196; punishment of enslaved, 83–84; reparations for, 202, 208, 209, 263; runaways, 82–83, 129, 157, 192; sale of enslaved, 80, 81–82, 185, 233
Slawson, Douglas
  259, 261
Smith, Harry
  69–70, 83
Smith, Levi
  69
Society of the Sacred Heart
  See Religious of the Sacred Heart
Sousa, Mathias de
  191
Spain
  223–24, 234; antislavery, 191–92; colonization by, 28, 189–90, 194, 213–14; control of Louisiana, 41, 194, 213–14, 218–19, 226, 230, 235; conversion of enslaved by, 192; and Holy See, 93, 95; participation in slave trade, 89–90, 99, 102, 189, 190, 192, 196
Spalding, John Lancaster
  67–68, 87
Spalding, Martin John
  87, 144, 150, 182, 187; "dissertation" on war and slavery, 177–79
Spalding, Richard
  85–86
Sprague, W. B.
  151
Springfield, Kentucky
  63, 67, 68, 72, 85, 87, 196
Springfield, Ohio
  201
Spring Hill College (Mobile, Alabama)
  26, 29
St. Augustine, Florida
  Catholic diocese of, 38, 85; ministry to Blacks in, 200; sacramental records of, 211, 259; slavery in, 190, 192, 193
St. Cristophe, Margueritte de
  226
St. Louis, Missouri
  Black community in, 31; Catholic (arch)diocese of, 131–32, 209, 265; ministry to African Americans in, 30, 55–56; sacramental records of, 211; slavery in, 9, 11–14, 18, 29, 40, 197, 198

St. Mary's Seminary (Baltimore, Maryland)
195
St. Mary's Seminary (Perry County, Missouri)
40, 259
See also Vincentians
Stevenson, Andrew
90
Stewart, Joseph M.
209
Stono Rebellion
194
Stowe, Harriet Beecher
141
Strahan, Charles, S.J.
2
Strong, George Templeton
170
Sugar Creek, Kansas
11, 12
Sulpicians (Society of Priests of Saint-Sulpice)
50; ministry to Blacks, 195; opposition to slavery, 51; as slaveholders, 40, 195, 260
Sumner, Charles
141, 159, 161

T

Taney, Roger Brooke
121–22, 206
Thebaud, Augustus, S.J.
17
Tighe, Paul
209
Timon, John, C.M.
43, 51, 198
Tolton, Augustus
201, 204
Toussaint, François Dominique
195
Toussaint, Pierre
194, 203
Towson University (Maryland)
208
Tranchepain, Sister Marie Saint Augustine
193
Treaty of Fontainebleau (1762)
194

Tremoulet, Marie Eliza (Sister Marguerite)
201
Tucker, John C.
114
Tyler, Charles H.
31–32
Tyler, Matilda
29–32

U

Uncle Tom's Cabin (Stowe)
141
Underground Railroad
82
See also fugitive slaves; slavery
Universities Studying Slavery (USS)
209
Urban VIII (pope)
37, 93
Ursuline nuns
198, 199; as educators, 193, 227; as slaveholders, 41, 50, 193, 227–28, 235, 260

V

Vales, Edmond
202
Van Buren, Martin
101, 103
Van Quickenborne, Charles, S.J.
1–3, 10, 13, 18
Vatican
See Catholic Church; Holy See
Veillon, Remi
232
Verhaegen, Peter, S.J.
12, 13, 18, 20, 197
Verot, Augustin
38, 85, 257
Verreydt, Felix, S.J.
2–3
Vianden, Philibert de
193
Vincentians (Congregation of the Mission)
ministry to enslaved, 55–56; as slaveholders, 40, 42, 43, 49, 51, 54, 198, 259, 261

Virginia
    anti-Catholicism in, 243; Civil
    War in, 169, 183; proslavery
    efforts in, 51; slavery in, 90, 183
Visitation Sisters
    reconciliation efforts by, 59–60,
    207; as slaveholders, 41, 49, 196–
    97, 260

W

Webb, Benedict
    69
Webb, R. D.
    107, 110
Welsh, Peter
    175
Weninger, Francis X., S.J.
    152
West Indies
    Code Noir in, 192, 216
Wheatly, James M.
    83
Whig Party
    101–3, 105
White, Charles I.
    239
White Marsh Plantation (Maryland)
    1, 3, 6, 10, 197, 210
Williams, Shannen Dee
    60, 208

women religious
    African American, 41, 50–51,
    197–98, 200, 201, 202, 203, 204;
    and ministry to enslaved, 50–51,
    197–98, 199, 200; opposition to
    slavery by, 54–55; reconciliation
    efforts by, 59–60, 202, 204, 205,
    207, 263–64, 266; as slavehold-
    ers, 12, 41–43, 47, 49–51, 60, 193,
    195, 196–97, 200, 227–28, 235,
    244, 246, 260
Woolett, Charles
    174–75
Woolfork, Austin
    233
Woolfork, Richard
    233
Woolfork, Samuel
    219–20, 233

X

Xavier, St. Francis
    8, 94, 97
Xavier University (Cincinnati, Ohio)
    27, 265
Xavier University (New Orleans)
    202

Y

Young, Josue
    167–68, 200

www.ingramcontent.com/pod-product-compliance
Lightning Source LLC
Chambersburg PA
CBHW020316010526
44107CB00054B/1863